THE DIVERSITY ILLUSION

What We Got Wrong About Immigration and How to Set it Right

Ed West

GIBSON SQUARE

First edition published by Gibson Square

Available as an e-book

    info@gibsonsquare.com
    www.gibsonsquare.com
    Tel: +44 (0)20 7096 1100 (UK)
    Tel: +1 646 216 9813 (USA)
    Tel: +353 (0)1 657 1057 (Eire)

    ISBN 9781908096050

Contents

Introduction

I was born in a multi-racial society, and one that prided itself on being multi-racial. My classmates and friends were the children of immigrants from every corner of the globe, from Pakistan, India, Iran, Armenia and the Lebanon, from Korea, China, the West Indies and Brazil, Italy, Portugal and Greece. So was I, my mother having arrived from Ireland in the 1960s. We grew up in a culture dominated by the BBC, and its cosy world of eccentric, gentle comedies, one that spoke to a diverse Commonwealth universe centred around London, and which projected a post-war British ideal of old-fashioned decency and modern liberalism. While Christianity was in steep decline, many of its values had seamlessly evolved into the new secular moral order.

Central to those values was the idea that racism was not only wrong, but the very worst evil. Our generation, born forty years after the start of the Second World War, lived in the long shadow of Auschwitz. Our history was framed by the wrongs of Nazism and colonialism, the Civil Rights movement in the United States, and the struggle against apartheid. There were anti-racist goodies and racist baddies, the Nazis, the Afrikaners and the Ku Klux Klan. Racism was not just illogical and unscientific, it was a sin, and the gravest sin; while diversity, the love of foreigners, the highest virtue. Racism was to us what sexual impropriety was to the Victorians, the wrong around which we defined our moral worth; this would make rational discussion of issues involving immigration and its after-effects very difficult.

Our other cultural influence was the United States, both looked down upon by the new British establishment and held up as an example of a multi-ethnic society. The US was a racially-divided capitalist empire run by people without England's metropolitan sophistication, but it was also a more diverse one, vastly more so than our parochial little island. And so the US was living proof that multi-racial, multicultural democracies were the norm and the highest goal of human societies. America had taken that epic journey from slavery and genocide towards universal suffrage and civil rights, a long battle against the forces of white racism, although the battle was not over.

Britain was also a multicultural nation of immigrants, or so we were taught. There were African soldiers in Roman York, and Eskimos (or Inuit, as we were corrected) in Elizabeth I's London. Asians and blacks played an important part in British history, although until the racial enlightenment prejudice had held them back. Like America, Britain had embarked on a journey from driver of slaves to cultural imperialists to a society of racial equality. The final part of this journey was its invitation to Commonwealth citizens to settle here, and its eventual acceptance of a multi-racial society, beginning with the sailing of the *Empire Windrush* in 1948. The British establishment had long ago disregarded the Whig theory of history, which saw our island story as a steady journey from Popish tyranny through to Parliamentary democracy, as too triumphalist; they replaced it with an anti-racist reinterpretation of the story. Robert Winder, author of *Bloody Foreigners*, summed up the nation's historic journey as 'a constant tussle between kind and cruel impulses, an exhausting two-steps-forward-one-step-back dance towards the Utopian idea of a pluralist, happy, cosmopolitan country'.

England had been a dull, drab, repressed place before the arrival of the *Windrush*, which heralded a more exciting, vibrant, diverse society enriched beyond measure, as immigrants brought new sounds, flavours and influences. Britain had become the chicken tikka masala society, after the name of the popular dish invented in Birmingham by South Asian immigrants. Anyone who disagreed was considered to be a moral degenerate, viewed in the same way that Victorians saw the highly sexed, and indeed many of the most vocal opponents, from Oswald Mosley to John Tyndall, were sinister and strange, and their followers the ill-educated and socially inadequate rabble from the depths of the British gene pool.

After all, Britain has always been a nation of immigrants; mass immigration brings great economic benefits; diversity leads to dynamism and cross-fertilises cultural development; communities blend together and segregation declines over time; and besides which, those differences between groups enrich our lives, making people more civilised and better behaved; while opponents of such diversity are motivated by deep psychological flaws or irrational hatred.

This is the consensus we grew up with, and it has gone almost unchallenged in the media for over four decades, accepted by the most articulate and educated (and nicest) members of society. And yet all these assumptions about cultural and ethnic diversity are unproven at best, and have only become orthodoxy because of the huge taboo that has grown up around this subject. In fact, Britain has historically had little large-scale immigration, and recent changes are unprecedented; the economic benefits are small and short term; diversity leads to illiberalism and reaction, atomisation, inequality and crime; and British segregation is drifting towards American levels as its demography emulates that of the United States.

Mass immigration in England happened largely by accident. The initial benefit from the British point of view was economic, immigrants filling gaps in the labour market, but as this argument faded, and as the British wished to avoid unkindness towards their new compatriots, a largely unpopular change was justified through a rationale of the cultural and moral benefits of ethnic, religious and racial diversity. Diversity became not just the side effect of immigration policy but an official good in itself. Several decades on this has been internalised by the population, so that today the media judges the value of institutions from schools and universities to political parties and football clubs by their 'commitment to' diversity. Every state department and quango, every charity and NGO, every local government body and major company in the country touts diversity not as a possible marginal benefit or just a quirk, but as a morally positive end in itself. And by law all bodies must ensure they promote 'equality and diversity'. 'Diversity', as the Unesco statement puts it, 'is the very essence of our identity'.

As time has gone by, the British people have come to accept these changes, assured that to do otherwise is morally repugnant.

And mass immigration, as an overarching change, has indeed been welcomed by many people, while less so by others, with most having mixed feelings. Yet it is hard to acceptably articulate *any* scepticism, and because it has become unsayable, the argument against mass immigration has been abandoned by the political mainstream, both Left and Right. It is perfectly consistent to believe in the sovereignty of nations and the legitimacy of national identity, even to the extent of not wishing to alter its fundamental nature through massive demographic change, while feeling comfortable with intermarriage and multiple loyalties. There is much to be said for the view, first articulated during the Enlightenment, that the branches of the human race may join up again; as French philosopher Joseph Marie de Gérando put it, what more 'touching purpose' could there be than 'to re-establish the holy knots of universal society, than to meet again these ancient parents separated by a long exile from the rest of the common family, than to extend the hand by which they raise themselves to a more happy state'. But this process can only work organically, over a very long time, and between countries of relatively equal development, not brought about by social engineering.[1] What is now touted as 'diversity' is a distortion of the Enlightenment idea of universal humanity, not a slow and peaceful international blending of people but a rapid one-way mass movement with profound social consequences.

The rate of change in British society has been astonishing. In 2009 25 per cent of births in England and Wales were to foreign-born mothers. By 2011 over 22 per cent of secondary school pupils were from ethnic minorities, and 26.5 per cent of primary school children.[2] A majority of infants starting school in Greater London two years earlier were from visible minority, while within London proper, inside the A406, 53.4 per cent of primary school pupils speak English as a second language. According to the 2011 census white Britons now constitute a minority in Greater London, and only 16 per cent in the borough of Newham, while in neighbouring Barking and Dagenham a third of the white British population had left the borough in the previous 10 years. Across Britain there are now 7.5 million people born overseas, officially. Even if immigration were to stop tomorrow, London in twenty years' time will look vastly different to today, let alone to what it was 30 or 50 years ago. This is neither cosmopolitanism, nor organic immigration as the country has witnessed before – it is a sweeping change unseen in modern history. As Kevin Myers wrote in the *Irish Independent*, London has 'undergone a demographic transplant unlike that experienced by any European capital since the Fall of Constantinople' in 1453.

To even question whether this is either ethically right or beneficial to society is viewed as immoral, and yet no one would argue that the peoples of Uganda, Iraq or Sri Lanka should become an ethnic minority in their capital cities or countries. If that were to happen, as a result of European immigration, Englishmen and women who loved those countries and their people would be horrified by the unsettling changes inflicted on them, while still finding some of the more zealot nationalists unpleasant. Why is it different for England?

Diversity has indeed brought many benefits. There have been stunning individual success stories, while Indian, Chinese and African-Asian immigrants today out-perform other members of British society in almost every sphere, from school results to average earnings; and by the turn of the century the top 100 British Asians were worth a combined £10.6 billion.[3] But while this is pleasing, we are less willing to stomach the fact that other immigrant stories have not been so mutually beneficial, and that there are heavy costs. Many people who experience the downsides of diversity – in frightening neighbourhoods marred by crime, isolation and even communal tension – simply do not understand why they should be forced to live in alien surroundings as part of some grand social experiment in which they had no say; nor why they are condemned for not possessing the saintly qualities required to withstand it.

Mass immigration began in 1948 when a few hundred Jamaicans landed in Tilbury. It was not expected that many would follow, nor even that those who came would stay. The idea that the descendants of Commonwealth immigrants would one day comprise almost 30 per cent of British births, and a majority in many parts of the country, would have seemed to Clement Attlee's generation alarming, if it were not so absurd.

The year the Windrush arrived, London hosted the Olympics for the second time. In 2012 it did so once again, a sporting event designed, as the Olympics always are, to showcase a particular idea of a society. London's bid was explicitly multicultural, winning with a video entitled 'I Believe', that suggested that British identity is, by definition, multi-racial and multicultural (and the opening ceremony of the Games emphasised Britain's multi-racial nature, and included actors playing Windrush passengers). Enjoyable though the event was, is the Britain of 2012 a happier, more pleasant or even more progressive nation than the one that hosted the Austerity Olympics of 1948? Many people are not so sure.

The latest projections suggest that white Britons will become a minority sometime around 2066,[4] in a population of 80 million, which means that within little over a century Britain will have gone from an almost entirely homogenous society to one where the native ethnic group is a minority. That is, historically, an astonishing transformation. No people in history have become a minority of the citizenry in their own country except through conquest, yet the English, always known for their reticence, may actually achieve this through embarrassment.

And, of course, the best possible motives. For whatever their drawbacks, the policies that have brought about this situation have been done with the most noble of intentions, and from humanitarian, liberal principles. Even people concerned about immigration, and about the changing nature of their neighbourhoods, are moved by the individual stories of people who have escaped oppression and poverty to find a new life in our country, most of whom feel the utmost gratitude. It would be a strange sort of patriot who did not feel proud about their country in such circumstances.

But while most people feel uncomfortable about such a prospect, they have lost the means to articulate why it is a bad thing. Two questions arise from that projection – is it morally acceptable to wish to prevent it without being considered a racist, and would it make the country a better place? I will argue that, not only is it ethical to oppose such a change, but wise, for such a society is unlikely to be the liberal, secular, peaceful and relatively egalitarian society that the elderly of 2066 grew up in. So why are we doing it?

1

'The Leftish Language of Social Justice'
Labour's immigration experiment

As a player in the British General Election of 2010, Gillian Duffy cut an unlikely figure. The Rochdale grandmother had only popped out to the shops to buy a loaf of bread when she was accosted by Prime Minister Gordon Brown, doing what came unnaturally to him, that is engaging an ordinary person in conversation.

'My family have voted Labour all their life,' Mrs Duffy told the PM as he grinned manically. 'My father in his teens went to free trade hall to sing the Red Flag. Now I'm ashamed to even say I'm Labour.' Having collared him about crime, the state's treatment of handicapped children, pensions and university education, she said: 'Look, the three main things that I had drummed in when I was a child was education, health service and looking after people who are vulnerable. There are too many people now who aren't vulnerable but they can claim and people who are vulnerable can't get claim [sic].' She then added: 'You can't say anything about the immigrants because you're saying you're [trails off]... but all these eastern Europeans coming in, where are they flocking from?'

Saying you're... racist? Brown, having smiled and been courteous to Mrs Duffy, got in his car and said to one of his aides 'You should never have put me with that woman. Whose idea was that? Sue's I think. Everything she said – she's just a bigoted woman.' The hapless Prime Minister did not realise that his microphone was on, and the episode, straight from the television satire *The Thick Of It*, became the highlight of the election campaign.

But it also pushed the sensitive subject of immigration into the media spotlight, highlighting two points: that society was split not down but through the middle over immigration, with the poor far more hostile than the rich, and that people felt they were unable to speak about it. In over sixty years of enormous change such debate had been restricted by taboo, fear and mockery. Immigration is the most thought about and least talked about subject in British history.

Some people were prepared to defend the Prime Minister's description, and yet Gillian Duffy could quite reasonably look around her neighbourhood and wonder why she could not discuss immigration. She had seen her town change dramatically both socially and economically as a result of Asian and eastern European immigration. In just 20 years Rochdale's ethnic minority population had doubled and in nine of its schools 70 per cent of pupils spoke English as a foreign language, while in one the figure was 100 per cent. And yet, as Douglas Murray noted in *Standpoint* magazine: 'Of all the huge demographic and economic changes that have occurred, none has happened with the consent of Mrs Duffy or anyone else. Nothing she could have done would have stopped it. And yet, like the rest of the British people, Mrs Duffy apparently accepted this wholesale change to her home without recourse to violence or obvious hatred.'

Meanwhile she had witnessed the collapse of the values she, and millions like her, felt to be at their core: education, the health service and the welfare state. And yet the two issues were not unconnected; for all of these values were products of a national culture and a nation-state that many in power had come to see as the preserve of bigots.

The Hans Christian Andersen fairly tale 'The Emperor's New Clothes' has become a dreadful cliché in political discourse, but only because the story explains a truth about human nature so well: that intelligent, decent human beings can sometimes delude themselves into thinking that an innovation is beneficial when in fact it is deeply flawed. This happens in the world of cinema, fashion, literature and any other area where most people are uncertain of what defines excellence, and so look to others for guidance. It occurs in politics, too, and it is often the most intellectually gifted and influential of people who will metaphorically gaze at a naked man and tell the world (and themselves) that he is dressed in the finest gold threads.

Two years before the General Election a BBC2 *Newsnight* poll of white British adults found that 77 per cent felt that they could not criticise immigration without being labelled racist.[5] Their fear is not unjustified. Throughout the past thirty years the term has been thrown about increasingly casually, and become completely detached from any workable meaning. This has silenced people even as their own interests were under threat. The trade unions, fiercely anti-immigration in the 1960s, barely spoke out as enormous numbers of new arrivals depressed the wages of their members during the 2000s. Indeed the TUC, Unison, the GMB and the Communication Workers Union all backed a Government-sponsored pro-immigration pressure group, the Migration Alliance,[6] when immigration levels were at their peak.

It is because of this fear, and of a fear of offending friends, that there has never really been a debate about mass immigration. You can say it has been a good or a bad thing, and there are arguments on both sides, but you can never say that the British people were consulted. Most of the supposed arguments one hears – that questioning mass immigration might make people feel unwelcome, that it could even inspire violence, and give comfort to racists – are arguments for not discussing the issue, not *for* the argument itself.

Never in modern history has a free population simply suppressed discussion of a major issue. As Kevin Myers noted, the people of Britain and Ireland 'have taken a secret, Self-Denying Ordinance not to discuss immigration or race in any meaningful way'. In living memory barely a newspaper article, radio or television show has seriously questioned the diversity orthodoxy, and even in the intelligent Right-wing press scepticism has had to be couched in such a cryptic way that the paper's horoscopes are more candid. Repression can be healthy, or at least healthier than explosive anger, but not when the underlying problem it masks is growing. The ideal level of diversity in any state may depend on any number of factors, but as we head for a society in which a quarter of all people are a member of a visible ethnic minority, the costs surely outweigh the benefits.

The previous October a former speechwriter for Tony Blair, as well as Labour Home Secretaries David Blunkett and Jack Straw, made a startling admission. Writing in his *Evening Standard* column, Andrew Neather said that the huge increases in immigration under Labour's rule had been part of a deliberate strategy to 'rub the Right's nose in diversity and render their arguments out of date'.

According to Neather, Labour's relaxation of border controls was a conscious plan to encourage mass immigration, but that ministers were nervous and reluctant to discuss such a move publicly for fear that it would alienate its 'core working class vote'. He said that as a result the arguments for immigration focused on economic questions instead.

He recalled that the 'major shift' in immigration policy came after the publication of a policy paper from the Performance and Innovation Unit, a Downing Street think-tank based in the Cabinet Office, in 2001. Neather wrote a major speech for Barbara Roche, the then immigration minister, the previous year, which was largely based on drafts of the report. The final published version of her speech contained only the economic case for immigration, but 'earlier drafts I saw also included a driving political purpose: that mass immigration was the way that the Government was going to make the UK truly multicultural'. As Neather concluded: 'it didn't just happen: the deliberate policy of ministers from late 2000 until at least February last year… was to open up the UK to mass migration'. This was at a time when the Conservatives had dared to raise the issue of immigration, increasingly a concern to the public, and were heavily criticised by the media and race relations industry; in 2001 the Commission for Racial Equality publicised the names of MPs who refused to sign its pledge promising to avoid the use of language likely to incite prejudice or discrimination, whether 'blatantly or covertly', a measure described variously as 'blackmail' and 'intimidation' by Tory MPs. Although many refused to sign, the party was cowed into downplaying the issue of immigration.

Neather's admission initially did not cause much of a stir, and nor did the announcement in the same newspaper that the Metropolitan Police would now be routinely armed in three areas of London: Brixton, Tottenham and Harringay, in response to the large number of young men using firearms, marking the end of the British tradition of the unarmed constable. Both stories were overshadowed by the appearance of British National Party leader Nick Griffin on the BBC's flagship discussion show *Question Time* that night. Griffin's invitation was a triumph for a group that in 2001 had won just 0.2 per cent of the vote in the General Election and had been on the very fringes of British politics, the epitome of the Gilbert and Sullivan outfit that George Orwell characterised of British Fascists. Yet earlier that year the party had achieved their best ever result when they won two seats at the European Parliamentary elections, with Griffin elected to the North-West Region. This success came in response to an enormous increase in immigration, and despite considerable incompetence on their part, and an inability to jettison the politically suicidal neo-Nazi language of their past.

Labour's 'conscious plan' to change Britain was in force from 2000 and since that time the country has experienced unprecedented levels of immigration, barely declining even after the system was changed in 2008. A House of Lords Economic Affairs select committee later concluded: 'The increase in immigration since the late 1990s was significantly influenced by the Government's Managed Migration policies.' According to estimates quietly released by the Government in September 2009, some 2.3 million migrants had been added to the population since 2000.

Gross immigration officially stood at 489,000 per year between 1997 and 2006, including 391,000 non-Britons, and from 1997 to 2009 about 1.6 million people were granted permanent right of residence, over two-thirds of them from developing countries.[7] Immigration in 2004 alone was somewhere between 582,000 and 870,000, in terms of proportion to the population as large as the peak years to the United States before the First World War, when the huddled masses of Europe poured through Ellis Island.

People were admitted through various channels. In 2006, for example, 59,810 were given 'leave to remain' as a family member or dependant of a permanent UK resident, including 42,725 partners, 9,290 children, and 1,470 parents and grandparents.[8] There were non-Europeans entering as students (309,000 in 2006 alone, up from 44,800 in 1992), bringing with them 17,000 dependants. Many of the colleges they attended were fronts for immigration through which people could work and never leave; the Home Office turned a blind eye to a system that was obviously being abused, with some 159,000 students currently overstaying. The number of work permits also shot up, from below 30,000 in 1994 to 167,000 in 2006, on top of 48,500 dependents. In some years migration was responsible for 80 per cent of Britain's annual population growth, and overall net foreign immigration – the number of non-British citizens arriving, less the number leaving – rose from 221,000 in 2001 to 333,000 in 2007.

There was also the issue of asylum. By 2007 there was a backlog of 450,000 asylum seekers waiting to be processed,[9] who under UN treaties had the right to 'freedom from persecution' and 'family reunion'. The UN treaties, based on humane ideas that worked in the mid-20th century when the world was home to 2 billion people, most of them ruled by a handful of empires, had become unworkable in a world of 6.9 billion people, 200 countries and countless civil wars, insurgencies and famines, far easier travel and established non-European communities in major Western cities. On top of this there were illegal immigrants, the numbers of which no mortal knows. In 2001 Professor John Salt of University College London's Migration Research Unit put the figure at between 310,000 and 570,000;[10] MigrationWatch UK, a pressure group set up in 2002 to counter Labour's policy, gave an estimate of between 515,000 and 870,000.[11]

The face of England changed with revolutionary speed. Between 1998 and 2007 two million people left London for other parts of the country, while the city experienced net international migration of 1.8 million. Throughout this period of rapid growth journalists compared the number of projected immigrants arriving in Britain to 'a city the size of', using such varied places as Milton Keynes, Leicester and Birmingham, until by the end of Labour's rule the only city it could be compared to was London, such was the rapid expansion in Britain's overseas population. It was a demographic change not just unprecedented in British history, but in almost any country that has not suffered cata-strophic military defeat.

A Nation of Immigrants

In September 2000, a month before publishing the paper which did not highlight the social objectives of mass immigration, Immigration Minister Barbara Roche gave a speech to the Institute for Public Policy Research (IPPR) in which she said: 'This country is a country of migrants and we should celebrate the multicultural, multi-racial nature of our society, and the very positive benefits that migration through the centuries has brought.'

This was indeed the version of history that had become accepted as fact; a few years earlier, in 1996, the Committee for Racial Equality, forerunner to the Equality and Human Rights Commission, had published a pamphlet, *Roots of the Future: Ethnic Diversity in the Making of Britain*, in which it commented that 'People with different histories, cultures, beliefs, and languages have been coming here since the beginning of recorded time. Logically, therefore, everyone who lives in Britain today is either an immigrant or the descendant of an immigrant.'

Precedence is justification; something is right because it has always been, so it is important for the advocates of diversity to backdate the process to before 1948. Britain should be a nation of immigrants because it has always been a nation of immigrants, from the Normans and Flemish to the Huguenots. And yet almost nothing could be less true than the statement 'Britain is a nation of immigrants' – this is what makes the changes of recent years so startling.

Daniel Defoe's poem, 'The True-Born Englishman', is often used to illustrate the truth of England's multicultural history, telling of a country marked by various migrations through the years, the true-born Englishman being a hybrid of races. It was written in defence of the Dutch-born King William III, who in 1688 had seized the throne from his father-in-law, the British (but unacceptably Catholic) James II. Despite being invited by the ruling clique, William was a charmless character whose favouritism towards Dutch friends at court caused much resentment. His opponents often used his nationality as a stick with which to beat him, and Defoe was making a valid point that as the English, like every nation, have foreign blood themselves, so William's

Dutchness did not make him an illegitimate ruler.

William (who was, it should be added, paying Defoe) was also unpopular because he used the English throne to pursue his lifelong obsession, fighting Louis XIV. The fanatically Catholic French king, although a grandson of the Protestant Henri IV, was locked in battle not just with Protestants abroad but at home. The minority Huguenots had been granted toleration with the Edict of Nantes in 1598, following a series of especially brutal civil wars that had drenched France in blood. But believing them to be a 'state within a state' and an obstacle to his goal of *un roi, une loi, une foi* ('one king, one law, one faith'), Louis revoked their rights with the passing of the Edict of Saint-Germain. Hundreds of thousands of French Protestants fled to England, Ireland, Germany, South Africa and the American colonies. But while the Huguenots' contribution to English society was considerable, their iconic status as Britain's multicultural forebears is somewhat over-emphasised. Most historians believe that between 40,000 and 50,000 arrived in England over a century, well below one per cent of the English population, and equivalent today to 500,000 people. And they were, proportionately, the largest immigrant group in Britain between 1066 and 1945.

Far from being a nation of immigrants, Britain's genetic make-up has barely altered in millennia. There have been many waves of immigrants, and a non-European presence on these islands for some time, but in minute numbers. Bryan Sykes, Professor of Human Genetics at Oxford and author of *Blood of the Isles: Exploring the Genetic Roots of our Tribal History*, wrote that most British DNA dates back to the first Palaeolithic and Mesolithic settlers who crossed the English Channel around 10,000 years ago and: 'By about 6,000 years ago, the pattern was set for the rest of the history of the Isles and very little has disturbed it since... Overall, the genetic structure of the Isles [suggests] descent from people who were here before the Romans... We are an ancient people, and though the Isles have been the target of invasion... ever since Julius Caesar first stepped on to the shingle shores of Kent, these have barely scratched the topsoil of our deep-rooted ancestry.'

Most British DNA was probably in place even before the

arrival of the first Indo-European-speaking farmers from the Middle East around 4000BC. In the words of Stephen Oppenheimer, author of *Origins of the British*, 'the ultimate numerical impact of the Near Eastern Neolithic invasion on Europe was generally underwhelming... [affecting] no more than a third of European gene lines, and usually rather less.' In north-west Europe that figure falls to 5 per cent of indigenous maternal DNA lines. The male line is rather more modern, for obvious reasons – male invaders kill native males and marry females. But even so, as Oppenheimer concluded, 'three-quarters of British ancestors arrived long before the first farmers. This applies to 88 per cent of Irish, 81 per cent of Welsh, 79 per cent of Cornish, 70 per cent of the people of Scotland and its associated islands and 68 per cent (over two-thirds) of the English and their politically associated islands.'

These recent studies overturned the previously-held view that the English were largely descended from 5th-century Germanic invaders who displaced the natives, a belief known as the Anglo-Saxon genocide theory. But this is unlikely. According to Oppenheimer the English are only about 5.5 per cent Anglo-Saxon, although this varies by region, Norfolk being the most, at 15 per cent. In Professor Jared Diamond's famous phrase, it was very hard to replace a population before the medieval period and the proliferation of 'guns, germs and steel'.

The Vikings, who invaded in waves between the 8th and 11th centuries, comprise a very similar proportion of English DNA. In the late 9th century the Danes had almost overrun the land, conquering all but one of the Anglo-Saxon kingdoms until Alfred the Great stopped their advances. His grandson Athelstan went on to unite England in 927, making it one of the oldest nation-states in the world. And as David Conway, author of *A Nation of Immigrants?*, points out: 'the term "immigrant" tends to be reserved only for those who move from elsewhere to somewhere that is already inhabited by a people among whom there have grown up sufficient mutual affinities, relations, and bonds to qualify them for being considered a nation, and enough political organisation and unity as qualifies their territory as a state'. The people who arrived before 927 were colonisers, invaders, settlers or slaves – but not immigrants. The English of 1927 were more than 90 per cent the descendents of the English of 927, which makes it entirely untrue to talk of 'a nation of immigrants'. Even the Normans, despite wiping out the English aristocracy (there were only two native major landowners by the time William I died in 1087), never accounted for more than 5 per cent of British DNA at the very most, and were almost certainly closer to 1 per cent.[12]

And then, in the words of G M Trevelyan in his 1926 *History of England:* 'Since Hastings there has been nothing more catastrophic than a slow, peaceful infiltration of alien craftsmen and labourers – Flemings, Huguenots, Irish and others – with the acquiescence of the existing inhabitants of the island.' This peaceful infiltration began with the Jews of Rouen, who never totalled more than 5 or 6,000 before the bloodthirsty King Edward I had them expelled in 1290. Between then and the Jewish return under Charles II in the 1660s there were small communities of Italian bankers, Flemish weavers and Dutch brewers, and little else. Even in the early modern period immigration was uncommon. As Conway says, from the 16th century until the Second World War, 'very little of Britain's net increase in population can be attributed to immigration. Virtually all of its increase was a purely natural one.'

As for non-European immigration into Britain, it was extremely rare. Around 10,000 Africans, mostly men, came to Britain during the era of Atlantic slavery. But despite there being black or certainly north African Roman soldiers in Britain – something even the most ill-educated British state school pupil comes away knowing – there is minimal pre-Windrush African DNA in Britain.[13] Asian immigration was minute until the 1950s; between the wars around 1,000 Indian doctors lived in Britain, part of a sub-continental population of under 7,000. An Indian, Dadabhai Naoroji, was elected MP in 1892, and a black footballer, Ghanian-born Arthur Wharton, played for Sheffield United before the First World War, but these were the exceptions. There was also a Chinese population of under a thousand, but generally foreign and exotic populations were concentrated in port towns, especially in London, Liverpool, Cardiff and Tyneside, which had a 3,000-strong Yemeni population from the 1890s, the first settled

Muslim community in Britain. Altogether there were 20,000 to 30,000 non-whites in the country at the outbreak of hostilities in 1939, around 0.04 per cent of the population, including 5,000 Africans and West Indians. All these migrations were vastly different to what happened after the 1948 British Nationality Act, which heralded the start of mass immigration and especially from 1997, when it intensified: almost all were northern Europeans, coming in small numbers, often over very long periods; nor did any newcomers retain connections with their homelands, forcing them to integrate out of economic and social necessity.

At the end of the Second World War over 70 per cent of British DNA dated back more than 6,000 years on these islands, and between them the Celts, Anglo-Saxons, Vikings and Normans made less of a genetic impact than post-war immigration has. Genetically the generation born the year Britain hosted the 1948 Olympics may have been closer to the Britain of 4000 BC, before work on Stonehenge was begun, than the generation born during the 2012 Games; the DNA of the British people has been changed more in one lifetime than in the previous 6,000 years.

The Chicken tikka masala society

Labour's attempts at creating a truly multicultural society have unquestionably succeeded. But why did the Government do this? What drove them towards imposing such an enormous change on England, one that will have profound, long-lasting and irreversible effects? And why did the entire political class go along with it? What, indeed, are the benefits of diversity?

It was not just idealism. Labour has consistently won the votes not just of immigrants but of British-born minorities in recent elections; 68 per cent of ethnic minorities opting for the party in 2010, compared to just 16 per cent for the Conservatives[14] (compared to 29 and 36 per cent respectively of the population in total). Commonwealth citizens legally resident in Britain can vote in general elections as soon as they put their names on the electoral register – and under Labour an additional one million people from the New Commonwealth arrived. One of Jack Straw's first acts upon becoming Home Secretary in 1997 was to abolish the primary purpose rule, making it easier to bring spouses into the country. This had previously denied entry to all non-EU citizens who had been unable to prove that their primary purpose in having married a UK resident was not simply to gain entry and residency rights. The rule mainly affected Pakistani and Bangladeshi-Britons, for whom 'fetching marriages' were common: the change caused both populations to grow rapidly, and to make assimilation harder, each generation injected with a top-up of the ancestral homeland's culture, language and attitudes (and spouses who cannot speak English).

Straw was MP for Blackburn, which was, by 2009, 30 per cent Asian Muslim. On *Question Time* with Nick Griffin he boasted about the size of his constituency's minority population, and talked about how Indian Muslim soldiers had fought on the Western Front in the First World War. Although no one would wish to dishonour their memory, those men did not fight and die so that their descendants might one day come to dominate Lancashire towns. What the men of Blackburn who fought in 1914 would have thought of developments a century later went unasked. Some of their descendants were making their feelings clear – the BNP won its first seat on Blackburn council in 2002. More people left the town altogether.

After newspapers picked up on the *Standard* article, Straw described the claims as 'nonsense', while Neather argued that the point had been twisted, and that the main purpose of immigration policy was economic. However three months later it was revealed that MigrationWatch UK had obtained an earlier draft of that policy paper, circulated in October 2000, which showed that six of eight references to 'social' objectives were indeed cut from the version later published.[15] A draft report from the Cabinet Office, published under the title 'Migration: an economic and social analysis', showed that ministers had 'social objectives' in their immigration policy, but the removal of significant extracts suggested that they were nervous about publicising them.

The original report, later cut, had stated: 'The emerging consensus, in both the UK and the rest of the EU, is that we need a new analytical framework for thinking about migration policy if we are to maximise the contribution of migration to the

Government's economic and social objectives.' Chapter 4 of the report, focusing on the Government's aim to regulate migration 'in the interests of social stability and economic growth', also showed that they had both economic and social objectives: 'The more general social impact of migration is very difficult to assess. Benefits include a widening of consumer choice and significant cultural contributions. These in turn feed into wider economic benefits.' Also cut was this: 'In practice, entry controls can contribute to social exclusion, and there are a number of areas where policy could further enhance migrants' economic and social contribution in line with the Government's overall objectives.' In other words having immigration controls, which would almost certainly involve barring some non-Europeans, would be seen as racist.

The paper also showed that ministers were more aware of the risks of high immigration than they let on. One of the sections missing from the final report said: 'There is emerging evidence that the circumstances in which asylum seekers are living is leading to criminal offences, including fights and begging.' A second section warned: 'Migration has opened up new opportunities for organised crime.'

Andrew Green of MigrationWatch UK wrote in the *Daily Mail*: 'Reading between the lines of these documents it is clear that political advisers in Number 10, its joint authors, were preparing a blueprint for mass immigration with both economic and social objectives. None of this was in the Labour manifesto of 1997 or 2001.' And yet, he pointed out: 'Labour had always justified immigration on economic grounds and denied using it to foster multiculturalism.'

Immigration minister Phil Woolas said there was 'no open door policy on migration' and denied there was a conspiracy. Certainly it was not a conspiracy in the sense of men sitting in smoke-filled rooms (not the least because New Labour was opposed to smoking in public buildings, and banned it altogether in 2007) but only because there was no need to create a conspiracy – as everyone in a position of power held the same opinion. Diversity was a good in itself, so making Britain truly diverse would enrich it and bring 'significant cultural contributions', reflecting a widespread belief among the ruling classes that multiculturalism and cultural, racial and religious diversity were morally positive things whatever the consequences. This is the unthinking assumption held by almost the entire political, media and education establishment. It is the diversity illusion.

As Andrew Neather later told David Goodhart, the editor of *Prospect* magazine, for a BBC radio programme, diversity was part of the 'leftist language of social justice' and they saw 'ethnic minorities as essentially the standard bearers of the sort of social justice rather than the working class and traditionally the white working class. And that's definitely something which emerged in this country in the 80s, 90s.'[16] On the same programme Ed Owen, a former advisor to Jack Straw, said: 'For some in the Labour Party, and perhaps for understandable historical reasons, the very notion of having an immigration policy was regarded as a rather unsavoury feature and would be then dismissed by some as being cow-towing to the Right or whatever. And so there wasn't enough space, I think in retrospect, for people who were thinking about this issue in a very serious way to think and to articulate. That space was severely restricted.'

The question is: why was it restricted? And who benefited from this?

The consensus of those in power was that diversity is good, characterised, in the words of one author, as 'fusion cuisine, American hip-hop picking up Caribbean reggae and Indian bhangra beats', which 'brings us into contact with different cultures and ways of thinking, making our lives more varied and rewarding, broadening our minds, and enabling us to learn from others'.[17] In Norway middle-class liberals, called *snillister*, 'do-gooders', use the phrase *fargerik felleskap* – 'colourful community' – to describe their new world. In Britain it is called the 'chicken tikka masala society'. Indeed the analogy of human and culinary diversity is made repeatedly, for as Theodore Dalrymple points out, 'intellectuals, when they talk of multiculturalism as a doctrine rather than as sociological phenomenon, are thinking of couscous today, chicken sagwalla tomorrow, cassoulet the day after, and sashimi the day after that'.[18] Peter Skerry of the Brookings Institution in

Washington christened this syndrome Sushiology for those who believe 'the extraordinary variety and quality of cuisine now available in the United States as evidence of the unalloyed benefits from our racial and ethnic diversity'.

Our views on diversity are used to mark our moral worth, which is why people react so publicly and ostentatiously on the issue of immigration, far more so than with any other issue. When two BNP candidates were elected as MEPs in 2009 there was an outpouring of 'not in my name' protests on social networking sites such as Twitter, a chance for middle-class Londoners to say, in effect, that 'I am comfortable and generous enough to share my country with others'.

A belief in the benefits of a multicultural, multi-racial society is an article of faith in today's largely atheist society; to not believe is to not be in communion. And yet mass immigration, like the related issue of European unity, is one where conservatives have clear majorities, for like many newly-established faiths, it has not been accepted by the population at large. In a YouGov poll commissioned by Channel 4 earlier in 2009, only 38 per cent of people agreed with the question 'Britain has benefited in recent years from the arrival of people from many different cultures and countries';[19] 38 per cent disagreed. A clear majority of Conservative voters said no, with Labour and Liberal Democrat voters very marginally in favour; only Green Party supporters were strongly in agreement, despite the environmental impact of migration. (And on their economic platform the BNP and Green party are not dissimilar: both would object to a typical London restaurant, the Greens for the distance the food on the plate had taken to travel, the BNP for the distance the person serving it had.) The 'Rivers of Blood' survey, held by Ipsos-MORI the previous year, suggested that a quarter of people felt that 'my area doesn't feel like Britain any more because of immigration', double the 2005 figure, and 58 per cent felt that 'parts of this country don't feel like Britain any more because of immigration'. 59 per cent thought that 'there are too many immigrants in Britain', while almost two-thirds agreed that racial tension will result in violence. A 2002 poll for the BBC found that only 28 per cent of white Britons agreed that immigration had benefited British society over the previous 50 years, and 47 per cent believed it had damaged it (a belief shared by 22 per cent of black and Asian Britons).[20]

What makes this scepticism striking is that such beliefs have been beyond the bounds of acceptable discourse for over four decades, during which time barely a single newspaper article has questioned the orthodoxy (even if they might criticise immigration levels), let alone the broadcasting media, which is committed to celebrating diversity. Never in modern British history has such a large percentage of the population, if not the majority, held a range of views officially considered immoral. How did this happen? And why did opposition to diversity become associated with racism, poverty, stupidity and violence?

2

Rivers of Blood
How diversity became a status symbol

We need to go back to the first wave of mass immigration, and to the last few weeks of the Second World War, when British troops advancing on Kiel in northern Germany captured a ship named the *Monte Rosa*. Built in Hamburg in 1930, following the Nazi takeover in 1933, the *Monte Rosa* was used by party members for 'Strength Through Joy', the Third Reich's official workers' holiday programme. Later it became a troopship for the invasion of Norway, where it remained until 1945, when the vessel was transferred to help with the rescue of Germans escaping from East Prussia. In January 1947, after the *Monte Rosa's* capture, the Ministry of Transport renamed it the *Emperor Windrush* (after a tributary of the Thames). Today Windrush Square in Brixton, south London commemorates a vessel as famous as any of the Royal Navy's great battleships.

The *Windrush* made its historic journey from Kingston, Jamaica to Tilbury on May 24, 1948, with 492 West Indian men and one stowaway woman. Also on board, but kept separate from the Caribbeans, were a group of 60 Polish women who had circumnavigated the globe, along with hundreds of thousands of their countrymen, during the conflict. These war-weary survivors had sailed from Palestine to Mexico, having escaped from Siberia via India, Australia and New Zealand, and were bound for England. The Poles did not mix with the Jamaicans and were disdainful of their fellow travellers, according to accounts.

They were not the only ones. A Privy Council memo of June 15 to the Colonial Office stated that the British should not help the migrants: 'Otherwise there might be a real danger that successful efforts to secure adequate conditions of these men on arrival might actually encourage a further influx.' However Arthur

Creech Jones, Colonial Secretary, replied: 'These people have British passports and they must be allowed to land.' But, he added confidently: 'They won't last one winter in England.'[21] The Ministry of Labour was also unhappy about the arrival of the Jamaican men, minister George Isaacs warning that if they attempted to find work in Stepney or Camden, areas of the capital where there was serious unemployment, 'there will be trouble eventually'. He said: 'The arrival of these substantial numbers of men under no organised arrangement is bound to result in considerable difficulty and disappointment. I hope no encouragement will be given to others to follow their example.'

Soon after, 11 concerned Labour MPs wrote to Prime Minister Clement Attlee, warning: 'The British people fortunately enjoy a profound unity without uniformity in their way of life, and are blessed by the absence of a colour racial problem. An influx of coloured people domiciled here is likely to impair the harmony, strength and cohesion of our public and social life and to cause discord and unhappiness among all concerned.' Therefore the Government should 'by legislation if necessary, control immigration in the political, social, economic and fiscal interests of our people... In our opinion such legislation or administration action would be almost universally approved by our people.' The letter was sent on June 22. That same day the *Windrush* arrived at Tilbury.

Jamaicans had performed heroically during the War, and many soldiers and airmen had been stationed in England, defending the island from slavery. Their experiences were mixed; there was friendship and incredible warmth from some English people, and hostility from others, but there was not the same colour bar as existed in the US Army. After their sacrifices, Jamaicans had every reason to feel they had a right to work in England. The Windrush passengers, including several RAF veterans, were unaware of the fear and apprehension facing them, nor that HMS Sheffield had been sent to monitor the liner, with orders to send them back if any passengers made trouble. None of them did. Many felt enormous joy at visiting England, a feeling described by one passenger, the calypso singer Lord Kitchener, real name Aldwyn Roberts, who wrote 'London is the Place for Me' on board. He later recalled: 'The feeling I had to know that I'm going to touch the soil of the mother country, that was the feeling I had. You know how it is when a child, you hear about your mother country, and you know that you're going to touch the soil of the mother country, you know what feeling is that? And I can't describe it.'

Attlee replied to his worried backbenchers on July 5: 'I think it would be a great mistake to take the emigration of this Jamaican party to the United Kingdom too seriously.' And Creech Jones wrote: 'I do not think that a similar mass movement will take place again because the transport is unlikely to be available, though we shall be faced with a steady trickle, which, however, can be dealt with without undue difficulty.' The *Windrush* passengers had no idea that they were at the forefront of the biggest social change in British history. None of Britain's political leaders, especially not from the Labour Party, had any notion that immigration would grow to massive proportions; it would have been inconceivable and appalling to them to imagine that white Britons would one day become a minority in Birmingham or London, even stranger that Labour would become the champions of such a development.

Besides which, Commonwealth immigration – the influx of imperial subjects who were owed natural rights by their mother country – was initially dwarfed by the 200,000 or so Europeans, the majority Poles, who had arrived since Hitler took power. Among them were tens of thousands of Jews from Germany, Austria and Czechoslovakia who had fled before 1939, as well as about 15,700 former enemy prisoners of war.[22] But Britain employed nothing like as many aliens as its enemy; foreigners held a third of all jobs in Germany during the war, seven million in total, the largest example at the time of mass immigration in European history. Yet even with European arrivals, Britain for the moment remained relatively unchanged. In 1951 only 3 per cent of the population had been born outside the UK, and this included half a million Irish – Britain was still, despite the turbulence of a conflict that had shaken the world, much the same. In 1949 only a further 39 Jamaicans came over.

Britain's first wave of mass immigration came about through a serious of unlikely and unintended events. The Old Commonwealth Dominions were in the process of clarifying their nation status, and in 1946 Canada passed a citizenship law, enacted on January 1, 1947. Previously, all Canadian nationals were de facto British citizens, but the new law forced Britain to clarify exactly which Commonwealth subjects were allowed to live here. And so the 1948 Nationality Act allowed entry to the British mainland for those 'who hold a UK passport or a passport issued by the Government of the United Kingdom'. It was partly sloppy lawmaking, partly a fading imperial paternalism which saw Britain as head of a family of nations, and it allowed the peoples of the doomed Empire free access. Although the law introduced a liberal immigration policy for the next 14 years, it was, according to historian Randall Hansen, 'never intended to sanction a mass migration of new Commonwealth citizens to the United Kingdom' and 'nowhere in parliamentary debate, the Press, or private papers was the possibility that substantial numbers could exercise their right to reside permanently in the UK discussed'.[23]

By 1951 some 1,500 West Indians were arriving annually. Many did not like their new home, as Daniel Lawrence found when he polled the immigrants of Nottingham in 1960s.[24] Among the responses were: 'We never realised that it would be so different... It was a big shock... We was told all lies back home... I was not expecting it.' In Andrea Levy's novel *Small Island* Jamaican war veteran Gilbert Joseph discovers on finally meeting the mother country that she is a 'filthy tramp': 'Ragged, old and dusty as the long dead... She offers you no comfort after your journey. No smile. No welcome. Yet she looks down at you through lordly eyes and says, "Who the bloody hell are you?"'

E R Braithwaite, a Guyanese-born RAF fighter pilot and author of an autobiographical novel entitled *To Sir, With Love*, deplored the British people 'demonstrating the same racism they had so roundly condemned in the Germans'. Braithwaite, despite a physics degree from Cambridge, could only get a teaching job at a sink school in east London. He remembered: 'I tried everything – labour exchanges, employment agencies, newspaper ads – all with the same result. I even advertised myself mentioning my qualification and the colour of my skin, but there were no takers. Then I tried applying for jobs without mentioning my colour, but when they saw me the reasons given for turning me down were all variations of the same theme: too black…' In a harrowing episode of *To Sir, With Love,* later turned into a film starring Sidney Poitier, he recalled how the only mixed race boy in the school lost his mother. The other children raised money for a wreath but refused to take it to the boy's home for fear of being seen. He wrote: 'It was like a disease, and these children whom I loved without caring about their skins or their backgrounds, they were tainted with the hateful virus which attacked their vision, distorting everything that was not white or English.'

In 1955 the British Government concluded that there was no race problem, but the colour bar was an embarrassment, not least for foreign relations. Back in 1943 cricketer Learie Constantine had been turned away from the Imperial Hotel, which sullied the atmosphere of a sport that was supposed to teach the peoples of the empire about gentlemanliness.

But there was a practical need to stay, despite the cold weather and even colder reception in some places, as remittances soon became Jamaica's second largest source of income. Elsewhere the economic benefits of emigration were even more pronounced; Montserrat in 1951 earned 10 times as much income from cotton as from remittances, but by 1960 remittances were worth four times as much as the island's principle crop. West Indian immigration had doubled in 1952, increased to 10,000 in 1954 and to 24,473 in 1955, peaking at 26,441 the following year. By 1958 the West Indian population was touching 100,000. From there it continued to rise, to between 210,000 and 250,000 in 1961, 400,000 in 1965 and more than 500,000 in 1971.

Old Debts

Whatever difficulties faced by both immigrants and natives adjusting to the changes, the successful establishment of such a community in a cold and distant island was something of an achievement for both. While many West Indians had a strong attachment to Britain, the feeling to many was mutual, especially in light of the common sacrifice that the peoples of the Empire and Commonwealth had made in forging a world where aggression would be replaced by mutual respect.

Indians could also claim to be owed a debt of gratitude. During the Second World War three million had fought for the British Empire, and many more had suffered, with three million in Bengal alone dying during the famine of 1943. In 1947 the Raj came to an end, as did a million lives, as the country was partitioned between Muslim Pakistan and predominantly Hindu India. Fourteen million crossed the border, while 30,000 Anglo-Indians, people of mixed descent, headed for England, many leaving palatial homes in the Raj for small, terraced houses in a cold, damp country where few spoke English as well as they did.[25]

Newly independent countries such as Pakistan were helped by the recently-established World Bank, which among other things loaned it money to build the Mangla Dam in Mirpur, in the northeast of the country, drowning 250 villages. This coincided with a labour shortage in the textile factories of Leeds and Bradford, a case of serendipitous timing for the Mirpuris who took leave of their new nation to make a new life in Yorkshire. The initial migration of men was followed by that of their families, so that by 1968 some 50,000 dependants had joined their menfolk, with the Indian, Pakistani and Bangladeshi populations in Britain all increasing ten-fold in the 1960s. Punjabi Sikhs settled in Birmingham and Leeds, the latter because of one man, Darshan Singh, who had arrived in 1938 and peddled goods around Yorkshire. Southall, Hounslow and other areas of Middlesex were a natural choice of destination for Punjabi and Gujarati migrants because of its proximity to Heathrow airport. Bengalis settled in Tower Hamlets, near the docks, 95 per cent of them from Sylhet, the region where the Royal Navy had recruited its chefs; there were Sylheti chefs in London as far back as 1873, and there were already twenty Indian restaurants in London in 1940, most of them run by Sylhetis.

Different immigrant groups had different mindsets. West Indians already saw themselves as British, and this made for both a greater level of integration and of disappointment. Before arrival 87 per cent of Jamaicans said they felt British, and 86 per cent said it was fine if their children felt English. Only 2 per cent of Indians and Pakistanis felt the same, and just 6 per cent were happy to accept their children as English.[26] When black immigrants experienced the colour bar it came as a greater psychological blow.

There were also 10,000 Hungarians fleeing Communism in 1956, and later up to 50,000 Greek Cypriots came over at independence in 1960, who were followed by 11,000 Turkish Cypriots from 1974. There were also 100,000 Italians and 40,000 Maltese, and on top of this several thousand Hong Kong Chinese. And further migration followed de-colonisation in Africa; Kenya became independent in 1963 under Jomo Kenyatta, a former student of Moscow University and a Left-wing intellectual at LSE, who had been imprisoned by the British for helping Mau Mau leaders. In 1967, just four years after independence, Kenyatta began the persecution of the country's 200,000 Asians, who were soon entering Heathrow airport at the rate of 1,000 a month, increasing to such an extent that some 13,000 arrived during January and February 1968 alone. The Asians were descendents of late 19th and early 20th century Indian merchants brought over by the British, and would have had the right to live in India. But under the terms of Indian independence Britain had agreed that Diaspora Indians could look to it for protection; it was argued, with good reason, that as Britain had moved them, the British should have responsibility for their safety. In 1963 Conservative Home Secretary Henry Brooke had said it would be out of the question to deny them entry, 'tantamount to a denial of one of the basic rights of a citizen, namely to enter the country of which he was a citizen'. Some 20,000 ended up in Britain.

The situation was even worse in neighbouring Uganda, where in January 1971 General Idi Amin Dada deposed President Milton Obolte and began deporting Indians as part of his all-round campaign to drive the country to ruin; he said he'd had a dream in which he had given Asians three months to leave, and dreams sometimes do come true. In August 1972 Amin declared 'economic war' against Uganda's 80,000 Indians and smaller number of Europeans. That month he expelled 60,000 Asians who were not Ugandan citizens, and who on independence had (wisely) retained their British passports. He later expelled most of the others. Some 28,000 settled in Britain, and others went to India, Pakistan, Australia, Canada and the US. As Robert Mugabe was to do to white Zimbabweans a generation later, Amin stole the Asians' property and handed it over to his supporters. The economy collapsed, and Amin grew increasingly eccentric, naming himself King of Scotland along with other grandiose titles,[27] and expressing his admiration for Hitler.

There were mixed feelings in England, pity and sympathy, resentment and fear. Leicester Council, which was already housing Kenyans, took out adverts pleading with Ugandans not to head there. But once again Britain felt morally obliged to offer them a new home. The *Economist*'s cover of August 19 presented an open letter to the immigrants: 'We know many of you didn't really want to leave your homes and jobs in Uganda. You know we didn't really want you to come before because we have problems with homes and jobs here. But most of us believe that this is a country that can use your skills and energies… You will find that we, like other countries, have our bullies and misfits. We are particularly sorry about those of our politicians who are trying to use your troubles for their own ends. And we're glad your British passport means something again.'

This was a stirring statement. As applied to a few thousand victims of chauvinism it represented the pinnacle of enlightened liberalism. As applied to the migration of millions upon millions, the majority of them, unlike the Ugandans, unskilled and unprepared for life in the West, it was an invitation to disaster. Indeed the Ugandan Asians were the sort of immigrants that most countries would be willing to kidnap. Only 12 per cent were not skilled, and while a Uganda Resettlement Board was established to help the new arrivals find their feet, it did not take long for them to stand up.

Between 1951 and 1991, the African-Caribbean and South Asian population of Great Britain increased from 80,000 to three million. As immigration rose governments passed various laws to restrict it, although it could be argued that they did not significantly stop the flow, while at the same time giving the impression to immigrants already here that they were not welcome. Other laws had unintended consequences. The Commonwealth Immigration Act 1962, which permitted only those with government-issued employment vouchers to settle, closed the door on automatic entry, but left it closing long enough for many more to rush in. Between 1960 and 1962 more immigrants entered Britain than between 1900 and 1959, including 80,000 in the six months leading to the act, rushing to cross the drawbridge before it closed. But far from being draconian, the act reduced the quota to 45,000 a year, with no country allowed to take more than twenty-five per cent of the vouchers, which still amounted to an extra one per cent increase per decade. By the mid-1960s there was considerable concern among the native population.

Opposition to immigration initially came more from Labour politicians than from Conservatives. Sir Harold Wiles, Deputy Permanent Under-Secretary, told a colleague in March 1948 that he felt that the implications of the decision to import 'coloured colonials' had not been thought through; he was in no doubt it meant that the 'coloured element will be brought in for permanent absorption into our own population'. TUC general secretary Frank Cousins said: 'We cannot afford that these people should be allowed unrestricted entry into this country.' And Conservative objections did not just come from Right-wing headbangers. Tory peer Lord Altrincham, who warned that a 'Borneo head hunter' might one day sit on the red benches, was a liberal Conservative who wished to abolish the monarchy, and who later became a *Guardian* columnist for 10 years.

As a party the Tories were generally relaxed about the prospect of further immigration. Quintin Hogg recalled: 'We thought that there would be free trade in citizens, that people would come and go, and that there would not be much of an overall balance in one direction or the other.' This, of course, was consistent with the classical liberal tradition of the Conservative Party, but it was out of touch with the realities of a world in which there were vast gulfs between rich and poor nations, an unprecedented population explosion, and where long-distance travel had become possible for the first time for hundreds of millions of people. Many others took the view articulated by Tory MPs David Maxwell Fyfe who said: 'We are proud that we impose no colour bar restrictions... We must maintain our great metropolitan tradition of hospitality to everyone from every part of the empire.'

All of this was historically accurate. Britons did not have the racial mentality of Americans, and many Americans were shocked by the lack of a racial consciousness among their hosts. As General Eisenhower remarked: 'The small-town British girl would go to a movie with a Negro soldier quite as readily as she would go with anyone else, a practice that some of our white troops could not understand.' In Britain racist ideas had also often met opposition from the traditional class system, a stronger division in a monocultural society tied to an international system of monarchy. This could be repressive, but it acted as a break on the worst aspect of racism. Douglas Lorimer, author of *Colour, Class and the Victorians,* wrote: 'Like their eighteenth-century forbears, the mid-Victorians accepted an individual black according to his ability to conform to English social conventions. A dark complexion did not necessarily signify lowly social status... In the absence of any consensus over the significance of racial differences, mid-Victorians simply treated each individual black according to their evaluation of his social standing.'

Britons might take pride in this, yet there is certainly a strong correlation between a society's racial ratio and its attitude towards race, a scale moving from Britain to Canada at one end to the northern and then southern United States to South Africa (and beyond that, the even more racist Rhodesia). British girls could take black guys to the cinema because, being so rare, they did not constitute a community or, therefore, a threat. But on the part of the British natives, the growing trickle of Commonwealth immigration became increasingly unpopular. By 1958 over 80 per cent of the population favoured immigration controls, and that figure changed little over the next decades. Few Britons may boast about this, but until that point no people in history had voluntarily welcomed such large numbers of different people into their homeland, and indeed their neighbourhoods, with any enthusiasm, and this is the same whether the natives have pale or dark skin. White liberals who experience friendliness in developing nations while on their travels lament that such people in Britain are not accorded the same warmth, yet a visitor – a rich one, especially – comes in a different guise to an immigrant.

Yet although these developments were unprecedented and unpopular, debate over immigration effectively ended on April 20, 1968, when Shadow Defence Secretary Enoch Powell gave a notorious speech in Birmingham, in which he warned that Britain's immigration policy was 'like watching a nation busily engaged in heaping up its own funeral pyre'.

Even without this and a second speech made in November that year, Powell would have been a controversial figure. A proto-Thatcherite – his monetarist views at odds with the Keynesian consensus – his opposition to Britain's membership of the Common Market, a subject over which he eventually resigned, would also have given him prophet status in certain circles. Instead he is most associated with his views on immigration, and his role as hate figure is part of the founding myths of multicultural Britain.

Powell was blamed for giving racism and racial violence a respectable face, and became a pariah. To British ears no Christian name aside from Adolf has become so associated with one man, and with the power to stir emotions; this obscure, Biblical name became shorthand for unacceptable discourse on race. Polite society especially disliked him because, unlike other prominent opponents, he could not be accused of being a Fascist or a crank, or of lacking intellectual weight. A classics scholar with a spectacular Army career, he was the only man to rise from private to brigadier during the Second World War, and had spent much time in India and was familiar with its people and culture. Powell had fairly strong anti-racist credentials; he saved a German-Jewish professor in 1939 by arranging a British Visa,[28] and as a young MP embarrassed his own government by protesting its inhumane treatment of Kenyan prisoners.[29] He once refused to stay in a colonial hotel until it allowed an Indian comrade to break its colour bar. But this made it all the more unacceptable that he had behaved in an indecent manner by appearing to pick on the underdog.

The address for which he became so reviled is known as 'the Rivers of Blood' speech, although he never used the phrase. His actual words, quoting Virgil's *Aeneid*, was 'As I look ahead, I am filled with foreboding; like the Roman, I seem to see "the River

Tiber foaming with much blood".' He was inspired to speak after meeting a middle-aged constituent who told him he wished to encourage his children to emigrate, for 'in this country in fifteen or twenty years' time the black man will have the whip hand over the white man'. He had also received a letter from a woman in Northumberland about a friend – a never-identified elderly lady living in Wolverhampton, Powell's constituency – who felt intimidated by immigrant teenagers. But he was also motivated to speak by the Labour Government's Race Relations Bill, which would have made it illegal for employers to discriminate on grounds of race. Powell felt it to be an unjustified, unprecedented intrusion into people's right to free association.

Powell received overwhelming support from the general public, with between 67 and 82 per cent of people in every national opinion poll expressing agreement,[30] and close to 90 per cent in some towns. Around 100,000 letters were sent to the MP, with only 800 expressing disapproval. Smithfield meat porters demonstrated in favour, hundreds of dockers marched on Parliament, and Wolverhampton factory workers expressed strong support for Powell's speech, as did members of the Transport and General Workers Union, which petitioned parliament in his support. On top of this 300 of 412 Tory constituency associations expressed agreement with his sentiments. According to Michael Heseltine, then a junior MP: 'If Enoch Powell had stood to be prime minister, he would have had a national landslide.'[31]

But the media, and most politicians, were outraged. The *Times* called it an 'evil speech' and an incitement to racial hatred. One Labour MP said he would refer Powell to the Director of Public Prosecutions, while Liberal leader Jeremy Thorpe said he should be arrested for incitement. Tory leader Edward Heath considered the speech 'racialist in tone' and forced him to resign the following day. Powell is still persona non grata in the party, so much so that in 2007 a Conservative candidate for parliament was forced to resign by David Cameron after writing an opinion piece for the *Wolverhampton Express and Star* in which he said 'Enoch Powell was right'.[32] And yet most Tory voters probably still agree with Powell's views, if perhaps not the tone in which he expressed them.

Afterwards, the words 'Enoch was right' became not just a

catchphrase for anti-immigration sentiment, but an ironic term used to mock bone-headed racism. And yet, whatever the incendiary nature of his words, in one sense he was right. He shocked an audience with a second speech later that year by quoting a projection that Britain's non-white population would grow from its current total of 1.2 million to 4.5 million in 2002 (in 2001 it was 4,635,296). In 1970 he went further, telling voters in Wolverhampton that between a fifth and a quarter of their city, as well as that of Birmingham and inner London, would be non-white one day. According to the 2011 census the figures were 27.5 per cent, 36.7 per cent and 45 per cent respectively.

Powell predicted that 'whole areas, towns and parts of towns across England will be occupied by sections of the immigrant and immigrant-descended population,' and warned of 'future grave but, with effort now, avoidable evils' – a duty which most politicians, as Powell said, 'knowingly shirk.'

But most people in a position of influence believed he should not have raised the subject, that he used violent language, and that his romantic vision of England would become dangerous in the hands of the less well-educated. His speech, in the words of Roy Hattersley, stirred some 'not very thinking people' – yet these were often Labour people, whose presumably leaden brains were also stirred by socialism. Powell himself predicted being blamed for 'self-fulfilling prophecies' when he said 'people are disposed to mistake predicting troubles for causing troubles and even for desiring troubles'. Yet while Powell viewed racial conflict through the prism of India, in which conflict and ethnic rivalry was the tragic consequence of different peoples living together, most intellectuals saw it through the recent history of Germany, where extreme, flag-waving nationalists had launched an unprovoked attack on an ancient and peaceful minority.

Diversity has never been seriously debated since, partly because of a fear of violence. Just a week after the airing of Powell's speech, the *Times* reported an incident in Wolverhampton where 14 white youths chanting 'Powell' and 'Why don't you go back to your own country' attacked a West Indian christening party. The child's grandfather, who was slashed across the face, told the press: 'I have been here since 1955 and nothing like this has happened before. I am shattered.' Powell's words certainly led to immigrants and non-whites feeling a heightened sense of anxiety, and some people took it as a green light to be as unpleasant as they wished. Yet there was no pogrom in England, and no other serious incident has been attributed to his speech. Supporters of Powell sent toilet tissue and bricks to his critics, including the local paper, but Powell was equally if not more harassed and intimidated. His constituency home was a target for attacks, policemen were forced to guard his house in London, family holidays had to be taken abroad, and swastikas were daubed on the constituency party office. His speech coincided with the student unrest of the late 1960s; there was a bomb threat at Essex University where he was due to address the university's Conservative Association, while another led to the withdrawal of an invitation to speak at Birmingham University, and a planned visit to his old school was abandoned for fear of disruption. An edition of *Any Questions* had to be moved, and outside opponents chanted 'disembowel Enoch Powell'.

However the divisiveness, the ugly racist sentiment, and the fear that the speech inspired, convinced many that any expressed opposition to change was too explosive. The logical conclusion of this argument was that it was better that the subject was never raised again, because the British are just too brutish to be allowed to discuss immigration.

It is partly for this reason that Far-Right parties are given a cordon sanitaire not applied to the Far-Left, and yet the idea that discussing immigration will lead some ill-educated psychopath somewhere to attack an Asian family relies on an almost chaos-theory view of hate crimes, one that is only ever applied to Right-wingers.[33] (In a similar way Evangelical Christians can be prosecuted for criticising homosexuality on the grounds that two hundreds miles away a gay man is murdered by some hoodlums, none of whom have darkened the door of a church or are familiar with Leviticus.) But if that's the case, does not the resentment espoused by Left-wing politicians lead to hate crimes against wealthy and middle-class people, from the countless incidents of student-bashing to vandalism against expensive cars? Many Islamic radicals are politically awakened by mainstream Left-wing

Western thinkers critical of the US and Israel, before their individual paths lead them to more extreme positions. It is itself totalitarian to dismiss peacefully-expressed views on the grounds that some unhinged mind might interpret them violently.

Status Signifiers

Racism has often inspired violence, yet one can have a principled opposition to demographic change, and still hate violence in all its forms. Nevertheless the association was cemented in the public consciousness by certain events. One of the most famous incidents, the Notting Hill race riots, occurred in 1958, when 400 Teddy boys descended on the west London slum to go 'nigger hunting'. Newspaper reports of the time show that the British public – most of whom were opposed to mass immigration – were disgusted by the hooliganism. But the riots helped to confirm the idea that because Teddy Boys and other social misfits hated immigrants, then mass immigration must in itself be moral, and to oppose it pandering to the worst elements in society. The *Observer* commented afterwards that to restrict immigration would be 'shameful' and 'the easy way out'. But it is still a fallacy to suggest that, because nasty or violent people oppose something, it should be supported. Among those objecting to bankers' bonuses one will find some of the most ignorant and violent members of society, whose hostility is based entirely on envy and ignorance. Does that nullify the case for controls on casino capitalism, in the same way that the ignorance of ill-educated racists nullifies any arguments against excessive immigration? The argument must stand or fall on its own merits.

Even the stereotypical image of the racist skinhead is misleading. Skinheads were often violent and unpleasant, but they were not necessarily racist. Emerging in the late 1960s, the skinhead movement was itself an example of cultural fusion, an import from Jamaica influenced by the rude boy subculture. Far from being racist, as skinhead photographer Gavin Watson recalled: 'There were black kids in our skinhead gang. My older brother was gay. My girlfriend was mixed race. We were as far from being Right-wing as you could get.'[34] It was not racism that motivated skinheads, but anger, criminality, poverty, alienation or a lack of education. Violent skinheads attacked outsiders, or people whom they viewed as weak; Pakistanis might easily fit the bill, but as with most racist attackers down the years, skinheads were just as happy to attack white people. Anti-social or violent individuals often show more hostility and aggression towards members of other groups, but they also display greater violence towards members of their own. This does not mean that diversity makes them less anti-social.

Indeed the skinhead craze was partly a consequence of white flight. The title of cultural critic Dick Hebdige's influential 1982 essay on the subject of skinheads and working-class alienation, 'This is England! and They Don't Live Here', was inspired by middle-class hypocrisy over diversity. As he explained later: '"They" does not refer to immigrants but educated, middle-class, white professionals who were deserting the rundown inner city areas skinheads shared with non-white immigrants.'[35] If anything skinheads were an example of how the fusion of two cultures can sometimes have negative effects, helping to heighten a sense of aggressive masculinity.

Opposition to immigration also came to be associated with poverty and failure. In the words of Tim Finch, head of migration for the Institute for Public Policy Research, people who thought mass immigration 'progressive' had a tendency 'to characterise our opponents as nasty, stupid and backward. By so doing, we give ourselves license to either patronise or ignore them.' The media characterised opposition to newcomers as largely coming from the poor and/or poorly educated, and partly out of embarrassment at being associated with such social deviants, intelligent people who opposed immigration for perfectly legitimate reasons kept quiet.

Certainly the poor have consistently shown more hostility to immigration. A survey of 2,000 adults in May 1948 found that only 19 per cent thought Britain had been 'selfish' towards colonials, but this figure was much higher among the more educated.[36] 'The guilt factor, in other words, was still the preserve of a privileged minority,' as *Austerity Britain* author David Kynaston wrote. A social survey in 1951 concluded that 'antipathy to coloured people in this country is probably considerable amongst at least one-third of the population', and that it was especially common among the elderly, the poor and those in low-status occupations. Opposition to immigration, and therefore racism, became associated with poverty partly because the poor suffer most of the downsides. But if mass immigration was retribution for Britain's colonialism, it was imposed on the descendants of the people who received the least from the sweat of slaves. As Julie Burchill once put it: 'That the working class might have a thoroughly legitimate reason for becoming more agitated about immigration than the tolerant middle class, with their health insurance, private schools and comfy cars, is never considered by these usually oh-so-caring types.'[37]

And the link between poverty and racism is not clear-cut; the poorest socio-economic class of whites are 12 times as likely to have mixed-race children as middle-class whites; typically working-class white Londoners have more black friends than the wealthy (in the case of Asian friends the reverse is generally true). Education and wealth does not make one less racist in our actual behaviour; it merely insulates from the worst aspects of diversity. In fact it is often the lower-middle class who express the most hostility to diversity, perhaps because racism can be the other side of the coin of respectability, and these are the people who most object to crime, noise, disruption and poor schools, all problems associated with immigration; they often come from areas with high levels of immigration, but cannot afford the wealthier areas where diversity is more of a blessing. Many of the Far-Right's leaders come from lower-middle class backgrounds. But despite poor whites being more likely to live in multi-racial neighbourhoods, send their children to multi-racial schools, and to have multi-racial children, the idea that there is a correlation between racism and poverty has stuck.

In Tom Wolfe's *The Bonfire of the Vanities* a New York couple with an inferiority complex towards their well-spoken British nanny are relieved when she makes a racist outburst. 'Kramer and his wife looked at each other. He could tell she was thinking the same thing he was. "Thank God in heaven! What a relief! They could let their breaths out now. Miss Efficiency was a bigot. These days the thing about bigotry was, it was undignified. It was a sign of Low Rent origins, of inferior social status, of poor taste. So they were the superiors of their English baby nurse, after all.'"

Liberalism on race (and many other subjects) is a status signifier. As Australian sociologist Katherine Betts found in her book, *Ideology and Immigration,* the university-educated are far more likely to favour immigration, and being pro-immigration was 'part of a cluster of values defining social status for Australian intellec- tuals'. The crime of that so-called 'bigoted woman', Gillian Duffy, was not to break any code of common decency. She did not say anything unpleasant or dehumanising about immigrants; it seems extremely unlikely that someone with her impeccable Labour credentials and history of working with the less fortunate would ever behave inhumanely to anyone on account of their skin colour or ethnic background. All she did was mention immigration, which in modern British society is the most non-U thing one can do, revealing low social status and lack of social nous. If *Pygmalion* were performed on the stage today Eliza Doolittle would not blurt out 'not bloody likely' but 'bloody immigrants'. That would be the most shocking thing to say in polite circles.

Liberal views have become what Geoffrey Miller in *The Mating Mind* called 'status signifiers' – a display of wealth and education. In this sense racial tolerance may be a fitness and wealth indicator, so that 'Where chimpanzees evolved leadership, humans evolved the more advanced capacity of moral vision, including the passionate articulation of social ideals concerning justice, freedom, and equality. Moral vision is sexually attractive, and may have been generated by sexual selection.' No undergraduate ever reduced his chances with the opposite sex by condemning racism. (Politics is highly social, which is why, once a stance becomes seen as unat- tractive, however logical its arguments, socially skilled men will begin to abandon it until it becomes associated with misfits and weirdos).

Anti-racist attitudes are the modern human equivalent of the peacock's tail. In contrast racism is very unattractive, which is why the vast majority of internet daters who only date members of their own race (a very large proportion) advertise a willingness to see anyone.[38] Personal diversity, in friendship circles, also suggests other qualities; cosmopolitanism and tolerance are signals of social success, and having friends from various different backgrounds suggests not only general popularity but also that people of other races are able to overcome their fear or hostility in your special case. And having the right attitudes to race, and being aware of the correct current terminology, also suggests contemporariness, a highly attractive quality.

Cultural self-denigration, towards British patriotism or Western civilisation in general, is a high-status signifier, since such attitudes are taught at universities and in higher cultural circles. Roger Scruton called such self-hate 'oikophobia',[39] from the Greek for home, and describes it as 'a stage through which the adolescent mind normally passes' but one in which 'intellectuals especially tend to become arrested'. Since the poor, the weak and the most socially inadequate rely on their attachments to institutions, disrespect for those social institutions – the monarchy, the Church, the nation – becomes a sign of high status. Admitting to pride in country, crown or faith is akin to admitting to needing a social crutch. (The one social institution that the middle-classes do not sneer at is football, although its social function as a crutch is similar.)

Opposition to mass immigration also became associated with neo-Fascism and racial supremacists. Some opponents of immigration are, of course, white supremacists, but most are not, and when the centre-Right gave up on the debate, the more racist elements, those who cared the most, came to the forefront. The National Front was formed in 1967, and led by A K Chesterton, cousin of G K, and a journalist who had been driven to drink by his experiences in the trenches. Chesterton had formerly led the pressure group League of Empire Loyalists, which actively campaigned against non-white immigration to the UK during the 1950s and 1960s. Although Chesterton was a former member of the British Union of Fascists, the LEL was more Colonel Blimp than Corporal Hitler. As leader he refused to ban Jews, crazy liberal that he was, leading to a walk-out from more extreme elements, including John Tyndall, who went on to form the first British National Party in 1960.

Such anti-immigration groups had always been a mixture of

'cranks and perverts', in the words of one NF organiser, but Tyndall was an open neo-Nazi who dressed up as a Brownshirt on weekends. He left the British National Party in 1962 to set up the National Socialist Movement, after which the BNP merged with the Empire Loyalists. While the leadership of the National Front had banned Nazis from joining the organisation, it was eventually taken over through entryism by supporters of Tyndall, who had by now split from the NSM and formed his own neo-Fascist group, the Greater Britain Movement. NF leader John O'Brien, a former Conservative and Powellite, grew disturbed by the rise of neo-Nazis in the party and severed his ties with it. He then did tremendous damage to the NF by revealing its true nature in a 1974 documentary.

By this stage the National Front had grown. It fielded 10 candidates in the 1970 election and 54 four years later; in the Newham South by-election in 1974 the party won 11 per cent of the vote. That year Kevin Gately, a 21-year-old maths student, became the first person killed at a political rally in Britain in 55 years, possibly as a result of being kicked by a police horse. The London demonstration against the National Front had been organised by the International Marxist Group, a Far-Left outfit that at the time supported the IRA, and like many of the groups that opposed the NF, was equally unpleasant (indeed, they enjoyed a symbiotic relationship).

But the violent protests of the 1970s further helped to make opposition to mass immigration illegitimate, while creating a martyrology of anti-Fascist activism that could trace its lineage back to the famous 1936 Battle of Cable Street, when police clashed with socialists demonstrating against a march organised by Oswald Mosley's British Union of Fascists. The Labour Party even claimed in its 2010 General Election broadcast that until Cable Street 'it seemed impossible to turn the tide of Fascism', set against images of Mosley's Blackshirts. Yet the BUF never even won a local council seat, had very little support, and at no point did it ever look like Fascism would remotely succeed in Britain except with a German invasion. The idea that the forces of anti-racism prevented Britain falling under the jackboot is about as historical as the claim that David Hasselhoff brought down the Berlin Wall with his song 'Looking for Freedom'.

Joseph Pearce, the leader of the Young National Front who later rejected the Far-Right after a conversion to Catholicism in prison, nevertheless says that the majority of violence at rallies was caused by Far-Left activists, but that the fights drove out any moderates. The 'Battle of Lewisham', another violent clash arising from an NF march in August 1977, was a 'watershed', he says. According to Pearce: 'Prior to that, the marches were mainly comprised of middle-aged, middle-class people. There were squadron leaders, Second World War veterans. And then with the increase of violence and the media interest before Lewisham a lot of the older people stayed away, because there was clearly going to be a riot and they didn't want to be part of it.' Instead 'the skinhead thing came back. Lots of football hooligan types who were racist came along for the fights. The violence from the extreme Left provoked violence in reaction. Then it got out of control, with thousands of football hooligans and skinheads, and then what you saw was 2,000 bald young men walking down the street doing Nazi salutes.'[40]

The National Front was killed off in 1979 by the election of Margaret Thatcher, one of the few shadow cabinet ministers in 1968 to oppose Powell's sacking. The party then descended into Monty Pythonesque in-fighting which eventually resulted in two National Fronts competing in the same districts and facing off each other at Remembrance Day services. John Tyndall left in 1980 to form the New National Front and then, in 1982, a second British National Party. He became representative of opposition to mass immigration, both sinister and pathetic, immersing himself with crazed Jewish world domination theories that, until the age of the internet, someone actually had to take the trouble to print. (Tyndall was so anti-Semitic that he had his successor Nick Griffin's ancestry probed for alleged Jewishness, an investigation we can safely say is unique in British political history.)

It was easy for the media to present opponents of immigration as ugly, violent and psychotic because, by and large, they were ugly, violent and psychotic, at least the ones who cared enough to make an issue of it. And the abdication of any debate by political moderates left it to skinheads and football hooligans. In turn a new generation of liberals, who were to take power towards the end of the millennium, came to see any opposition to mass immigration as extreme, and a love of diversity as the mark of political morality. This mentality would lead to immigration on an unprecedented scale, once the effects of a profound and radical cultural revolution had set in.

3

The Shadow of Auschwitz
The universalist illusion

Such radical change could not have become accepted were it not for the intellectual justification provided by the idea of universalism – that races and ethnic groups are just meaningless social constructs, nations artificial creations, and therefore states cannot be drawn along any ethnic lines. As Mario Vargas Llosa wrote in *The Culture of Liberty*: 'The notion of "collective identity" is an ideological fiction and the foundation of nationalism.'

Once someone accepts this premise, opposition to immigration is morally impossible to justify. Philippe Legrain argued in *Immigrants: Your Country Needs Them* that 'The idea of a single, unchanging national community... is a myth' and therefore 'The case for excluding foreigners cannot rest on their ethnic or racial difference, because the national community already includes people of diverse ethnicities and races: you cannot, for instance, legitimately exclude blacks from Britain on the basis that Britain is a wholly white country, because it no longer is. Instead, the basis for exclusion must be their foreignness, which in turn implies a Britishness that is based not on race or ethnicity, but on a broader sense of community expressed through a willingness to obey the same laws and accept government by a majority. That community may be very diverse, not only ethnically but in value terms, yet still bound together by a common identity, common habits and common interests.'

But can there be a nation-state based on nothing but 'common identity, common habits and common interests', rather like a stamp-collecting club? And how can one 'legitimately exclude' anyone in that case?

Fifty years ago the idea that there was such a thing as a national community based largely (but not necessarily exclusively) on ancestry was almost uncontested, and it still goes uncontested outside of the West. Humans have always lived in groups based on kinship, but the philosophical basis of the nation comes from 18th-century German thinker Johann Gottfried von Herder, who developed the concept of *volk*. It is a word which might have acquired, shall we say, a slightly sinister air in recent years, but the peoples he thought of were distinct because of *Kultur* rather than biology. The nation was a natural entity and societies worked best when states reflected natural national entities; for Herder 'the most natural state' was 'one nation, with one national character'. In contrast nothing 'appears so directly opposite to the end of government as the unnatural enlargement of states, the wild mixture of various kinds of humans and nations under one sceptre'. Herder thought artificial polyglot entities like the Hapsburg Empire absurd monsters, 'a lion's head with a dragon's tail, an eagle's wing, a bear's paw [sewn together] in one unpatriotic symbol of state'. God only knows how he would have described the European Union.

But Herder was not a racial supremacist; he hated the racial theories that were gaining currency at the time, believed in human equality, and his idea of the nation was neither explicitly racial nor non-racial. And the relationship between nationhood and blood has varied from country to country; in Germany it has tended to be close, while in France and the United States nationality was tied to citizenship, which allowed in theory for any man to become a Frenchman or American, although in the latter being of European descent was effectively essential until the 1960s. In Britain, as with many things, it was ambiguous; Britain never thought to answer the question 'what does Britishness mean' not because it was necessarily colour-blind but because the answer seemed self-evident, largely because it had never had much immigration.

Attitudes have radically shifted in a short space of time. Today arguing in favour of a nationhood based even partly on blood or other forms of exclusivity is like answering a blasphemy charge in a court where the judge, jury and lawyers all believe in the literal truth of the Bible and view any argument against it as itself evidence of blasphemy ('How can we believe what this man says? Why, he doesn't even believe in diversity'). Many people feel some unease at the prospect that London or Birmingham or even Britain might have a white minority, yet are unable to articulate why, without committing one of the secular deadly sins. Why should it be white? What's wrong with non-whites? You don't have to be white to be British. What's skin colour got to do with it? Arguing against people who control the terms of debate is a hard task, and in a way exponents of diversity have achieved a tremendous success in making opponents have to justify their objections, when the burden of proof should be against those advocating the radical change. Until relatively recently it would have seemed strange to justify why minority status should alarm. Indeed in no place or time except for today's Europe, and the other nations settled by Europeans, would any ethnic group have been morally condemned for objecting to becoming a minority in their native city or country. This is actually quite revolutionary; and its origins lie in the traumatic events of the past century.

Bunk, bunk, bunk

The classicist Goldsworthy Lowes Dickinson noted in his 1931 work *Plato and His Dialogues* that: 'I have never met a young man who passed through [the Great War], or grew up after it, who has any belief in progress at all.' The deaths of 10 million people in the First World War shook the West's confidence in mankind and civil-isation, but most of all in patriotism. However the view that the Great War was a senseless waste of life only became universal towards the end of the 1920s; many veterans at the time had believed that it was a bloody but necessary conflict to halt German aggression. The changing attitude was highly influenced by three plays performed in London around 1930, which attacked not just the war, but everything it was fought for: Noel Coward's *Post-Mortem*, RC Sheriff's *Journey's End* and *For Services Rendered* by Somerset Maugham.

In one powerful speech in Maugham's play Sydney, a promising young man blinded by the Great War, says: 'I know that we were the dupes of the incompetent fools who ruled the nations. I knew that we were sacrificed to their vanity, their greed and their stupidity. And the worst of it is that as far as I can tell they haven't learned a thing. They're just as vain, they're just as greedy, they're just as stupid as they ever were. They muddle on, muddle on, and one of these days they'll muddle us all into another war. When that happens, I'll tell you what I'm going to do. I'm going out into the streets and cry, Look at me: don't be a lot of damned fools; it's all bunk what they're saying to you, about honour and patriotism and glory, bunk, bunk, bunk.'

Sydney's speech reflected a widespread sense of disillusionment with all that had been fought for in 1914. When Hitler began to rearm, the British people were unwilling to face another war; that they got one was seen as proof not of the failures of appeasement, but of the fundamental evils of national feeling, and the Holocaust further undermined Europeans' faith in their civilisation. As Danish writer Helle Merete Brix wrote, the wars were proof 'that our culture was worthless. It was basically destroyed. And that prepared the way for two sorts of totalitarianism' and for 'atrocities of a magnitude that is hard to imagine'. In turn the Nazis 'made Europe think it is doomed and sinful… and deserves what it has coming.' This certainly influenced its attitude to immigration. As Christopher Caldwell wrote in *Reflections on the Revolution in Europe*, 'it is possible to say that Europe's decision to welcome millions of foreigners was made at a time when it was not of sound mind and body.' Looking on the presence of jihadists able to operate freely in Belgium, Caldwell suggested: 'An immigration of the sort that brought Muslims in such numbers to Europe would have been unthinkable without the anguished moral self-examination the Holocaust brought in its wake.'

While the war ended with Marxist armies in control of Eastern Europe, Marxist and other radical ideas also made huge gains in the West. Among these was a belief in a world without borders or nations. At the end of *The Great Dictator*, Charlie Chaplin's ultra-black 1940 comedy about Adolf Hitler, the famous silent film actor spoke for the first time on screen. Playing a Jewish barber in one of the first movies to break the taboo about anti-Semitism in Germany, he tells the camera: 'Let us fight to free the world, to do away with national barriers, do away with greed, with hate and intolerance. Let us fight for a world of reason, a world where science and progress will lead to all men's happiness.'

Universalism, the idea that any form of political or social separation between nations or groups is wrong, is a product of horror and guilt, a reaction to the collective memories of colonialism (and especially slavery) and the Final Solution. This has made it very hard for Europeans to discuss race, ethnicity or anything that involves in-groups and out-groups. Ever since the 1960s, a period where greater Holocaust-awareness coincided with decolonisation in Africa, the Civil Rights movement and the start of the ANC's struggle against apartheid, issues of race, racism and immigration have become highly-charged moral questions almost devoid of any practical considerations. As conventional British morality - largely Protestant, prudish, hostile to shows of extravagance, violence or emotion – was overturned, anti-racism became a central moral issue, rather than merely a question of how best to order a society. Throughout the 1990s and the arguments about asylum, the Holocaust loomed over the debate.

It also overshadowed and inspired the other great utopian post-War venture, the project to create a new Europe without nation-states. In May 2005, at the site of Theresienstadt concentration camp in the Czech Republic, European Commissioner Margot Wallstrom warned that hesitation in surrendering national sovereignty could risk another Holocaust. Dutch Prime Minister Jan Peter Balkenende told the electorate the following year that if they voted no to an EU treaty, then there would be dire consequences: 'I've been in Auschwitz and Yad Vashem. The images haunt me every day. It is supremely important for us to avoid such things in Europe'. One expects first year students on internet message boards to use Godwin's Law[41] so crudely, but perhaps not a prime minister.

After the war Europe's elite set out to purge the continent of nationalism through 'the European project', the name given to the creation of a unified European state. Jean Monnet, the architect and first president of the European Coal and Steel Community, conceived the idea of a united states of Europe after the First World War in order to create permanent peace through a new empire in which nationalism was cured. Many of its great advocates, including British Prime Minister Edward Heath, had seen fighting in the European wars. Alexandre Kojeve, who set up the embryonic European Union, but more importantly established the intellectual rationale behind it, believed a united Europe would represent the 'end of history', when national boundaries and exclusive communities will wither away. The logical conclusion to this thinking is that there should be no borders or restrictions, and that nations become mere geographic entities from which people can move freely from one to another. In the minds of universalists, immigration controls are therefore immoral, variously described as a 'Berlin Wall', 'apartheid,' compared to medieval serfdom and North Korean Communism.

National identity was heavily undermined by post-war academia, with nations recast as mere by-products of 'print capitalism', in the words of Benedict Anderson; Ernest Gellner deconstructed nationalism as a way for bureaucrats to legitimise their rule; Marxist historian Eric Hobsbawm popularised the term 'invented traditions'. Nations are, as philosopher AC Grayling put it, artificial constructs, 'their boundaries drawn in the blood of past wars'. Meanwhile, it was argued, national cultures were not homogenous; rather countries are home to more than one different but usually coexisting cultures. And in the more pluralist and wealthy post-war era, national identity has indeed given way to lifestyle subcultures which cross political boundaries, and have become more important to many people than outdated, artificial nations: more important because they are willing associations. Meanwhile expressions of national pride, such as flag-waving and anthem-singing, became associated with the petit bourgeoisie and *lumpenproletariat*. In the universalist world there would be no more nations, no more ethnic groups, no more divisions, and no more national history. To continue with nationalism would, in the words of EU president Herman Van Rompuy, 'lead to war'.

But does it? His view, Roger Scruton wrote, 'identifies the normality of the nation state through its pathological examples. As Chesterton[42] has argued about patriotism generally, to condemn patriotism because people go to war for patriotic reasons, is like condemning love because some loves lead to murder.' Besides which, men have killed in large numbers for faith and class – the crusade for equality has put more men in their graves than all religions combined – why single out nationhood?

Opposition to any form of national identity partly explains the disproportionate amount of hostility Israel attracts from the European commentariat. Many on the European Right once feared Jews as rootless agents of internationalism; today the Left dislikes Israelis for being agents of nationalism, or 'Israeli apartheid', Zionism being the ultimate endorsement of national identity. The idea that 'Zionism is racism' was given concrete form in a 1975 UN Resolution, yet Zionism simply refers to a belief in the right of the Jews to a state; it is racist only in the sense that all national independence movements are racist, in that they recognise a people united by a common culture, language or ancestry who wish to form their own state. In fact most Arab and African leaders who condemn Zionism share the same nationalist beliefs, yet do not have Israel's demographic insecurity; indeed, among the sponsors of the 1975 resolution were the Libyan *Arabic* Republic and the Syrian *Arabic* Republic. Israel is 'racist' because it will not award Palestinians the right to return; yet aside from the practical issue that a 50:50 Jewish-Arab state would be fatally unstable, a Jewish state is not a Jewish state unless it is Jewish. That is not racism; it is at worst ethnocentrism (and in Israel's case, motivated by a justified historical fear of minority status). Former prime minister Yitzhak Rabin, by no means an extremist, once said that Israel had to be no less than 80 per cent Jewish. If Palestinian leaders in a fairly partitioned Holy Land wanted their country to be 'at least 80 per cent Arab', few would think it an unreasonable expression of national self-determination.

Racism and anti-racism

Universalism was a reaction to the scientific racism of the late 19th and early 20th century. Today the term racism has come to mean almost any recognition of race (and at the same time, not recognising it when appropriate) and of differences (or average differences) between groups, as well as its original meaning of racial supremacy. And without any recognition of race, or ethnicity, there can be no logical opposition to immigration.

The word 'racialist' first entered the English language in the 1900s, followed by 'racist' in the 1930s, but it was only in the 1960s that the latter began to be used widely.[43] The term comes from the French word for breed, as in dogs, and both racists and anti-racists have used this scientifically questionable comparison. Although xenophobia and tribalism are as old as man, actual racism – the belief in overwhelming biological differences between groups – is a relatively recent phenomenon, and replaced a Christian worldview divided between the religious and savages. Race was first articulated by Immanuel Kant, who wrote in 1775: 'Blacks and Whites are not distinct types of people, for they belong to one tribe, and yet to two different races'.

Medieval Europe sometimes had a positive image of blacks, who were often portrayed as kings, as in Leonardo da Vinci's *The Adoration of the Magi*. Historian Felipe Fernández-Armesto says that before the modern era 'Negritude carried associations of regality, wisdom and the privilege of one of the earliest of divine revelations about the nature of Christ.' Maps of the late medieval period, he wrote, 'gleam with Europeans' high expectations of the black world and the civilised habits of its people. Black Africa appears dotted with gilded cities and richly arrayed monarchs'. That Europeans later developed a less positive attitude to Africa was because this stereotype was overcome by reality; Africa was not dotted with gilded cities and biblical kings.

Since the first Europeans made contact with non-Europeans, they debated whether such people were less advanced because of their environment, or nature. Many early philosophers of the Enlightenment expressed a hope that, if man was equal underneath, science and reason would allow us to one day break down the walls. German philologist Wilhelm von Humboldt provided as much as a definition of a liberal view of race as anyone when he wrote that the highest goal of humanity would be 'that of establishing our common humanity, of striving to remove the barriers which prejudice and limited views of every kind have erected amongst men, and to treat all mankind without reference to religion, nation or colours, as one fraternity, one great community, fitted for the attainment of one project, the unre-strained development of the physical powers'.

But at the time the evidence suggested to most intelligent

people that such a dream was unattainable, and racialist ideas developed during the 19th century. Thomas Henry Huxley, the English liberal biologist nicknamed Darwin's bulldog, wrote in *Emancipation: Black and White* that: 'The highest places in the hierarchy of civilisation will assuredly not be within the reach of our dusky cousins, though it is by no means necessary that they should be restricted to the lowest.' Charles Darwin is perhaps unfairly blamed for the growth of scientific racism; polygenism, the idea that the races are essentially separate sub-species, became influential from the 1840s, long before *The Descent of Man*, while Darwin himself was a monogenist, believing that all humans are descended from a single group of hominid ancestors. Alfred Russell Wallace, Darwin's unsung co-discoverer of evolution, thought the 'inevitable effects of an unequal mental and physical struggle' was extermination: 'It must inevitably follow that the higher – and more intellectual and moral – must replace the lower and more degraded races.' This was a positive thing as eventually 'no individual of which would be inferior to the noblest specimens of existing humanity'. Wallace later changed his mind, but his comments are telling, not just in their brutal Darwinism, but also in the belief that, for equality and homogeneity to be achieved, all diversity must be removed.

After the defeat of the Nazis it was agreed that, for racism to be eradicated, the scientific hinterland that gave credence to the Final Solution must be destroyed. The year after the end of the war saw the creation of the United Nations Educational, Scientific and Cultural Organisation (UNESCO). Its founding constitution declares: 'Since wars begin in the minds of men it is in the minds of men that the defences of peace must be constructed.' Peace, therefore, must be founded 'upon the intellectual and moral solidarity of mankind'. UNESCO brought together a group of scientists, led by the British-born American anthropologist Ashley Montagu, to articulate the new world view of race. Their proclamation of 18 July 1950 declared that: 'The likenesses among men are far greater than the differences. For all practical purposes "race" is not so much a biological phenomenon as a social myth.' Since then any findings challenging this belief have been deemed beyond the bounds of acceptable discourse. So if race was just a 'social myth', and nations imagined communities, what justification could there to oppose universalism and its logical conclusion of open borders?

In reaction to the racist consensus of the pre-war period there grew up an alternative theory of race. The radicalism that emerged in 1968 as the dominant cultural force in the West included among its doctrines what later became known as 'anti-racism', or the Marxist interpretation of race. To call anti-racism the bastard child of Communism would be doing it a disservice; it is the favourite son and heir to Communism, and bears an uncanny resemblance to its father.

The New Left movement that emerged in the 1960s shifted the aims of Marxism from the economic to the social sphere. While European socialists were traditionally concerned with the plight of the workers, following the increased prosperity of the 1960s the emphasis moved towards the 'New Social Movements', feminism, gay rights, third-world liberation struggles and the plight of minorities and immigrants in the West. The African-American Civil Rights movement caused a major shift in the Left, with non-whites in and outside the West replacing the workers as the agents of social revolution. Chris Dillow, author of the *End of Politics*, wrote: 'Inspired in part by Hobsbawm's essay, *The Forward March of Labour Halted?* many on the Left gave up on the idea of the working class as a revolutionary force, and looked instead to what they called "new social movements", women, blacks and gays. Allied to this was a growing lack of interest in economics, and a rise in interest in cultural theory.' This new emphasis on social rather than economic issues could bypass Marxism's obvious economic failures and instead focus on cultural revolution. This was a far more attractive idea for the middle-class radicals who comprised the bulk of the New Left. Economic radicalism is not just evidently unsuccessful, but involves financial sacrifice, and shunning wealth is often necessary for personal credibility. Political radicalism costs nothing; the benefits are to middle-class cultural revolutionaries, while the risks and costs are usually borne by people far away. A western European can show solidarity with Latin American or African guerrillas, knowing that were they to actually take power and bring their nations to abject ruin, it would affect him not one bit. The promotion of cultural diversity at home, which affected the working classes to a far greater extent, was a milder manifestation of this.

These ideas took time to become established. In the 1920s Marxist philosopher György Lukács said that revolution had failed in the West because of 'false consciousness', and so revolutionaries needed to seize 'the means of mental production' in the media, entertainment industry, education and the arts. It was not until the 1960s when an expansion in the university system and a popularisation of Marxist critical theory allowed this to happen. Universities helped to popularise the work of thinkers such as Herbert Marcuse, the Marxist philosopher who argued that liberal Western society was in reality 'repressive tolerance' and who believed that working men were dupes, and that the barbarian within society should be assisted because the true barbarism may well be the 'continued empire of civilisation itself'. In Marcuse's view whoever defies society and the state is not to be brought under control, but is society's saviour, and prominent among Marcuse's revolutionary 'outcasts and outsiders' are 'the exploited and persecuted of other races and colours'.

Anti-racism transferred the struggle of the workers onto non-whites and women, and with Marxist dogmas transferred too. Works such as Oliver Cox's 1948 study *Class, Caste and Race* helped to spread the idea that race was a fictitious concept which was created and used to help 'a practical exploitative relationship' between one group and another. In Marxist thought race is a construct used to justify the exploitation of cheap immigrants, who can be scapegoated for economic problems when hard times fall. Racial prejudice divides the working population and prevents class consciousness from forming. This is a wonderful theory which ignores the unfortunate fact that working-class people might actually have agency and functioning brains of their own and do – genuinely – feel uncomfortable about their territory being taken up by another group, a fact increasingly shown by neuroscience. Marxist thinkers such as Immanuel Wallerstein even suggested nationalism and racism to be part of the evolution of capitalism. Such ideas were orthodoxy in the Soviet Union in the 1930s, and were necessary to explain the failures of Communists to shift peasant loyalties. Likewise the Marxist interpretation of racism is necessary to explain the shortcomings of diversity, including the failure of the state to create equality of outcomes.

Because Marxist ideas about class exploitation came to pre-eminence, so anti-racism as an ideology holds that racism is by definition only racism when it is 'dominant groups' doing it. In English schools it is quite normal for children to be taught that racism is the legacy of slavery, segregation and white people in general, as if racism was the result of some genetic flaw that arose in Neolithic Europe. Under the Oxford English Dictionary definition for racism it reads, '*white racism*: SEE WHITE'. The dogma that racism can only be felt and expressed by dominant groups side-steps the fact that what is now defined as racism – xenophobia, hostility to outsiders or ethno-centrism – is common to humanity. In fact anti-racists have often embraced black nationalists whose attitudes mirrored those of white racists; while 'anti-racism', and its obsession with a wealthier group who are accused of attaining greater success by nepotism and other nefarious means, can more closely resemble pre-war anti-Semitism than typical white anti-immigrant racism does. Yet racism, or what anti-racists understand as racism, is a universal part of human nature, 'as human as love' as novelist Thomas Keneally put it. Racial *hatred*, however, is different, a pathological variation of that human preference for sameness and kinship. One might regret that, just as one might regret that greed, lust and violence are part of human nature, but building a society based on the assumption that they can be driven out through re-education is an optimistic idea.

The popularity of the Marxist theory rests not just on its moral superiority but on its irrefutability; by its own logic it can never be disproved. For anti-racism shares with Soviet Communism a Utopian worldview in which every problem is caused not by the implementation of anti-racist policies, but through a lack of them. In the USSR every failure in the system was blamed on bourgeois capitalist tendencies or insufficient instruction in Soviet socialism, not on the intrinsic weaknesses of the idea behind the system. Any failings of a multi-racial state can be blamed on racism, rather than on the innate weaknesses of diverse societies. Likewise, because racism is this indefinable vice which can and does infect almost everyone, the solution to any problem of human interaction is more anti-racism measures. So if mental illness increases in diverse areas,[44] it must be the fault of racism, not an instinctive human sense of discomfort with diversity. If one group does less well on average than another, it must be a result of racism rather than individual behaviour or cultural trends. If there is a rise in racial tension because of high immigration, it must be because of racism and the false consciousness it has caused. The fight against racism is therefore an open-ended war which, like all unwinnable wars, comes to drain, obsess and demoralise the nation waging it.

Like in any Utopia, those who point out the system's faults are castigated for being immoral and blamed for the Utopia's failings, so that 'the millions dead or enslaved do not refute utopia, but merely give proof of the evil machinations that have stood in its way', in the words of Roger Scruton. Scruton cites mass immigration as an example of 'unscrupulous optimism' at work, a policy driven by an unthinking hope rather than calculated logic. It is 'an unachievable goal chosen for its abstract purity, in which differences are reconciled, conflict overcome and mankind soldered together in a metaphysical unity, [which] can never be questioned, since in the nature of the case it can never be put to the proof. All the crimes committed on the way to it are deviations, perversions or betrayals, things that the ideal was designed to prevent.'

That Marxist Universalism went unchallenged was largely due to the collapse of Western conservatism after 1945, and the monopoly that liberalism has held in the intellectual sphere. In the post-war period, Harvard sociologist Daniel Bell wrote, the entire conservative project was marginalised. Since 'World War Two had the character of a "just war" against Fascism, Right-wing ideologies and the individual and cultural figures associated with those were inevitably discredited'. After the 'preponderant reactionary influence in pre-war European culture', he said, 'No single Right-wing figure retained any political credibility or influence'. Scruton, one of the great Right-wing philosophers of the 20th century, recalled that when he took a permanent lectureship in Birkbeck College in 1971 the only other conservative in the entire university was the Neapolitan cleaning lady: 'In

1970s Britain, conservative philosophy was the preoccupation of a few half-mad recluses.'

And on top of this ideological utopianism one can add a particular English, northern European arrogance, which holds that just because no society in history has ever produced a, liberal, multi-ethnic democracy free of racial tension, somehow England will, because it is somehow uniquely tolerant and morally superior.

Media Bias

In Britain the state-run broadcaster wields enormous power, and this accentuates the liberal bias of the media, although it is not alone; one study found that in Denmark the media applied the word 'extremist' seven times as often to Right-wing as to Left-wing politicians. British rules governing impartiality also ensure that there is only one opinion allowed in broadcasting – the default centre-Left one. As the *Observer's* Will Hutton put it: 'Europe acts to ensure that television and radio conform to public interest criteria' – and the definition of public interest is defined by a fairly narrow liberal patrician circle. But across Europe and the United States there is very little diversity of political thinking at the top, whether in broadcasting, the universities or in the wider political class. One poll of professors in the US found that just three out of 1,000 identified as conservative, a bias that leads to what evolutionary psychologist Jonathan Haidt calls a 'tribal-moral community' united by 'sacred values'.[45]

Members of what is usually critically called 'the liberal elite' (an overused and slightly caricatured term, but a valid one) have a habit of speaking to people with political views similar to theirs (and those who do not may not have the courage to voice their opinions). An enclosed social circle can quickly evolve political views, and the concentration of Britain's intelligentsia within small networks predominantly in west and north London helped to radically shift accepted ideas and prevent dissenting voices emerging. As Cass Sunstein noted in *Going to Extremes*: 'Social networks can operate as polarisation machines because they help to confirm and thus amplify people's antecedent views.' Our attitudes to any subject can be moved by the company we keep, so that 'white people who tend to show significant racial prejudice will show more racial prejudice after speaking with one another. By contrast, white people who tend to show little racial prejudice will show less prejudice after speaking with one another.' Interactivity between a group with political leanings of a certain bent acts as an echo chamber, progressively radicalising them even more.

In its most dangerous form this can drive young men towards extreme radicalisation, especially in the age of the internet. But the echo chamber can act in less violent ways. Within the British political arena the inhabitable zone of acceptable, mainstream views has shifted rapidly in a generation; what was orthodoxy 30 years ago and mainstream 20 years ago becomes taboo today and criminal tomorrow. Radical changes usually occur from the top down, driven by ideas that develop in universities and other intellectual hubs, and the universalism that had become widely accepted by the turn of the 21st century was based on new ideas that spread in intellectual circles before and after the Second World War. Only small numbers of people supported the idea of a truly multicultural society, but they were among the most intellectually confident and high-ranking, and so the idea gradually became accepted. Indeed studies of controlled group-think have shown that, as Sunstein puts it, 'low-status members of groups become ever more reluctant, over the course of discussion, to repeat privately held information'. This is why the British media shifts the country leftwards, even though, judging from a newspaper stand, it appears to be incredibly Right-leaning; tabloid newspapers, despite being able to voice anti-immigration sentiment to a large readership, have little intellectual clout or influence on ideological trends.

This is the story of the Emperor's New Clothes interpreted by modern social psychology. Cascades, where people start to believe something, and to express a view, because they think other people will express this view, are often behind these shifts. This is why ideas taught by lecturers in the 1960s and 1970s have been able to have such influence, despite seeming wildly radical and unattractive to most people outside of academia.

Even though conservatives had greater public support on key issues such as immigration, crime and Europe, when conservatism began to recover it took the path of least resistance through economic liberalism, rather than harder cultural battles over national identity. Besides which, economic liberals are happy with the free movement of peoples, which is consistent with their worldview, and has tangible economic benefits for the wealthy. And since conservatives believe that individuals are largely responsible for their own success and failure, it is harder for them to sympathise with poor natives who resent incomers, many of whom are hard-working and devoted to family and education. Even when they felt uncomfortable with the rise of radical ideas, conservatives became unable to articulate reasonable and moderate scepticism, because they had lost confidence in their own beliefs and the ability to express them in the language of the day.

In a television-dominated culture where emotion plays an important part in political discourse, it is very difficult for the immigration sceptic to present an argument without appearing uncaring or inhumane. Where tolerance has become the most important virtue – more so than honesty, intelligence or integrity – debates are not always logical. If we were to take a subjective, anthropological view of our behaviour in recent years, rather than voice opinions that might make us appear compassionate, we might conclude that diversity is not in our best interest. But in the television age people want their politics, like their religion once did, to make them feel good about themselves: warm, welcoming sentiments about the universality of man make us feel morally valuable and provide a serotonin hit; facing up to uncomfortable truths about the potential darker sides of human nature does the opposite. Those who oppose such grand changes can easily be portrayed as being heartless or discriminating (and the word is now almost only used in a pejorative sense) about their fellow humans.

In *The Righteous Mind* Jonathan Haidt argues that human beings have developed certain moral foundations, and among these care for the vulnerable and opposition to oppression are stronger among self-identified liberals. These instincts, which evolved to allow humans to work in large, non-kin groups, help us to identify with vulnerable groups such as migrants, which makes many people instinctively react to anyone who appears to harm them.

The television-dominated media has played a large part in presenting the diversity debate in stark, almost religious terms. Just as the media can be used to appeal to our basest xenophobic impulses by spreading hate for out-group members – for example, in Rwanda – so it can be used to manipulate people's more noble xenophile urges, with harmful results. The way in which the immigration debate has been emotionalised has certainly benefited the pro- lobby; anyone can cite a real or anecdotal hard-working, law-abiding and family-loving immigrant to argue for fewer restrictions, but no decent opponents wish to highlight the examples of people who steal, claim benefit on arrival or take part in organised crime. Yet both these types are real, and both arguments are as anecdotal and irrational as each other – and such an anecdotal argument used in any other debate would be dismissed as naked emotionalising.[46]

The moralisation of diversity is reflected in the fact that almost across the board churches in the West are pro-immigration, even though their congregations are not (in the US self-described Christians are more hostile to immigration than non-believers). In a sense secular universalism has grown on and replaced Christianity, which is also universalist and stresses sacrifice for the sake of humanity, although in Christianity altruism is voluntary, and comes with heavenly rewards (and religions have their own out-groups, of non-believers). Because diversity is framed in such morally polar ways, it is very hard to argue against it from a Christian standpoint, and few do. While churches have often spoken on behalf of individual asylum seekers, they have gone further in promoting the diversity agenda. The Catholic Church in England has even put its weight behind asylum amnesties that would have resulted in half a million people being legalised, even though similar schemes in Spain have encouraged further illegal immigration (and resulted in many deaths, of Africans drowned trying to reach Europe). And as social diversity has increased the churches have become increasingly dependent on immigrants filling the pews, to replace natives who have lost their faith.

The changing language, and the identification of native Europeans as 'whites', a word that carries overtones of colonial oppression and bullying, made universalism irresistible, for as Susan Sontag put it: 'the white race is the cancer of human history'. The French philosopher Pierre-André Taguieff coined the term *immigrationisme* to describe the ideology that immigration is always 'both inevitable and good', a good that would cleanse Europe of its guilt.

This discomfort makes it morally unacceptable to define Britain as a 'white country', which in itself makes philosophical opposition to change impossible. Yet until recently Britain was a white country. Recognising this, the 1961 Immigration Act restricted immigrants from the New Commonwealth but not from Ireland, despite Ireland having left the Commonwealth by this stage. A Government working party explained: 'it cannot be held that the same difficulties arise in the case of the Irish as in the case of coloured people… The outstanding difference is that the Irish are not whether they like it or not a different race from the ordinary inhabitants of Great Britain.' This was clearly racialist, in that it recognised racial differences, but it was not inaccurate. The Oxford English Dictionary defines race as 'A group or set, especially of people, having a common feature or features… Any of the major divisions of humankind, having in common distinct physical features or ethnic background.' Today, while many people have moved away from the social science idea that race is a 'social construct', a view held by few biologists, the area is still contested, and emotionally charged.

Was it wrong to offer more relaxed immigration rules for people who were ethnically related? If one cares more about a principle than the practical best interests for a society and its inhabitants, then yes; but pragmatists would say no. And until then no one on earth would have found it strange, nor would anyone today in India, China or across Asia.

And whatever the meaning of race, and whatever its insignificance to a man's worth and his soul, it exists, for no other reason than people act like it exists. When American politician Pat Buchanan famously said that it would be easier to integrate a group of Englishman than it would the same number of Zulus,[47] it was considered a typically beyond-the-pale comment from someone who lived among the wild Gaels of politics, yet in a white neighbourhood they undoubtedly would integrate more easily. Immigrants to a country where the natives largely share recent common ancestry are easier to integrate, and so immigration has fewer social costs. We would rather phrase it differently because colour-based racial grouping sounds not only unpleasant, nasty and supremacist, but also petty, yet it is nevertheless factually true. Of course barriers to integration can be and are overcome, as the rise of the mixed-race category testifies to , but the level of such integration depends on the size and structure of the minority population. A colour-blind immigration policy ultimately leads to a more colour-conscious society, and vice versa. The stricter the rules on the door, the more relaxed the club can be with its members.

When people say that Britain is a multi-racial society and that the typical person is not white, what they are saying is that it is what they want it to be, and how they see the future. Historically it is not the case, and one only has to look outside at our dreary, soul-sapping climate to be reminded that we are in northern Europe. People referred to as 'white British' overwhelmingly descend from the original inhabitants of this island, mixed with more recent invaders and, sharing a common gene pool which has been shaped by natural selection pressures, tend to exhibit a number of typical physical characteristics, the most ubiquitous being pale skin; there is nothing offensive in pointing that out, anymore than it is to say that ethnic Yoruba are black or the Han Chinese are East Asian.

The discomfort attached to colour-based racial markers is the main reason for the introduction of the term 'indigenous British'. The phrase as a substitute for 'white British' was first used in Far-Right circles, but it is not historically incorrect. When American playwright Bonnie Greer told Nick Griffin on *Question Time* that 'there are no indigenous British people', Griffin asked whether anyone would say the same thing about Aborigines or American Indians. It is considered bad form for journalists not to argue that if Griffin says it's raining outside, it must be sunny, but his point was valid. No one would suggest that a white man, even one claiming descent from the *Mayflower*, was a 'Native American', but that is not to say that whites cannot be Americans, or that ethnic minorities cannot be British without being 'indigenous'. Liberals object to the term only because 'indigenous' has a moral cache, being usually applied to threatened peoples, and carries an air of paranoia, but it is perhaps little surprise that people feel paranoid when they are told they must welcome minority status.

Writing about Tibet, liberal blogger Dave Osler once stated that China 'has resettled Han Chinese colonists there to the point where Tibetans are at risk of becoming a minority in their own homeland'. On his own country he declared that 'further mass immigration obviously has the potential to rejuvenate the population of this island once the politicians can get their head round the idea'. Tibetans becoming a minority in their country are a threatened species; the English are being 'rejuvenated'.[48] Of course the Tibetans have no choice in becoming a minority, yet when the British express their opposition to 'rejuvenation' they are condemned as racists.

Looking at the situation in reverse one can see how un-universal the universalist idea actually is. Imagine if Pakistan's political elite had encouraged immigration to such an extent that their largest city, Karachi, had a non-Pakistani majority, and their second largest, Islamabad, was on the point of having a non-Asian majority. And that in all their major cities some large districts were almost totally devoid of Asians and that predominantly white Christian, secular immigrants openly displayed their increasingly Christian, secular identity. As Christopher Caldwell writes: 'If one abandons the idea that Western Europeans are rapacious and exploitative by nature, and that Africans, Asians, and other would-be immigrants are inevitably their victims, then the fundamental difference between colonisation and labour migration ceases to be obvious.' Indeed one of the curious aspects of current immigration debate is that the groups calling for a world without borders are entirely confined to the West. India, China, Japan, Taiwan, South Korea and the Philippines all have strict, largely ancestry-based immigration rules that are clearly racial in their intention and effect; anyone in those countries suggesting substantial levels of non-Asian immigration would be considered a lunatic. And while any white American who expresses concern about projected minority status is labelled an extremist, the same does not go for their colonies. In the 1990s the US Congress granted five US Pacific Island territories – American Samoa, Micronesia, Marshall Islands, Northern Mariana Islands and Palau – local control over immigration to protect their ethnic majorities.[49] In two of these territories US citizens who don't belong to those majorities cannot even own land. Why shouldn't Samoans be rejuvenated too?

Such one-way movement can only be justified because, as so many advocates of diversity suggest, mass immigration is punishment for and purification of past sins. One of Britain's most famous imports and perhaps its greatest post-war novelist, the Indian-born Salman Rushdie, told viewers in a television documentary called *The New Empire Within Britain* in 1982 : 'It sometimes seems that the British authorities, no longer capable of exporting governments, have chosen instead to import a new Empire, a new community of subject peoples of whom they think, and with whom they can deal, in very much the same way as their predecessors thought of and dealt with "the fluttered folk and wild".'

Rushdie blamed British racism on hundreds of years of colonialism and argued that the country needed to be put through a form of de-Nazification: 'Britain isn't Nazi Germany. The British Empire isn't the Third Reich. But in Germany, after the fall of Hitler, heroic attempts were made by the people to purify German thought and the German language of the pollution of Nazism. Such acts of cleansing are occasionally necessary in every society. But British thought, British society, has never been cleansed of the filth of imperialism. It's still there, breeding lice and vermin, waiting for unscrupulous people to exploit it for their own ends.

'For the citizens of the new, imported Empire, for the colonised Asians and blacks of Britain, the police force represents that colonising army, those regiments of occupation and control. If you are liberal, you say that black people have problems. If you aren't, you say they are the problem. But the members of the new colony have only one real problem, and that problem is white people. British racism, of course, is not our problem. It's yours. We simply suffer from the effects of your problem. And until you, the whites, see that the issue is not integration, or harmony, or multi-culturalism, or immigration, but simply the business of facing up to and eradication the prejudices within almost all of you, the citizens of your new, and last, Empire will be obliged to struggle against you.'

Whether or not racism is entirely a product of imperialism that can be indoctrinated out of us, one could argue that the shadow of imperialism lingers only because of the multicultural society that followed the British home.

The last 40 years has indeed seen a sort of de-Nazification process, with Britain making amends for its past sins; even our role in destroying actual Nazism has been re-written to suit the new moral order. This is the country, as most school children are now taught, which fought the Second World War to rid the world of Fascism and racism, or as Billy Bragg put it: 'When Churchill talked of "their finest hour," he meant 500 million men and women of different languages and cultures, all coming together on our small island to fight Fascism.' Does it matter that this is not remotely true? That Britain did not declare war on Germany to rid the world of racism, as it is currently understood? That none of the politicians, let alone the servicemen, had any notion they were fighting for immigration into England. Indeed, to put it bluntly, they were fighting to keep certain foreigners out of their country. That is not to say that the racism of the Nazis did not disgust people, which it did, and that they did not want to build a society and world more free and equal, and less violent; and when the United States joined the war the Allies did draft war aims to spread liberal democracy around the world. But the freedom to cross borders was never part of the package.

The mood in Britain had become increasingly anti-imperialist by the end of the war, and it was widely believed that the Empire's peoples should be free of colonialism. The main desire on the part of most Britons was that, following the collective sacrifice and hardship of the war, they would create a more equal society, one where the strong would help the weak and where the principles of social democracy would thrive. These were the values of the Labour movement and ethical socialism, the values that Mrs Duffy, and millions like her, believed in. So why are they now in tatters?

Because just as the Left won all the social arguments, the Right was triumphant in the economic sphere.

4

Doing the Jobs Brits Won't Do
Does mass immigration benefit the economy?

The poor man's take on immigration, 'They come over here and take our jobs', is much parodied as an example of economic illiteracy, giving guilty middle-class types their one chance to mock the ignorance of the less well-off – when it involves crude racism.

Whatever the social costs, immigration surely brings great economic benefits, as hard-working and enterprising newcomers do the jobs Brits won't do, and without them our economy would collapse. Yasmin Alibhai-Brown, writing for the *Independent*, declared: 'I have long had this fantasy. With millions of true-born Brits reviling immigrants and blaming incomers for everything – unemployment, poor public services, crime, violence, social unease, widespread rape even – why not have an annual day called "Immigrants Out". We who are thus pilloried, and our progeny, previous arrivals and their descendents too, should put down tools, shut up shop and march in our best clothes to show the many unappreciative citizens just what we do. We could pick the birthday of Mary Seacole, the Jamaican who nursed our soldiers in the Crimean War. In all the hysterical, anti-immigration debates a question hangs like an eagle looking down from the clouds above. What would happen if the immigrants left?'

A Radio 4 programme asked just this question. *The Day the Immigrants Left* looked at Wisbech, near Peterborough, new home to over 9,000 eastern Europeans who work in factories and fields. Although 2,000 locals are out of work, employers in the region argue that without Poles and Lithuanians to pick the crops, and the local unemployed refusing to, the fruit would rot in the fields. When the BBC took out a dozen foreigners and replaced them with native Brits, half of them either failed to show up or turned up late on the first day.

Immigrants, it is always argued, are needed because they will work for non-market-clearing wages, as their expectations are lower. Mary Riddell, a native of the East Midlands, wrote in the *Telegraph*: '[Gordon] Brown should say the politically unsayable: that immigration has and will be a boon. He should recognise the hospitals and care homes staffed, the potatoes picked and streets swept by incomers filling jobs, even in a recession, that the indigenous workforce cannot do or will not take.'[50]

The idea that immigrants fill labour shortages is certainly widely-held. Tony Blair, speaking to the CBI just before EU enlargement in April 2004, when the Home Office confidently expected some 15,000 migrants to arrive from eastern Europe a year (just below the actual figure of 447,000 in two years),[51] expressed it clearly: 'There are half a million vacancies in our job market and our strong and growing economy needs migration to fill these vacancies... some [of which] are for unskilled jobs which people living here are not prepared to do... [moreover] a quarter of all health professionals are overseas born... 23 per cent of staff in our higher education institutions are non-UK nationals... our public services would be close to collapse without their contribution'.[52] This became the basis of Government policy. And yet the argument that mass immigration benefits the economy is arguably as weak as that of the skinhead blaming the Indian for taking his job. In fact any economic benefits brought about by mass immigration are small, short-term and mostly felt by the wealthy, and dwarfed by the long-term social costs.

Certainly some economists believe that immigration benefits the economy. In the *Economic Costs to International Labor Restrictions* Jonathon Moses and Bjorn Letnes estimated the gains from free migration to be 'as high as $55 trillion', while the US Academy of Sciences estimated that the average foreign-born resident in America was a net $3,000 recipient of public funds while their kids were on average net contributors of $80,000. One study of European countries found that a 1 per cent increase in the population through migration is associated with an increase in economic activity of between 1.25 per cent and 1.5 per cent. But just as many economists argue to the contrary. According to the

National Institute of Economic and Social Research, eastern European immigrants into Britain increased the output of the UK by a mere 0.38 percent from 2004 till 2009, despite adding 1 per cent to the population, concluding that it had an 'insignificant' impact on growth. Cuban-born Harvard Professor George Borjas concluded in *Heaven's Door* that the net economic benefit to the US was probably less than $10 billion a year, and this did not take into account the costs of welfare, schools and hospitals.[53]

In Holland the WRR, a scientific council for government policy, concluded: 'The net benefit of total immigration for an economy like that of the Netherlands is small in current circumstances, if not neglible'.[54]

In Canada Herbert Grubel, Fraser Institute senior fellow and co-editor of *The Effects of Mass Immigration on Canadian Living Standards and Society*, estimated that immigrants who arrived in the 12 years before 2002 imposed a fiscal burden of $18.5 billion on all Canadians in the year 2002 alone. And immigrants to Canada are far more likely to be skilled than those who arrive in Europe.[55]

One thing is almost certain – the costs or benefits to the economy are small. According to a House of Lords inquiry from 2008, which generated more than 70 pieces of written and 35 pieces of oral evidence, from a wide range of people and institutions in and outside Britain, including academics, think tanks, employers associations, trades unions, NGOs, local government and government departments, the economic benefits are almost non-existent. The Lords declared that the biggest beneficiaries from international migration are 'migrants themselves', but, it argued: 'We have found no evidence for the argument, made by the Government, business and many others, that net immigration – immigration minus emigration – generates significant economic benefits for the existing UK population.'

Immigration boosts GDP, but this only measures the size of the economy, not income per head of the population. Instead, the Lords argued, 'both theory and the available empirical evidence indicate that these effects are small, especially in the long run" and that it brought 'relatively small costs and benefits for the incomes of the resident population.' Neither, they concluded, did immigration reduce labour shortages, because by increasing labour demand, it creates new vacancies. Immigration leads to an endless cycle of immigration. According to the ITEM Club, one of Britain's best-known independent economic forecasting organisations, the impact of the most recent wave of immigration on GDP per capita has been neutral or even slightly negative. The Government's claim that immigration has contributed £2.5 billion to the Exchequer was also questioned, the Lords finding that the impact 'is likely to be small'. They concluded that the economic benefits of positive net immigration were 'small or insignificant', and suggested that policy should be based on other criteria, 'including diversity and social cohesion and the advantages or disadvantages of a growing population'.

The real argument is not so much economic as political and moral, for diversity helped to match the social goals of the radical Left with the economic aims of the radical Right. Although the Left won most of the social arguments of the late 20th century, the Right won the economic ones, and the two are not incompatible. Free-marketeers dislike nationalism for impeding the free movement of goods, capital and labour, and the combination of cultural radicalism and economic liberalism was very attractive to the post-1968 generation. Since the cultural revolution of the 1960s, the fall of Communism and the deregulation of the money markets in the 1980s, cultural radicals have applied (traditionally 'Right-wing') economic liberalism to argue for unrestrained trade not just in goods and services but in people too. It is a tempting idea that promises: do good and get rich. The developing world presents an almost endless supply of workers, workers who the West needs to do the dangerous, difficult, dirty and demeaning jobs. And giving them such work is ethical, offering a better life to millions living in squalor through no fault of their own. Why not help them escape their miserable lives while providing us with cheap workers?

The huge flaw is that labour shortages are usually short term, while immigration is often permanent. Many Commonwealth immigrants were originally brought to Britain to perform the jobs natives didn't want, and when these jobs disappeared the immigrants stayed. But while industry might desire cheap labour, it is not the same as needing it; in the 1960s the textile industries of Japan and Britain both demanded increased immigration, but the Japanese government refused. Their textile industry instead invested in more efficient machinery and outsourced its unskilled work, while Britain imported a cheap Pakistani workforce. But those Pakistani migrants, like the Turks in the Ruhr valley and Algerians in France's linen mills, were recruited into industries that were already on their last legs. (Strangely, while British trades unions object to outsourcing jobs to Asia, they rarely mention cheap immigration, even though these are effectively the same economic processes.)

Despite intending to be temporary, immigrants often then find themselves stuck, unable to return home but unhappy in their new homeland. It has been true of every group from the Huguenots, many of whom still believed they would return to France right to the end, to the Irish homeless of Camden Town too ashamed to go back. This is why guest worker systems never operate as intended because, as the Lords put it, 'there is nothing more permanent than temporary migrants'. It is nonsensical to train someone who will be forced to return home just as he or she is returning the labour investment, and unethical to make an immigrant leave once they have established a family in a new country.

This is where neo-liberalism as utopia fails. Globalism has many benefits, but mixed with universalism it can become an ideological dogma that ignores the human consequences. Phillippe Legrain asks: 'Why can computers be imported from China duty-free but Chinese people not freely come to make computer here? Why is it a good thing for workers to move within a country to where the jobs are, but a bad thing for people to move between countries for the same reason?' That is because human beings are not computers. Goods can be freely moved about only because they can be discarded when they are no longer useful; humans cannot. Immigration is long-term and has permanent effects for everyone involved. Besides which, globalisation has reduced the need for importing workers, since free trade allows for firms to move to where the cheap labour is, not vice versa, with far less disruption and homesickness attached.

Economists, when it comes to immigration, routinely ignore

the social costs; would they do the same when measuring, for example, the growth of the alcohol industry or, for that matter, fossil fuels? Open borders – especially while much of the world has high fertility rates – have enormous non-economic effects. So while big business might want an endless supply of foreign labour, since when were the interests of big business put above any potential social cost of their practices? When it involves diversity. And yet the social costs of immigration are a form of market failure, problems created by businesses which enjoyed the benefits but do not have to pay for the migrants' welfare, housing or schools once they are no longer needed.

When New Labour came to power there were significant skills and labour shortages, both in the private and public sectors, and many employers were lobbying the government to open the gates. Labour, keen to be friends with business, found that for once this new relationship could chime with their commitment to a progressive policy: diversity. It also allowed them to sidestep a serious obstacle facing the government – welfare dependency.

Welfare traps

Commentators who hail the work ethic and dynamism of immigrants often use it as a stick with which to beat the natives, without ever looking at the comparative incentives offered to the two groups. Yet Britain's supposed 'need' for cheap labour appears odd when one looks at the statistics. By the end of Labour's rule a total of 5.8 million people in Britain were claiming benefits, while a majority of new jobs during the period had been filled by immigrants,[56] and over 95 per cent of the 750,000 or more Poles who arrived in Britain had found work. And although many of the unemployment hotspots are in the north of England or south Wales, among the worst are in inner London, where there was, until the banking crisis, no shortage of unskilled or semi-skilled work, and within walking distance of the City of London, the economic centre of the universe where hundreds of thousands of low-paid workers are hired from sub-Saharan Africa and South America.

Upon coming to power Tony Blair had appointed Birkenhead

MP Frank Field to 'think the unthinkable' on welfare; he did, and so they offered him a job in another department . But without a reform of welfare the labour shortage could never be filled, because it makes no economic sense for many claimants to seek low-paid work such as picking fruit; so the Government chose immigration instead.

This they justified on humanitarian grounds, both for migrants and natives. When works and pension secretary Iain Duncan Smith suggested in 2010 that the unemployed might move to a neighbouring town, Hackney MP Diane Abbot said it was 'cruel' and 'unworkable'. Yet her own parents had come all the way from Jamaica, while her Government had encouraged millions of people to traipse across the globe to carry out demeaning jobs serving Britain's rich. Are British people above such work? The Labour Party certainly wins, since both benefits-claimants and immigrants are more likely to vote for them, but it is a short-term solution that creates two long-term problems – the problems associated with diversity and long-term unemployment.

But there is one group who undoubtedly lose from this system – the working poor. Incomes since 2004 have fallen for people in the bottom 20 per cent, probably as a result of high immigration. A study by Professor Christian Dustmann of UCL found that while immigration had a positive wage effect, it also 'lowers wages of those workers employed in the lowest paid jobs'. Each 1 per cent increase in the ratio of immigrants to natives in the working age population ratio led to a 0.5 per cent decrease in wages at the first decile (the lowest 10 per cent of wage earners), a 0.6 per cent increase in wages at the median, and a 0.4 per cent increase in wages at the ninth decile. The House of Lords suggested that 'immigration has had a small negative impact on the lowest-paid workers in the UK, and a small positive impact on the earnings of higher-paid workers. Resident workers whose wages have been adversely affected by immigration are likely to include a significant proportion of previous immigrants and workers from ethnic minority groups.' In Slough Pakistanis resented the 'incoming Polish community, which is higher skilled and prepared to work for lower wages', while black leaders have complained that eastern Europeans were taking jobs that would otherwise be done by young black men. So the more immigration there is, the less that immigrants and their children benefit from it.

Professor Dustmann also pointed out that the presence of cheap labour 'is good for large corporations who get cheap non-unionised labour', as well as 'homeowners who see property prices rise, and middle-class professionals who don't compete with immigrants but employ their services. This is the reason why big business and its agents of opinion – the CBI and the chambers of commerce, the *Financial Times* and *The Economist* – are without exception supporters of more open borders.' The Lords added: 'Most of our witnesses agreed that there is some negative effect of immigration on the wages of low-skilled workers.' And the City of London Corporation concluded that the concentration of immigrants in low-paid jobs in the capital had led to 'significant downward pressure on wages at the bottom end of the market'. In America, George Borjas has estimated that immigration reduced the wages of the poorest native workers by over 7 per cent between 1980 and 2000.[57] The US government's Bureau of Labour Statistics estimated that 50 per cent of real wage loss among low-skilled Americans was due to competition from low-skilled immigrants, while the National Academy of Sciences stated that 44 per cent of the decline in wages among high school dropouts was accounted for by immigration.

Native workers also receive lower wage settlements because the fear of unemployment increases, and cheap immigration allows employers to charge below the minimum wage, by imposing various charges on foreign workers ignorant of their rights. It also affects youth unemployment, which increased by about 100,000 during the boom years of 2004-2008, school leavers being in direct competition with immigrants for low-paid jobs. And there are few union worries either, since labour movements are weaker in ethnically diverse workforces. By reducing labour costs, immigration may even have contributed towards the runaway salaries of company executive during the last 30 years; in the US CEO salaries went from forty-two times the average blue-collar worker's pay in 1980, to four hundred and thirty-one times in 2010. No wonder that major American corporations spent $345 million lobbying for just three pro-immigration bills between 2006 and

2008, including $23 million from Philip Morris and $12 million from Exxon Mobile.[58]

And no wonder that wealthy liberals find diversity so enriching. Caitlin Flanagan noted in her essay *How Serfdom Saved the Woman's Movement* that females were able to break through the glass ceiling because their menial work was done by immigrants. 'The new immigrants were met at the docks not by a highly organised and politically powerful group of American women intent on bettering the lot of their sex,' she wrote, 'but, rather, by an equally large army of educated professional-class women with booming careers who needed their children looked after and their houses cleaned. Any supposed equivocations about the moral justness of white women's employing dark-skinned women to do their shit work simply evaporated.'

Until relatively recently it was rare for upper middle-class couples to both work; today it is not just considered right for women to have a career after childbirth, but the cost of living (housing especially) makes it a necessity. Having a regular supply of domestic help is almost essential. Yet the continued importation of people to service the wealthy further adds to the main driver of rising living costs for the middle class – runaway house prices, immigration accounting for 10 per cent of the increase this century.[59] Between 1991 and 2006, 989,000 non-Britons moved to London and another 200,000 to the South East; during the years 2004 and 2006 alone 230,000 people from overseas settled in the capital. Goldman Sachs have estimated that a 1 per cent increase in the number of households raises house prices by 8 per cent in the short run and by 6 per cent once house-building has responded. From 2000 to 2008 the ratio of average house prices to average annual earnings rose from four to seven; it is estimated that at current rates within 20 years it will reach 9.3 per cent with zero net migration, but 10.5 per cent with current levels.

Where mass immigration has been found to bring economic benefits, people often ignore the attached infrastructure costs. Even a Treasury statistic suggesting that immigrants spent more in tax (£31.2 billion) than they received in benefits (£28.8 billion) was made without taking into account other services that immigrants used, such as transport, health and education. And after the IPPR think-tank suggested that immigrants cost the treasury on average £700 less than the British-born in 2003-04, the Government used this to back up claims that the 'exchequer is better off with immigration rather than without it'. Yet these figures were flawed, because the health care, education and other public service costs of children born to one immigrant and one UK-born parent were all allocated to the UK-born population, rather than being split. MigrationWatch calculated that that the migrant population actually had a net fiscal cost of £100 million in 1999–2000 compared to the £2.5 billion surplus figure in the Home Office study, and that migrants made a smaller net contribution than British-born people.

The long-term structural costs of immigration would include an extra 64,000 primary school places from 2013 in England and Wales for the children of immigrants, at a cost of £130 million a year. In the 2000s the number of births by foreign-born mothers increased by 64 per cent to over 170,000 a year, placing a significant strain on education. When in 2009 the Government announced there was a chronic shortage of primary school places in London, the Cross Party Group on Balanced Migration said the figures suggested that the pressure on primary schools was intimately connected to a lack of border controls. Furthermore Labour MP Frank Field and Conservative Nicholas Soames said that the Government had lied about the truth that immigration was the main driver, instead referring to 'local circumstances'. This was 'deliberately misleading'.

A fair economic assessment would also have to include the £283 million annual cost of imprisoning foreign criminals in Britain since 1997; between 1999 and 2009 the foreign inmate population grew by 5,962, an increase of 110 per cent compared to a rise of 20 per cent among British prisoners.

A third of new households are a result of immigration. This brings with it pressures on the countryside, and the need for more roads, railways, airports and car parks, all of which bring social, economic and environmental costs. Greater population density, which creates sprawl and congestion, may also reduce productivity.[60] England's population density of 395 people per square kilometre is already the highest of any European country above a million people, and seventh in the world. By 2029 Britain's population will be 70 million, a rise of 10 million in just 24 years.[61]

On the notorious *Question Time* episode featuring Nick Griffin, Jack Straw said that we could not guarantee that population would not hit 65 million because it would involve forcing people to have fewer children, which went unchallenged despite being patently false. The British fertility rate is well below 2.1 children per woman, and has been for many years, so in the long term all population increase is due to immigration. Britain's native population will decline once the baby boomers start to die off, and by the end of the century Britain's population – now 62 million – would be down to 57.3 million if it had no immigration, compared to a population of 64.3 million with balanced migration; if it continues with its current level it will be 91.9 million. That is the difference of 34.6m immigrants and their descendants, the majority of them from outside Europe.

It would be an interesting place, and added to the physical cost of immigration one must add the cost of integration, which together, according to Oxford Professor of Demography David Coleman, amount to £12.8 billion per year. Professor Coleman says we must include 'the total cost of the integration process, and of the associated immigration and race relations businesses, the cost of meeting the special education, health, and housing needs of immigrants, the net effect upon the education of ordinary children in immigrant areas, the permanent need to "regenerate" urban areas of immigrant settlement instead of demolishing them, issues of crime and public order, [and] the multiplier effect on future immigration'. What about the cost of the Department for Communities and Local Government's role in 'community cohesion', or that part of the £80m cost of the Equality and Human Rights Commission which deals with race and religion? Post 7/7, the British taxpayer spends a fortune funding 'community cohesion'. Yet perversely some immigration costs actually appear as an economic growth in official figures. As Professor Coleman pointed out: 'The income of a "diversity consultant"… shows up in national statistics as part of that gain in economic output. But couldn't it just as well be deducted as a cost of managing diversity?' That is how the *Government* calculates the benefits of immigration – yet we make fun of people who say 'they're taking our jobs'.

And diversity has not even made Britain smarter. The economic reasoning behind open borders is that it brings the best together, a brain trust on a global scale, and yet in Europe's case this has not happened. Rather than being the grammar school of the world, Europe has become a struggling comprehensive. The EU attracts 85 percent of all unskilled migrants to developed countries but only 5 percent of the highly skilled, with the US and Canada receiving 55 per cent of the world's academically qualified immigrants. And the UK has a net brain loss, with 1.4-1.6 million British graduates working aboard, compared to 1.2-1.4 million highly-skilled foreigners here. The 'immigration equals dynamism' argument rests on the assumption that immigrants are most likely to have drive, energy and brains. Certainly the earlier settlers to the American colonies were weeded out in brutal Darwinian fashion, while later migrants to the United States tended to be more determined than those who stayed home (and as the US had no welfare, 40 per cent returned home penniless or were deported). But while many face perilous journeys, immigration is certainly not so hard in the 21st century, surviving in a welfare state even less so.

An IPPR report in 2007 concluded that 'hundreds of thousands of immigrants are a drain on Britain and its economy, not a benefit',[62] with migrants from wealthy countries being a boost, and those from the developing world costing more than they contribute. It found that fewer than half of Britain's 650,000 Somalis, Bangladeshis, Turks and Pakistanis have jobs and the four communities have the highest levels of benefit dependency. Almost no Americans and 1 per cent of Poles and Filipinos in Britain claim income support, compared to 39 per cent of Somali immigrants, and overall people from only 13 countries paid more tax than the average British citizen. The overall employment rate of immigrants, at 68 per cent, is lower than that of natives, about 75 per cent, as of 2008, so the stereotype of the hard-working immigrant supporting idle white trash is a middle-class fantasy. What these figures show is that the ideal sort of immigration, from the host country's point of view, is between countries relatively equal in wealth.

Immigration certainly benefits the home country in the short term, and is arguably the most efficient and humane way of helping the developing world to develop. According to the World Bank, in 2006 migrants sent home $250 billion in remittances, three times what developing countries received in aid from rich nations, and also exceeding the $200 billion of net foreign direct investment (£4 billion is sent back from Britain, compared to £2.3 billion sent to Britain from ex-pats). In Tajikstan, Moldova and Tonga, remittances account for a third of the economy, in Honduras a quarter, and in Sri Lanka it brings in more than tea exports. The Philippines even has a Migrant Workers Day, where the president gives a *Bagong Bayani* ('modern-day hero') award to 20 outstanding emigrant workers with a track record of sending money home. And remittances are more effective than aid, with the money in some urban areas ten times more likely than other forms of payment to affect a child's chances of remaining in school.[63] Remittances, in other words, are a good example of the conservative argument that people spend money more wisely on their families than government officials do.

This improves humanity's overall lot, which is why economists tend to approve of it. Yet this process also robs developing nations of their most energetic people, and as a result there is an acute shortage of medical staff in many parts of the globe, Western countries having recruited them without having to pay for their training. It is hard to see why this is ethical; indeed the UN passed three resolutions, in 1967, 1968 and 1972, condemning the West for stripping the developing world of its talent.

More recently, 16 African countries have asked Britain to stop recruiting their nurses, who their governments have often paid to train, and the brain drain is so pronounced that economists from Addis Ababa have concluded that African's loss of 20,000 professionals a year costs the continent $4billion annually.

As well as the brain drain, mass immigration also creates a dissident drain, allowing dictators to seamlessly remove opponents, a trick used by Communists rulers such as Fidel Castro and Tito. Neither does it ease population pressures in the developing world, as emigration encourages higher birth rates.[64]

Of course there is the argument that immigration allows skilled professionals to hone their skills in the first world, send remittances and then return home with added skills, yet this happens more in theory than in practise, and usually only once the economic situation of their homeland drastically improves – migration from south Asia to Britain is 12 times the rate of movement in the opposite direction, with many of those heading east elderly people returning home.

And if there is one debate more sentimentalised than that of immigration, it is the argument over the National Health Service, an institution that, as former Chancellor Nigel Lawson once remarked, is the closest thing the secular British have to a religion.

It is a common refrain that without foreign staff the NHS would collapse, and indeed a visit to an NHS hospital today is the closest thing anyone of my generation will get to witnessing the British Empire in action, with English consultants and managers ruling over various Indian doctors, Australian nurses and African midwives. In 2003 a third of all doctors were born overseas, and even in our diverse society the NHS is exceptionally cosmopolitan. But why is that? The clue is in the name, for this jewel of the national welfare state is dependent on foreign staff precisely because it is nationalised. The NHS's virtual monopoly of healthcare means that doctors, nurses and other health care professionals are paid below the market rate, the NHS using its market dominance to suppress wages. Britons are simply not willing to work for wages set by a socialised state medical monopoly. Even in the United States, which is far more diverse and which allows medical professionals fairly easy entry, only 15 per cent are born overseas, half the NHS proportion.

Of the five professions with the greatest proportion of foreign-born workers, two are in healthcare, and another – scientist – is overwhelmingly state-dominated. Even if the skill and hard work of Indian doctors is very much appreciated and a benefit to the country, immigrants often replaced British doctors who went abroad to receive better wages, usually in North America; meanwhile there are 100,000 fully-trained nurses in Britain not nursing because the pay and conditions are not good enough, and a third of trainee nurses drop out. (And the diversity of the NHS does not necessarily improve quality – foreign-born doctors are four times more likely to be suspended or struck off by the General Medical Council as their British colleagues).[65] It is paradoxical, for Britain only has socialised medicine because of the high levels of social solidarity it had achieved by the mid-20th century, and this partly because it was so ethnically homogenous. Without a strong sense of national identity people will not willingly pay for their fellow citizens' healthcare bills. This, of course, presents us with three options – either the status quo, whereby we continue to depend on previously-trained staff from the developing world, privatising the NHS, or ensuring that doctors and nurses receive the market rate, in tandem with restrictions on the number of non-UK nationals who can work in each healthcare category.

In recent years Britain has had a shortage of plumbers and other skilled tradesmen, largely because of the decline of apprenticeships and in the quality of state education in general. But the market had begun to rectify itself, partly because some tradesmen were by 2004 earning up to £80,000 a year, considerably more than many of their middle-class graduate customers. Newspapers even ran reports of professionals retraining as plumbers and electricians. Meanwhile the Government had reintroduced apprenticeships, and was actively encouraging firms to hire young people. So while householders appreciated the arrival of Polish workmen that followed the country's accession in 2004, who quickly gained a reputation for hard work, diligence and honesty, the market was already correcting itself.

Given a choice, firms are far more likely to employ cheap, fully-trained and hard-working Poles than take a chance on British youngsters straight out of school. If I were running a company, I probably would. But immigration designed to address short-term shortages may have the unintended consequence of creating the conditions that encourage them in the longer term, because young people are put off going into those trades. Able to stick its underclass on welfare while employing newcomers, the state is spared having to deal with the problems of illiteracy and unemployability, and without immigration Britain would have to address this failure. It is easier to snatch educated, well-socialised workers from abroad; easier in the short term that is.

Immigrants as replacements

But there is a deeper and more existential labour shortage. At the core of the economic argument for immigration and diversity is a belief that Europe needs replacements. As the historian Timothy Garton Ash put it: 'The populations of Europe are ageing fast, so more immigrants will be needed to support the pensioners, and these will largely be Muslim immigrants.' Stefan Theil warned in *Newsweek* that 'the surge of intolerance' in Europe was a disaster. 'The continent is heading for serious long-term economic trouble unless it learns to manage immigration intelligently.'

Europe's population is ageing and will eventually contract, and that means a shrinking ratio of the number of working-age people to retirees, so that within a generation the former will have an unbearable burden supporting the latter. Europe's problem is that its people want to enjoy the lifestyle that leads to a sub-replacement level fertility rate, a life of thirty-two hour weeks, five-week annual holidays (plus two weeks at Christmas), free health cover, retirement at 60 or 55, 20 years by the sun-lounger and another ten in care. Europe wants to sit back, and its post-1945 history has in many ways been one long quest for continent-wide retirement, its civilisation too tired to fight any more

But there are no 'optimum' birth rates, as such. If a country wishes to decrease its population, having a total fertility rate below 2.1 is not necessarily bad; the retirement age will have to rise, and the economy would most likely contract, but GDP per capita would not, and in the longer term there may be benefits from a reduced population (the Population Matters think-tank argues that Britain's optimum population is between 20 and 30 million).

Yet even if Europeans were to accept levels of immigration that would make the most lurid Right-wing fantasies come true, it would not help, for the problem with replacements is that they eventually grow old and need to be replaced. And the numbers required would be stunning. The United Nations population division calculates that replacing the EU's age structure and support ratio would require 670 million immigrants by 2050, including almost 60 million for Britain alone, which would dwarf Western Europe's current population of 400 million.[66] And the National Center for Policy Anaylsis calculated that in order to keep America's Social Security payroll going, the US would have to double its immigration over 20 years, the equivalent of half the non-elderly population of Latin America.[67] Another report, by the C D Howe Institute in Canada, concluded that 'the number of young people Canada would have to attract' to pay for its future welfare bill would be 'preposterously large'.

And most immigrants to Europe pay *less* tax than the natives, so even the most outlandish immigration figure actually underestimates the level needed. Furthermore, once immigrants become European they, and their children, no longer want to do the jobs Europeans won't. As Christopher Caldwell says: 'So the moment immigration is successful socially, the main economic reason society thinks it "needs" immigrants in the first place vanishes. At that point, to ensure that those jobs-nobody-wants get done, society must recruit a new reserves army of foreign-born grunt workers, which sounds like the capitalism of Karl Marx's worst imaginings.'

How much people are swayed by the thin economic arguments, and how much by the concept of diversity itself, is hard to say. A 1991 study by the Economic Council of Canada found that even a theoretical doubling of immigration to 1 per cent of the population a year would make only a 1.4 per cent difference to the economy compared to immigration of 0.5 per cent a year, but then advocated that it should be done anyway because it would 'make Canada a more interesting and exciting society' (is that possible?). Imagine if Europe was next door to a continent full of white-skinned, English-speaking Christians famed for their conservative views on women and gays, who were also fecund and could provide lots of cheap labour. Would the collective voices of the intelligentsia be insisting we import a million a year?

Most of the 'economic' arguments for movement are really only arguments for universalism, which are shared by few outside the western intelligentsia, and not by immigrant themselves; after all, people do not migrate from Somalia or Pakistan to Britain for the sake of 'diversity', but come with the far more noble intention of feeding their families. As the Pakistani-born writer Sarfraz Manzoor pointed out: 'They seek to come for the simple reason that it is better to live here than where they came from. That is an entirely honourable and understandable reason. But it is ludicrous to suggest that the only impact this has on our country is economic.' The natives respect this motive, but most do not receive any obvious advantage from the exchange, which is why they have come to make themselves believe in some vaguely pseudo-spiritual rewards instead.

Immigration is a form of social debt, offering small short-term financial benefits with long-term social costs to future generations, and the social effects are considerable. The economic argument is a red herring convenient for both sides, since liberals do not want to raise the clearly unpopular social implications of immigration, and conservatives cannot honestly discuss the issue without being accused of racism. And yet those social implications are enormous, and most damaging to the poor and vulnerable.

5

Diversity and inequality:
The social costs of mass immigration

What sort of country do we want to live in? Most liberals, it is reasonable to say, aspire to a Scandinavian-style society where people use public transport, the state looks after the weak and poor, and the middle class actively want to send their children to the local comprehensive. A tolerant, progressive and egalitarian society, Sweden is often cited as a template, a happy place despite, as Labour MP Alan Johnson once pointed out, all the Ingmar Bergman films. But liberals also want the dynamism of the United States. They love America's racial diversity while despairing of its hostility to socialism and welfare, not to mention its violence. And yet these two desires – for diversity and egalitarianism – are contradictory.

Conservative politician David Willetts christened this the 'progressive dilemma', and in a 1998 *Prospect* magazine roundtable suggested: 'The basis on which you can extract large amounts of money in taxation, and pay it out in benefits, is that most people think that benefit recipients are people like themselves facing difficulties which they too could face. If values become more diverse, lifestyles more differentiated, it is harder to sustain the legitimacy of a universal, risk-pooling welfare state. This is America versus Sweden.' In the same magazine two years later political academics Alan Wolfe and Jytte Klausen suggested that solidarity and diversity are both desirable, but 'unfortunately, they can also conflict. A sense of solidarity creates a readiness to share with strangers, which in turn underpins a thriving welfare state. But it is easier to feel solidarity with those who broadly share your values and way of life. Modern progressives committed to diversity often fail to acknowledge this.'[68]

In one of the most influential books of recent years, *The Spirit Level*, epidemiologists Richard Wilkinson and Kate Pickett argued that inequality is linked to most indices of social deprivation, such as poor health, obesity, depression and crime, and that these problems affect the rich as well as the poor. While their theory and methodology has been questioned,[69] most people would agree with the premise that vast inequality is a bad thing, and yet the authors glossed over a massive elephant in the room: that a society's ethnic and racial diversity correlates strongly with its inequality levels. The most egalitarian countries tend to be the most homogenous, or at least homogenous until very recently, with Denmark, Japan, Sweden, the Czech Republic and Slovakia topping the latest UN Gini index of inequality. Behind those are the more multi-ethnic European states, Holland, France and Britain, followed by the semi-European Canada, and then the truly diverse United States. At the extreme end are the fantastically exciting, sexy, carnival-mad, grossly unequal and violent Bolivia, Colombia, Brazil, South Africa and Paraguay.

Despite the *Spirit Level's* call for huge government action to equalise society, the level of state spending on wealth redistribution does not hugely affect inequality levels. As the authors conceded, New Hampshire and Vermont have the third and fourth lowest levels of income inequality in the USA, and yet the former is one of the least redistributive states and the latter one of the most. But both are among the most ethnically homogenous regions in the Western hemisphere, as are most of the other egalitarian US states, Alaska, Utah, Wyoming and Idaho, while the least homogenous states also tend to be the most unequal.[70] Overall there is a medium-strong correlation of 0.453 between a US state's inequality levels and the size of its minority population. If Vermont or New Hampshire were as diverse as Alabama or Louisiana, it is highly unlikely that they would have the high levels of solidarity necessary to bring about greater equality, however much they spent on welfare. And the *Spirit Level* authors' argument that inequality leads to general increases in negative indexes among both rich and poor also applies to diversity; mixed white-black states in the US have worse health outcomes, and higher murder rates, both for blacks and whites, than overwhelmingly white ones.

The roots of social equality lie not in financial but social capital, the term used by sociologists to describe social trust and solidarity, and the degree to which interpersonal relations can be seen as capital just as any other form. Although first coined in the early 20th century by L.J. Hanifan, it was popularised in *Bowling Alone*, Professor Robert Putnam's bestselling 1999 study of American society, which analysed why people had become more inward-looking, lonely and unhappy. Social capital has value, just like physical capital, and is closely related to the idea of civic virtue. A society where people trust each other, and as a result are more likely to be honest, politically engaged and law-abiding, will be wealthier, happier and freer as a result; and these are not things that the state can legislate for. In the US levels of social capital and equality rose and fell in tandem throughout the 20th century. Social capital affects not just inequality levels but levels of social solidarity, trust and happiness, which is why more diverse societies and areas tend to be both more unequal and less trusting.

So while socialism can temporarily reduce inequality, for redistributive policies to work there must already be high levels of social capital. Sweden is not egalitarian because it is socialist; it's socialist because it's egalitarian, and it's egalitarian partly because it is, or was until very recently, ethnically homogenous. In contrast diverse societies, and diverse areas of the United States in particular, lack the capital and civic engagement necessary to reduce inequality.

   European liberals are horrified in particular by the small size of the American welfare state, which strikes many as positively Darwinian. Yet welfare spending is a reflection of civic engagement, and correlates strongly with diversity. In their 2001 paper *Why Doesn't the US Have a European-style Welfare State?* Harvard economists Edward Glaeser, Alberto Alesina and Bruce Sacerdote suggested that American welfare stinginess was a result of too many recipients being black or Hispanic, and too many taxpayers being white. The paper also found that US states that are more ethnically fragmented than average spend less on social services.[71] And in a 2005 study called *Fighting Poverty in the US and Europe: A World of Difference,* Glaeser and Alesina suggested that roughly half of Americans' antipathy towards European-style socialism could be accounted for by the ethnic diversity of the US. Glaeser later wrote: 'The redistribution gap between the United

States and Europe could best be explained by America's greater ethnic heterogeneity and more conservative political institutions. Countries with more ethnic diversity generally spend less on social programs.' Glaeser's colleague Erzo Luttmer also found that 'people in the United States who live around poor people of a different race are more likely to oppose welfare spending'.

Even when they don't leave a diverse area, whites vote for lower welfare spending. Robert Putnam[72] found that 'across local areas in the United States, Australia, Sweden, Canada and Britain, greater ethnic diversity is associated with lower social trust and, at least in some cases, lower investment in public goods'. There is also evidence to suggest that diversity erodes faith in institutions that rely on pooled resources. In Britain researchers at Mori found that levels of satisfaction with local authorities decline steeply as ethnic diversity increases, even allowing that areas of high ethnic mix tend to be poorer.[73]

This affects politics, too. According to the pre-eminent American historian C Vann Woodward, racial divisions have often been used to reduce the appeal of redistributionist political movements in the US and abroad. America's only two periods of welfare expansion, Franklin Roosevelt's New Deal and Lyndon Johnson's Great Society, both came during the long break in mass immigration between 1924 and 1965.

In that same period income inequality steadily declined, so that by the 1960s America 'was more egalitarian than it had been in more than a century', after which it began a sharp rise upwards. As Putnam says: 'the last third of the twentieth century was a time of growing inequality and eroding social capital... The timing of the two trends is striking: somewhere around 1965-70 America reversed course and started becoming both less just economically and less well connected socially and politically.' Nineteen-sixty-five was also the year that the United States opened its borders to non-Europeans with the Immigration and Nationality Act.

Both the United States and Britain have become steadily more unequal as they have become more diverse. One report, 'An Anatomy of Economic Inequality in the UK', indicated that by 2007-8 Britain had reached the highest level of income inequality since just after the Second World War. Political philosopher Phillip

Blond noted in *Red Tory* that 'in 1976, the bottom 50 percent of the British population had 12 percent of the wealth (excluding property). By 2003, that percentage had fallen to 1 percent.'

Prospect magazine editor David Goodhart, in one of the most influential essays of the early 21st century, wrote about the problems of a welfare state in a diverse society, noting that 'sharing and solidarity can conflict with diversity. This is an especially acute dilemma for progressives who want plenty of both solidarity (high social cohesion and generous welfare paid out of a progressive tax system) and diversity (equal respect for a wide range of peoples, values and ways of life).' This 'suggests that the left's recent love affair with diversity may come at the expense of the values and even the people that it once championed... Progressives want diversity, but they thereby undermine part of the moral consensus on which a large welfare state rests.'

A functioning welfare system relies not just on people being intimidated into paying tax and behaving altruistically, but feeling that they have a moral duty to do so. Without a sense of civil duty, and a wider reserve of social and moral capital, the state begins to rely on force.

Goodhart was one of the first on the Left to question the orthodoxy that diversity was in itself a good thing, noting: 'The Left is reluctant to acknowledge a conflict between values it cherishes; it is ready to stress the erosion of community from "bad" forms of diversity, such as market individualism, but not from "good" forms of diversity, such as sexual freedom and immigration.' Conservatives, he noted, ignored the issue because they were not as interested in solidarity, but were trying to prove their diversity credentials. Although two British academics, Bhikhu Parekh and Ali Rattansi, argued in response that the welfare state arrived at the same time as mass immigration, as Goodhart later replied, this assumes that the welfare state suddenly arose from nowhere.

In fact it came on the back of a century of slowly-changing and mutually-agreed social reform, and on top of centuries of nation-building by teachers, social reformers, vicars, ministers and various other individuals and groups who built up the nation's social capital reserves. In contrast, attempts to impose modern democracies and welfare systems on countries with little civic engagement have all failed. Social capital, just like any other kind, requires generations of careful saving and hard work, and can last long after its original source dries up. Perhaps we are currently running on the reserves that were built up by our ancestors. Indeed people who claim to be above such attachments, and who argue that nations and religion are outdated, may be social capital free riders, living off the trust built up by those same institutions they disdain.

A Society of Strangers

Britain's social capital probably peaked during and after the Second World War, the threat of outside danger tending to heighten group solidarity. Britons have looked back fondly on the 'Blitz spirit' ever since, as solidarity steadily declined with greater wealth, inequality, mobility, cultural change and immigration.

The British welfare state, plans for which were finalised during the conflict, was the fruit of this social capital. National Insurance was based on the mutual or friendly societies of the 19th century, where groups of working people, often from the same church, pooled their money as a form of insurance should one of them fall sick. These institutions were built on trust, and when the British welfare state was created it was understood that a national welfare state would be hard to maintain without a feeling of nationhood. William Beveridge, architect of the welfare state, said in 1942 that social insurance would require 'a sense of national unity overriding the interests of any class of section'. This was not a 'Right-wing' idea by any means. In a 1931 book *Equality*, the Christian socialist R.H. Tawney wrote that 'what a community requires... is a common culture, because, without it, it is not a community at all'.

Perhaps nations did begin as imagined communities, with mythologised histories built around the person of the sovereign and military victories, but that myth-making helped to create real communities. Living in societies that enjoy the benefits of nationhood, we easily forget that it is not the natural state of affairs. Before the advent of modern nations men and women owed their loyalties to their extended families, clans or, in certain contexts, their religious communities. The clan was needed for protection, to enact justice and to ensure contracts were met. The creation of nations, under which common law ensured that justice was dealt out by disinterested magistrates, allowed the radius of trust to expand and, even where the authorities were not close at hand, mutually-understood norms of behaviour were built up. And so, with enormous increases in social capital, people living in nations, social solidarity maintained by a deliberately-encouraged patriotism, were able to speed ahead of societies where men still owed their loyalty and protection to clan and tribe.

And while some academics argue that Britain has always had multiple identities of class, region and religion, these have never been strong enough to threaten the integrity of the nation. It was the strength of what Sir Arthur Bryant called 'the legal and spiritual association of men of different creeds, callings, and classes in a nation' that helped to create political structures. As Scruton put it: 'Thanks to national loyalty citizens were able to set religion, family and personal networks in the background of politics, and make common cause with strangers in the election of their government. They were able to acquire that strange habit – unknown in most of the world – of regarding people whom they intensely disliked and would never vote for as nevertheless entitled to govern them.' Once able to govern collectively, the nation-state was able to create that fantastic testimony to man's capacity for good – the welfare state.

The national community is the only environment in which democracy has thrived, for democracy requires a citizenry that feels itself part of the political process, even when in opposition to the government. National history and national identity also promote trust and solidarity within a society, something that liberal ideals fail to do, precisely because they are so vague and un-exclusive. That the international institutions favoured by liberal universalists, the United Nations and European Union, tend towards corruption and waste, reflects the failings of these ideals.

So one can believe in the nation-state because of some romantic ideal, or just pragmatically see it as the most effective way for producing a fair and democratic system that helps the weakest. But welfare systems work less well if people do not identify with the nation; they must feel that the people they are supporting with their hard-earned money are people like them, and who would help them too. Welfare was created as a quasi-contractual agreement between state and citizen, the very term 'National Insurance' expressing the understanding that welfare is, in Scruton's words 'part of being together as a nation, of belonging with one's neighbours, as mutual beneficiaries of an ancestral right'. The language of public debate has made universalism difficult to argue against, with terms such as 'discrimination' and 'exclusion' now shorn of their original morally-neutral meaning.[74] Yet the nation-state, and its benefits, is by definition exclusive, just as any membership is; nationality must be discriminating if it is to create social trust.

Social housing represents the largest investment in the collective pot. It is also the most explosive issue in areas with high immigration, and it is not just a perceived grievance. In the years 1999-2009 the number of foreign-born tenants in social housing increased from 800,000 to 1.1 million, a 38 per cent rise. At the same time, the number of UK-born social tenants fell by about 1.2 million.[75] And because the total social housing stock decreased, the proportion of foreign-born increased by 54 per cent to over 11 per cent of the total. Meanwhile the waiting list over the years 1997-2010 rose by over 50 per cent (and 87 per cent in London).[76]

Because the cost of social housing comes out of a shared pot, rather than individual wealth, shortages aggravate communal tension far more than private housing does. This does not matter so much in the United States, where social housing accounts for only about 2 per cent of all housing stock, compared to 25 per cent in Britain. Diversity is less problematic where the role of the state is small, and a large social housing sector may be incompatible with a multi-ethnic democracy, causing too much resentment, segregation and identity politics.

The United States is unusual in having an 'elective nationality', yet the US has always been strict about newcomers adopting an American culture that was explicitly not universalist, revolving around the English language, English law, Scots-Irish folk music and a range of cultural influences from Germany, Scandinavia, the Netherlands and France. And elective nationality brings with it certain pressures, so that the US has traditionally been less tolerant about 'foreignness'. Norman Tebbit's famous cricket test – would the children of immigrants support England or their parents' countries? – was shocking to English liberals because dual loyalties have never been an issue, but perfectly intelligible to Americans, for whom such attachment to the old country is less sympathetically viewed. (Until recently Americans could not even hold dual nationality.)

The universalist ideal rests on the belief that human beings are willing to share such a collective system with the rest of humanity. But evolutionary psychology suggests that humans have developed kin selection, those tribes with the strongest sense of in-group altruism being the most likely to survive. Although modern nations are not as compact as tribes and individuals probably have little genetic interest in helping compatriots, evolution has caused us to adopt innately different attitude towards in-group and out-group members. No universal altruism has evolved because a sense of universal altruism would have no evolutionary advantage. Garrett Hardin argued in a 1982 essay, 'Discriminating Altruisms', that a world without borders or distinctions is impossible, because groups that practise unlimited altruism will be eliminated in favour of those that limit altruistic behaviour to smaller groups, from whom they receive benefits.

An extreme example of this is the white liberal environmentalist who decides, for the good of the planet, that he or she should remain childless – the result being that future generations will contain fewer white liberals (some might argue that that's not a terrible thing). Another is the country that opens its borders based on a universalism not shared by other nationalities. Hardin called universalism 'altruism practised without discrimination of kinship, acquaintanceship, shared values, or propinquity in time or space… To people who accept the idea of biological evolution from amoeba to man, the vision of evolution from egoism to universalism may seem plausible. In fact, however, the last step is impossible… For three billion years, biological evolution has been powered by discrimination.' In the words of 19th-century French philosopher Pierre-Joseph Proudhon: 'If all the world is my brother, then I have no brother.'

For two and a half thousand years men have tried to overcome their nature through various political structures, with disastrous results. Plato advocated abolishing the family and having the state raise everybody as children, to which Aristotle responded: 'That which is common to the greatest number has the least care bestowed upon it... How much better it is to be the real cousin of somebody, than to be a son after Plato's fashion!' The universalism that opposes all discrimination, on the basis that there are no in-groups and out-groups, follows in the Platonic tradition of utopia; morally impossible to argue against, once you accept its definitions and language; unworkable in reality.

This aspect of human nature is unlikely to be overcome, and it may be necessary to have in-groups and out-groups, and to treat people differently from within and without. Hostility to and warmth to strangers, xenophobia and xenophilia, may be competing and balancing drives in the human mind, with a surplus of either a danger; too much of the former and a tribe becomes warlike, too much of the latter and the incentives for altruism decline.

The diversity illusion rests on the premise that humans will abandon nations, ethnic groups or religious communities for wider loyalties, yet greater diversity probably has the opposite effect. In-groups and out-groups of race and tribe are contextual, and affected by demography. A lone Asian boy in a school of whites, or a lone Protestant in a school of Catholics, will not form an out-group, nor even will a small sprinkling of minorities; he'll be an exotic curiosity. Groups form only when a minority becomes large enough to develop a group consciousness. The argument that immigration rules should overlook ethnic background ignores the fact that people do not always act as individuals. In every area of life, whether it's a propensity to have children, get married, divorced or go to church, people's behaviour is influenced by their peers. People think and act as 'Christians' or 'Muslims' or 'blacks' or 'whites' or any other group identity depending on the number of like-minded people around. An immigration policy that ignored an individual's (potential) group identity would ignore the effects it had on wider society; a colour-blind immigration policy certainly does not lead to a colour-blind society. The question should be asked whether theoretical opposition to discrimination is more important than living in a harmonious, and less racially conscious, society.

Liberalism developed within fairly homogenous national communities, and flourished best in those parts of the West with the least diversity. Even the great liberal political movements of the 1960s might not have happened had the US not been so high in social capital after its 40 year's immigration pause, a period when America was as un-diverse as it has ever been. And liberalism still flourishes best in the most monocultural parts of the US. Author Aaron Renn, an 'urbanophile' aiming to rejuvenate American cities, and by no means on the Right of the political spectrum, noted a similarity between the most progressive cities in the United States, among them Portland, Seattle, Austin, Minneapolis and Denver. 'But look closely at these exemplars and a curious fact emerges. If you take away the dominant Tier One cities like New York, Chicago and Los Angeles you will find that the 'progressive' cities aren't red or blue [Republican or Democrat], but another color entirely: white. Why? Progressive policies work better when there is high social trust. Lack of diversity in a culture makes it far easier to implement "progressive" policies that cater to populations with similar values; much the same can be seen in such celebrated urban model cultures in the Netherlands and Scandinavia... It is much more difficult when you have more racially and economically diverse populations with different needs, interests, and desires to reconcile.' The paradox is that while liberals love diversity, diversity turns people into conservatives; liberalism depends on trust, which relies on external barriers.

At the other end of the Gini index to Sweden is Brazil, another country famed for its attractive women (indeed the beauty of Brazil's people is used as a half-serious pseudo-scientific argument for multi-racial societies). But while it may have sexy women, Brazil also has a murder rate twenty times that of Britain. Most of the most murderous countries are highly diverse, including Honduras, Sierra Leone, Venezuela, El Salvador, Guatemala, Trinidad, South Africa and Colombia; the most homogenous countries, such as Japan and South Korea, tend to have the lowest crime rates. No wonder that throughout history less homogenous societies have tended to require a harsher justice system. In *Babylon: Mesopotamia and the Birth of Civilisation* Paul Kriwaczek attributed the brutal penal code of Hammurabi of Babylon to the new diversity of its society,[77] likening it to the differences between the United States and Europe: 'The draconian Babylonian laws, like the similar legal provisions of the Hebrew Bible, both reflect and attempt to limit the potential for discord and violence that always haunts a fragmented society.'

None of this bodes well for the future of European liberalism and European welfare systems, which by their very nature depend on trust. And already attitudes to the poor are becoming Americanised, according to the annual survey conducted by the National Centre for Social Research. The number of people who think the Government should spend more on benefits dropped from 58 per cent in 1991 to 27 per cent in 2009, and while newspapers called it the 'Thatcher Effect' it may have less to do with the former prime minister, and more the inevitable consequence of diversity. And as our society increasingly resembles that of the United States we can be sure that appeals to fight inequality with taxpayers' money will increasingly fall on deaf ears.

In the past few years, social democratic states in Europe have begun to reduce the size of their welfare states, including Sweden, which has recently begun a diversity experiment bolder than Britain's. On current demographic trends the Scandinavian nation will be the most Islamic country in Western Europe by mid-century, with a Muslim immigrant-descended population somewhere over 20 per cent. Its great welfare institutions and its high level of equality may hold up – but history does not suggest so.

6

Happiness
Atomisation and diversity

The benefits of diversity are often expressed in the language of youth, immigration bringing vibrancy, dynamism and regeneration. But while London may have all those qualities, it is lacking the most youthful and dynamic of social demographics – teenagers. In 2008, 50,000 children celebrated their first birthday in inner London, compared to only 26,000 who turned 14, a similar pattern being found in Manchester and Birmingham, the three cities between them containing the 20 most teen-free boroughs in England,[78] according to the Office for National Statistics. The exodus of families from the cities peaks in the years just before the children enter primary and secondary schools, with the most popular counties of destination being Devon, Dorset, North Yorkshire, Worcestershire and Cumbria.

Why should this be? Newspaper articles explain this 'chicken run' in terms of 'better quality of life', 'a sense of community', 'lower crime' and 'better schools', but a less delicate term might be 'white flight', as the middle-classes flee problems aggravated by immigration and diversity. Many middle-class liberals remember how their childhood experience of ugly racism towards the class's only non-white pupil influenced their politics. Now there is a completely different dynamic in their child's school and they find themselves talking about a 'better quality of life', unable to express their anxiety in a society where English sexual hypocrisy has been replaced by new collective white lies.

What later became termed 'white flight' pre-dates the arrival of non-whites, and has socio-economic as well as racial factors – sociologists call it 'secondary migration'. In the 1860s Walworth, a prosperous if unspectacular area of south London, experienced a rapidly changing population when the middle-classes escaped from the path of poor rural migrants, especially but not exclusively Irish. Walworth's well-to-do fled to Peckham, Brixton and Clapham, and the area never really recovered (a century later it experienced a far more pronounced movement following West Indian immigration). Exodus from the city has been a feature of civilisation for some time, but in England it has markedly accelerated in recent years. So if diversity is such a good thing, why do so many people vote with their feet to avoid it?

Confronting this taboo leads us to the question of whether someone can be a good person and want to live in an area with people largely of the same ethnic group. Reluctant BNP voters, when questioned by journalists, often find it hard to articulate why, aside from economic pressures, they do not want foreigners and minorities moving into their neighbourhood. Or in David Goodhart's words: 'is it ever acceptable to be racist? Why do people feel more comfortable around people like them? Is this a permanent feature of society or passing? Can it be educated out of existence?'[79] The evidence suggests that, if it can, it is only to a certain degree.

After *Bowling Alone*, Robert Putnam, a self-declared liberal whose daughter is married to a Central American, went on to look at social capital in neighbourhoods across the United States. The paper that resulted, *E Pluribus Unum: Diversity and Community in the 21st century*, made uncomfortable reading. Putnam found that ethnic diversity had an extremely negative impact on social life, so that 'in the short run… immigration and ethnic diversity tend to reduce social solidarity and social capital'. After detailed interviews of nearly 30,000 people, in the largest ever study of civic engagement in America, he concluded that in diverse communities people tend to 'distrust their neighbours, regardless of the colour of their skin, to withdraw even from close friends, to expect the worst from their community and its leaders, to volunteer less, give less to charity and work on community projects less often, to register to vote less, to agitate for social reform more but have less faith that they can actually make a difference, and to huddle unhappily in front of the television'.

Among the most trusting places were New Hampshire and Montana, poor, rural areas of West Virginia and East Tennessee, and cities such as Bismarck, North Dakota, and Fremont, Michigan, all homogenous, while the least trusting were ethnically diverse cities such as Los Angeles, San Francisco and Houston.

'People living in ethnically diverse settings appear to "hunker down" – that is, to pull in like a turtle,' Putnam wrote, adding that 'immigration and ethnic diversity challenge social solidarity and inhibit social capital' and 'across American census tracts, greater ethnic heterogeneity is associated with lower rates of car-pooling, a social practice that embodies trust and reciprocity'. Overall, he said: 'In the most diverse communities, neighbours trust one another about half as much as they do in the most homogenous settings.' Such is the discomfort that this subject inspires that Putnam delayed the report's publication for five years, hoping to find proposals to compensate for negatives which it 'would have been irresponsible to publish without'.

Putnam recounted other examples of diversity weakening trust, such as among Peruvian micro-credit cooperatives, where ethnic heterogeneity is associated with higher default rates; in Kenyan school districts, where ethno-linguistic diversity correlates with less voluntary fundraising; and in Pakistan, where clan, religious and political diversity is linked with failure to maintain collective infrastructure such as roads and schools. Even studies of prisoners' dilemma have suggested that people are less likely to betray a member of their own ethnic group. In the game two 'suspects' are offered a deal; if one testifies and the other remains silent, the defector goes free and the silent accomplice receives a long prison sentence. If both players betray each other, they each receive a five-year sentence, but if both remain silent they both receive a mild punishment. Within experimental game settings players who are more ethnically diverse (regardless of whether or not they actually know one another) are more likely to defect. Such results have been reported in many countries.

Putnam is far from being the only academic to have noted the downsides of diversity. A study by Harvard's Alberto Alesina, New York University's William Easterly and Reza Baqir of the IMF found that municipal spending on roads, education and rubbish collection was lower in racially diverse cities. Economists Matthew Kahn of the University of California in Los Angeles (UCLA) and

Dora Costa of the Massachusetts Institute of Technology (MIT) reviewed 15 recent studies in a paper published in 2003, all of which linked diversity with lower levels of social capital. They found that greater ethnic diversity is associated with lower school funding, census response rates, and trust in others.[80]

Putnam's report also contradicted the accepted idea that diversity was good for the workforce, noting that 'international heterogeneity (in terms of age, professional background, ethnicity, tenure and other factors) is generally associated with lower group cohesion, lower satisfaction and higher turnover'. This is certainly not the only study to find this; among others a CBI-backed survey by the Policy Research Institute on Ageing and Ethnicity (which, as one might guess by its name, is not a hotbed of white supremacism) found that only a third of businessmen thought that diversity helped business, while more disagreed.[81] Studies in the US have shown that, where firms do have ethnically diverse workforces, they benefit from playing down such difference and emphasising what workers have in common.[82]

Although Putnam was horrified by the messages of support he received from racists, his study certainly put into the language of sociology what many people feel intuitively, but are unable to express, that they are happier in neighbourhoods among people like themselves. People in Britain appear to feel the same; a report by the Home Office suggested that 'the more ethnically diverse an area is, the less people are likely to trust each other'. Trevor Phillips of the Equality and Human Rights Commission accepts that people are happier if they are with people like themselves: 'We've done work here which shows that people, frankly, when there aren't other pressures, like to live within a comfort zone which is defined by racial sameness.' Alas, as we shall see, government's solution to the problems of diversity is never 'less diversity' but always 'more government'.

People have a preference for cultural and ethnic sameness. English people are quick to see expansive body language as aggression, and the behaviour of outsiders with different behavioural norms adds to the stresses of life. In the context of lowered community trust, even diversity's advantages are doubled-edged. One of the most visible benefits of diversity is in sport, where immigrants have vastly improved Britain's sporting power. Yet sports such as football are a substitute for community spirit and identity, and especially attract people who feel a great sense of atomisation, those same feelings which are aggravated by immigration.

The difficulty we have dealing with this issue is reflected in the number of euphemisms attached to immigration. The most commonly-used cliché about multi-ethnic areas is that they are 'vibrant', a synonym for exciting which stems from the Latin *vibrans,* 'to shake'. It is often used by rural-based writers who extol the virtues of exciting London on their days out to the capital, and it is true: visually, sartorially, musically, cosmetically, aromatically, and in many other ways, London is vibrant and fun to explore, precisely because of the mark that immigrants have made on local culture. Yet few people choose to settle down in vibrant areas, and most people don't necessarily want their neighbourhoods to be 'shaky'. Calling in on a non-stop Freddie Mercury-style orgy with bare-buttocked dwarves walking around with trays of cocaine might be some people's idea of fun; living above someone who holds such parties less so. 'Vibrant', often estate agents' slang for 'non-white', has now mostly come to be used ironically, like so much of the language of multiculturalism. The use of another diversity jargon word is telling; 'community' only became popularised just as the thing it described began to decline, and is most commonly used by local government officials in those multi-ethnic areas where such a sense is most lacking. Later 'community' came to be used exclusively as an ethnic term, 'the black community', 'the Asian community', and generally 'communities' as a substitute for 'non-whites'. The Government even has a 'communities' minister whose job it is to look after race relations and 'community cohesion'.

Diversity can make people unhappy; it may even drive them mad. In London studies have shown higher incidence of schizophrenia, suicide and self-harm among ethnic minorities living in neighbourhoods with fewer people of the same group, than in areas where they are dominant, even when they are more affluent.[83] Under the Marxist consensus this was always explained as a product of discrimination and prejudice, which could be solved through anti-racism measures. The mental health profession is even accused of racism because it disproportionately sections members of some groups. When in 2007 psychologist Swaran Singh co-published a systematic review pooling data from all British studies of detention of ethnic minorities under the Mental Health Act, and found no evidence that higher rates of detention were due to racism, he was denounced in public. And yet, he wrote, 'careful studies in different countries have shown that rates of serious mental illnesses are high in all migrant ethnic minorities, indicating that this is a function of migration rather than ethnicity. Researchers have used culturally neutral assessment scales devised by the WHO, rated the assessments blind to ethnic origin of the patients, and even had psychiatrists from the Caribbean recheck the diagnoses. The findings stand'.[84]

Mental illness is a part of the immigrant's experience, a process that can be sad, stressful and isolating, sometimes even more so for the second generation. In 1932 Ornulf Odegaard, a Norwegian psychiatrist, reported high rates of schizophrenia among his countrymen in Minnesota, and it seems unlikely that this can be explained by the racism of American natives towards blue-eyed Nordic immigrants. And higher rates of psychosis in migrants have since been reported in several countries. A 2011 University of California report found that levels of mental illness were far higher among Mexicans in the US than Mexicans back home. As Dr Singh said: 'Childhood exposure to economic adversity, family breakdown, social exclusion and living in areas with poor social cohesion all increase the risk. Ethnic minorities have higher rates of psychosis as they are much more likely to suffer these adversities.'

The idea that mental illness is explained by racism is undermined by the variant rates in immigrant groups. In the Netherlands Moroccan and Turkish immigrants have higher than average rates of psychosis but the levels in Moroccans are far higher, which Singh suggests may be because Turks mostly migrated as families, while Moroccans came as single men. In Britain African-Caribbeans, a visible minority but one without the same levels of self-segregation or religious and extended family structures as Asians, are 44 per cent more likely to be sectioned, 29 per cent more likely to be forcibly restrained, 50 per cent more likely to be placed in seclusion than the population as a whole, and make up 30 per cent of inpatients on medium secure psychiatric wards. The Dutch do not discriminate against the Moroccans anymore than they do Turks, and the English do not discriminate against blacks or Irish (who also suffer higher rates) anymore than they do Asians. High mental illness rates are caused by the shock of dislocation and diversity, a shock that can be sustained with community support. As Dr Singh explained, in minority groups 'values and beliefs, family structure and community norms... can bolster resilience and reduce the impact of adversity'.

And it is a trauma that affects natives too. Novelist Tim Lott recalled how his mother explained in her suicide note: 'I hate Southall, I feel so alone.' As he wrote: 'In case anyone dare accuse her of any racism, she may have hated Southall, but my mother was incapable of hating people. She worked in the last years of her life as a dinner lady in an all-Asian school and was much loved. But she was lost. Her world had disappeared.' It is a feeling many Britons share.

Social structures provide protection against mental collapse, which is why the decline of institutions hits the poor hardest. Psychologist Martin Seligman has suggested that modern individualism and consumerism has led to unprecedented depression because we can no longer fall back on the institutions of religion, country and family. He wrote: 'When you fail to reach some of your personal goals, as we all must, you can turn to these larger institutions for hope... But in a self standing alone without the buffer of larger beliefs, helplessness and failure can all too easily become hopelessness and despair.'

As those institutions have weakened, British society has become more atomised and unhappy. Richard Laylard, author of *Happiness*, one of many books that in recent years has addressed the subject, suggests that the decline of social trust brought about by migration may also lead to rising crime: 'Crime rates are high when there is geographical mobility. Indeed, the best predictor of crime in a community is the number of people each person knows within 15 minutes of their home: the more they know, the lower the crime rate. So we should try to sustain communities and not rely on "getting on your bike" or international migration to solve our problems, as free-market economists often urge.'[85] He noted that crime had risen in every industrialised country between 1950 and 1980, with the sole exception of Japan, 'and its causes are not completely understood'. There may be many, but Japan is the one industrialised country not to have embraced diversity, and it has certainly retained a very high level of moral capital, as was demonstrated by the absence of major looting in the days following the 2011 tsunami.

Community feeling is strongest in areas in which kinship is valued. Regions with lower levels of mobility, and in which a large percentage of the population has lived in the area for many generations, have higher levels of social capital and trust. Yet this horrifies diversity enthusiasts. When residents in an area of Shropshire known for its strong sense of community, where over a third of residents had been in the vicinity for three generations or more, inquired about the possibility of building social housing for the children of long-standing residents, they were told that it would break race relations laws. In Greenwich, south-east London, the local council's 'sons and daughters policy', of giving preferential treatment to people with long-standing roots and relatives in the neighbourhood, has been a persistent target of anti-racist campaigners.

Across the river in Tower Hamlets, researchers at the Young Foundation discovered that hostility to Bengali settlement was linked to how rooted an individual was to the area, in terms of length and 'local commitment'. They found: 'The people who are most put out by Bangladeshi settlement are precisely those with the longest involvement in the community and greatest stake in the area. Conversely, those who mind least about Bangladeshi settlement are those with least local commitment... Hence it was among the "yuppies" that we found the most reliably positive attitude towards Bangladeshis, commonly tailing off quite quickly into an indifference to the issues, or gentle suggestions that the respondent was above such matters.' For middle-class settlers the Bangladeshis gave the locality 'an exotic aspect and cheap, agreeable eating spots – rather like being on a permanent foreign holiday'. In contrast people with children in the area were far more racially hostile, and there was strong correlation between racism and an individual's Local Family Network Density index (LFND). The person who finished top of this index turned out to be the one supporter of the BNP in the survey.

Londoners take pride in their apathy to race, and disdain more traditional parts of Europe where minorities find it more difficult to settle, yet in this sense our atomisation could be our strength (and many like the anonymity that comes with big cities). But how much atomisation do we want?

In turn white flight increases suburbanisation, which further atomises, being a flight not just from the cities but also from civic life. Urban planners Andrew Duány and Elizabeth Plater-Zyberk call suburbs the 'last word in privatisation, perhaps even its lethal consummation and... the end of authentic civic life,' where people no longer shop at local stores with familiar faces but choose impersonal supermarkets. Suburbs damage community life because sprawling disrupts 'boundedness', so people end up living in areas of endless, homogenous housing rather than in communities with a village-like quality. But thanks to runaway house prices, most Londoners who wish to start a family have the choice of either living in a high-crime inner-city area with poor schools, or moving out to dormitory towns where they often have no connections, spending thousands of pounds a year to commute up to four hours a day (Britons have the longest average commutes in Europe, and the most expensive railways). It is important to stress that immigration has not caused these problems, but it has certainly made them worse. The environmental impact on the country, not just from the population increase but the need for more transport infrastructure and suburban building, must also be taken into account. While another little known casualty of Britain's diversity drive may be the Welsh language; post-war immigration has caused perhaps the biggest shift westwards since the Anglo-Saxon invasion, as Londoners and Brummies flock to the West Country and Wales, including Welsh-speaking areas. Children in London's schools may speak up to 150 languages, but what impact will it have on Britain's oldest native tongue?[86]

*

Bonding v bridging

The major weakness of a diverse society is that bonding social capital – within a group – tends to conflict with bridging capital – between groups. This may be a mildly humorous inconvenience for southerners wishing to become part of the community in the close-knit Yorkshire Dales, but the stakes are raised in an ethnically diverse society. As Putnam says: 'A society that has only bonding social capital and no bridging social capital looks like Beirut or Belfast or Bosnia... tight communities but isolated from one another.' So where diverse societies are concerned, community spirit may actually be a bad thing; in Birmingham the riots of 2005 started because a tight-knit Asian community came into conflict with a tight-knit black community.

So in order to prevent a society fracturing into sectarian strife, it must sacrifice some community spirit, because the only logical way to increase low bridging capital is to reduce bonding capital; but aside from the costs involved in terms of personal happiness, if we believe in the freedom of movement and association, then we must also accept that voluntary segregation is a fact of life in a free society. Harvard Professor of Political Science Eileen McDonagh once asked: 'Is it better to have neighbourhoods legally restricted on the basis of race, but with everyone having everyone else over for dinner, or is better to have neighbourhoods unrestricted on the basis of race, but with very little social interaction going on between neighbours?' However this is not quite the question being asked by most. Very few people believe that legal restrictions should be imposed; the real question is whether the government should force diversity upon communities.

The most famous example of this was the desegregation of American education, and the busing in of children to neighbour-ing schools. The civil rights movement was, says Putnam, 'aimed at destroying certain exclusive, non-bridging forms of social capital - racially homogenous schools, neighbourhoods, and so forth'. What they replaced it with was the harder part. 'Proponents of bussing believed that only through racially integrated schools could America ever generate sufficient social capital – familiarity, tolerance, solidarity, trust, habits of cooperation, and mutual respect – across the racial divide. Opponents of busing replied that in most parts of America, neighbourhood schools provided a unique site for building social capital friendship, habits of cooperation, solidarity. The deepest tragedy of the bussing controversy is that both sides were probably right.'

Although the majority of poor and middle-class whites had opposed integration, they were defending the morally indefensible. Judge J Skelly Wright summed up the mood of the time when he wrote in a 1967 court decision: 'Racially and socially homogenous schools damage the minds and spirits of all students who attend them.' And yet the controversial predictions made by opponents that integrated schooling would lead to whites leaving Washington DC and other urban areas turned out to be true. While the civil rights movement was unquestionably just, and bussing one of its iconic moments, in terms of actual results bussing was a failure. Educational standards declined, and white flight followed on an enormous scale, which resulted in segregation levels remaining the same in many areas. This was not bone-headed bigotry on the part of white parents; integrated schools had higher levels of disruption and conflict, and lower grades. Even Judge Murray Schwartz, who had overseen bussing, took his own children out of state schools three years later and sent them to private academies.

Schools are a major driver of secondary migration; for while diversity may well increase bridging capital, and improve race relations up to a point, it does not necessarily make for better-educated young citizens. The worst boroughs in England for education are Hackney (47.1 per cent white British), Haringey (47.6 per cent), Southwark (52.6 per cent) and Leicester (under 60 per cent). But where the authorities consider segregated education a serious threat to society, they may choose integration over education. After race riots in Burnley in 2001 and the subsequent election of BNP councillors in the Lancashire town, blame was placed on its divided schools. The Government spent £250 million on closing down (and mostly demolishing) its eight largely segregated schools and building five new ones, gerrymandered to have a suitably mixed Asian and white intake, 'so the kids now have the chance to grow up together', in the words of one politician. Hameldon Community College was created by merging Ivy Bank

High (41 per cent A–C GCSEs in the 2001 tables) with Habergham High School (the borough's leading state school, with a 66 per cent pass rate), yet produced only a 40 per cent pass rate, and was wracked by violence; police were called to the school 19 times in its first five weeks, attendance dropped to 25 per cent, and the trouble only abated after CCTV was installed in corridors. The school was in special measures within eighteen months. A second Burnley 'superschool', Shuttleworth, soon joined it. A third, the aptly named Unity College, was on 'notice to improve', and was placed in the bottom 5 per cent of the country in terms of value-added performances.

Two parents meetings at Hameldon attracted just 40 and 20 people for a school of 1,700 pupils. As the blogger Laban Tall put it: 'Just as any country with "Democratic" in its name is a dictatorship, so the word 'Community' in any institution should set alarm bells ringing. You know at once that whatever you'll find in the area, it'll certainly be uncontaminated by community.'

The council then sold one of the old school buildings, Burnley College, to the Al-Ehya Trust, which hopes to turn it into a private Islamic girls' school. In contrast nearby Blackburn is home to a Muslim girls' state school, which draws pupils from among the poorest wards in England, and yet regularly achieves among the best GCSE results in the country. Indeed one of the rarely mentioned aspects of the debate over faith schools is that their popularity in urban areas, such as east London, is partly due to parents wishing to send their children to schools where minorities do not constitute a majority.[87] Despite this the perceived need to close down high-achieving faith schools in the name of integration may become too compelling to resist.

Elsewhere the increase in diversity has led to greater segregation and in turn to the call for state action. Fewer than half the children in schools in inner-city Bristol now come from white British backgrounds, and where Somalis make up the bulk of two primary schools, segregation has become pronounced. After a report into the city's schools, council leader Barbara Janke said: 'One of Bristol's great strengths is its diversity… The report says that without rapid and effective action, like many similar cities in the UK, we could find ourselves in a situation where schools are increasingly socially and ethnically divided. We are committed to taking action to prevent this happening.' A 'strength' that is divisive? We can only assume the 'action' will be detrimental to bonding.

But can different communities be bridged? The debate about immigration and segregation is built upon the contact v conflict question. Contact theory holds that once brought into contact, people from different groups will become more tolerant as they become friends, lovers and eventually relatives. Conflict theory holds that greater contact will make people more hostile and racially conscious. There is some truth in both.

Contact theory is vital to the hope that, with time, and with the state's help, ethnic rivalry can be eliminated. It is a hope held by many; a draft paper drawn up for the Home Office in 2000 declared that 'anti-immigrant sentiment is closely correlated with racism' and that 'education and people's personal exposure to migrants make them less likely to be anti-migrant. The most negative attitudes are found among those who have relatively little direct contact with migrants, but see them as a threat.' But people who live in and around migrants are a self-selecting group in terms of attitudes to outsiders, since many of those who do not like immigration and have the means to leave have already left. Those unhappy about it get out, often replaced by more immigrants; those who are content, or too poor to move, come to accept it. Hostility tends to peak in those areas immediately outside areas of immigrant concentration; in France maps illustrating support for the Front National show its greatest concentration in districts forming a circle around North African areas, a phenomenon known as the 'Halo effect', which suggests that diversity inspires understanding in some, but higher hostility in others. A similar pattern emerges in England with support for the BNP.

On the other hand Putnam's findings suggest that diversity causes people to withdraw from everyone, since levels of trust are lower intra-racially as well as inter-racially; rather than making racist bigots open their hearts to their neighbours, diversity probably causes them to stop talking to anyone. This also jars with the assumption that once an area becomes more multi-racial, the people become more civilised and less oafish, a view widely believed without any evidence. This was epitomised by actress Emma Thompson when she complained about the bigotry her black adopted son had experienced at university in Exeter, unpleasantness which she believed was due to the town's lack of diversity. But would her son, who was verbally abused in the town, have been less likely to experience unpleasantness in Manchester or Birmingham? Has diversity made Moss Side and Aston pillars of gentlemanly behaviour? (Thompson had been asked in a Q&A session: 'What can we do to change the whiteness of Devon and Cornwall?' Would anyone ask the same thing about a region of Nigeria and its 'blackness'? Exeter University is over 12 per cent non-white and Devon over 3 per cent – what percentage would satisfy Thompson and her audience?)

The negative experiences of black or Asian students are not necessarily the result of racism so much as individual criminality and societal breakdown. In 2009 two Asian BBC reporters posed as a Muslim couple on a council estate in Bristol for a documentary, the woman wearing a headscarf, and between them they were racially abused more than 50 times, with 'Paki', 'Taliban' and 'jihad' all shouted at them. Yet Southmead, the area in which it was filmed, is a notoriously crime-ridden district with high levels of social pathology. In the same month in the same area a female police officer was scarred for life after being hit in the face with a pint glass, nearly blinding her. Would any respectable-looking white man in a suit and glasses on the estate have gone unmolested, or for that matter anyone who appeared to be strange, different, weak or vulnerable? Probably not. Diversity is unlikely to improve such behaviour; it might only make the local hooligans more wary of using racial slurs for fear of retribution from their Asian counterparts. But in a race-obsessed society people are much more likely to focus on the racist aspect of such abuse rather than on the general rudeness and anti-social behaviour found among the British population. As a result 'tolerance' of other cultures, a message with pro-diversity, pro-immigration undertones, is promoted at schools as a remedy for such incidents, when simply teaching a politically neutral concept of good behaviour and basic humanity would do just as well.

By the logic of some anti-racists any area that is overwhelm-ingly white must be thuggish and dangerous for any outsider, yet pretty much anyone can walk around Scotland or Ireland today without harassment. Despite Britain being an overwhelmingly white country in 1966, there was no recorded racism towards foreign players when England hosted the World Cup. Some 51,000 working-class Liverpudlians packed Goodison Park to watch Portugal beat North Korea in one of the most thrilling matches in the tournament's history without feeling the need to racially abuse Eusébio or the Koreans, despite the city having a chronic shortage of diversity sensitivity trainers at the time. They just had common decency.

Besides which, to classify people as either 'racist' or 'non-racist' is overly simplistic, if not inaccurate, as these are spectral feelings found across the population. It may be that the arrival of one exotic family in a white neighbourhood unsettles a tiny proportion of people, those in the 100th percentile of social anxiety, with hardened hostility to outsiders. The arrival of a second and third family may discomfort people in the 90-99th percentile. We may view all these people as racist by the general definition, but there comes a critical mass when those in the 70th, 60th, 50th and 40th percentiles all feel unsettled, threatened, unhappy or depressed about their changing neighbourhoods. Most people are in those middle bands, and are happy with diversity up to a point. Researchers such as Isaac Marks at London's Institute of Psychiatry have suggested that it is not possible to neatly divide the population between a small group of xenophobes and 'the rest'. Feelings of suspicion and hostility towards outsiders are found in almost all of us.

Conventional anti-racist logic dictates that anyone who feels uncomfortable about diversity must be morally bankrupt, misguided or in some way indoctrinated in colonial racism, but it is most likely that those at the median point have considerable feelings of unease. The extent to which this is learned is still not known, but studies of children aged 3 show that racial stereotypes and preferences are ubiquitous by that age, and in all races; the only children who display no racial prejudice are those suffering from Williams syndrome, a brain disorder caused by the deletion of 26 genes from chromosome 7. Evolutionary psychologists such as E O Wilson have found much evidence showing that tribal feeling is innate, and that this leads people from an early age to express a preference for those like them in language and appearance.[88] So while it is despicable to act unpleasantly to someone because of their origins, to feel uncomfortable about large numbers of different people moving into one's neighbourhood is just human. We may be repeating the mistakes of Marxist regimes in believing that human nature can be essentially changed through ideology. In the Soviet Union overt expressions of capitalism rarely came to the fore, but in their acquisition of better housing, cars, food and school places, people's actual behaviour rarely conformed to the greed-free ideology that the state promoted. People just did not admit to it for fear of being labelled as 'capitalist'.

Money plays a big factor, which is what makes diversity rather hypocritical. Middle class areas of London are often pleasantly mixed, and the local primary schools a mish-mash of different nationalities, but to send a child to such a multicultural paradise one needs to be able to afford a £500,000 property. With lower levels of trust and higher crime, poorer communities depend on more clearly defined social norms and stronger networks, since they do not have the barrier of wealth to shield them. Rich, diverse neighbourhoods such as Kensington, west London (perhaps the most cosmopolitan area in Britain), or fee-paying schools for that matter, suffer less in the way of reduced social bonding because wealth in itself is a form of segregation, and ensures a certain norm of behaviour. A white Englishman living in a £1 million house next door to an Indian immigrant in a £1 million house will have a very different experience to a white Englishman in an East End council flat next to a Bangladeshi immigrant. With little cost to group solidarity, the wealthy man can truly enjoy the individual benefits not just of his neighbour's friendship but also perhaps the experience of learning about Indian culture, history, language and – yes – cuisine.

And just as Soviet citizens failed to live up to the state's beliefs, so do citizens of multicultural states, for often the loudest yelps for diversity come from the drivers of Range Rovers. Even the most outspoken anti-racists often move out of London when their children reach school age, or when they wish to settle down permanently. The Clash's Joe Strummer, having been at the forefront of anti-racism in music, left London for rural Somerset. Billy Bragg, the folk singer and anti-racism campaigner, is known as the 'Bard of Barking' despite the fact that, as Garry Bushell put it, he 'live[s] in a lovely big house in West Dorset'. Bragg campaigned against the BNP in his native town, yet lives in one of the whitest places in Europe. Of course he can argue that he has a right to speak about the subject, as he did not leave Barking because of immigration, but because he's wealthy and wanted somewhere nice and spacious. Mick Jagger grew up across the river in the still very white but poor Dartford, but has not stuck around, choosing to spend his time in the south of France or Martinique, as any sensible person would. But Bragg's hard-earned wealth does mean that he has what philosophers call moral luck, while poor people in Barking do not. Bad moral luck means fate forcing you into making immoral decisions between the lesser of two evils; accept a social change that makes you unhappy, or be a racist. After it was revealed that Bragg had been the subject of a hate mail campaign by some demented BNP supporters who called him a hypocrite, he told the press that 'even in a sleepy village like ours, people reject the politics of racism'. And yet rejecting the politics of racism is not especially difficult for people living in a sleepy village, since they experience little of the downsides of diversity.

But hypocrisy is not necessarily a bad thing in practice, depending on how it affects those being lectured to. A religious leader who cheats on his wife and drinks while commending sobriety and monogamy to his flock may still be a force for good, if those parishioners find that sobriety and monogamy help their lives (which they probably will). That their pastor has fallen to temptation does not mean that abstinence is any less beneficial, only that temptation is strong. But a politician who extols the benefits of immigration on his poor followers, immigration he will not experience to any large degree, is somewhat different, if his flock does not necessarily benefit from the lesson.

7

Dynamism and Ghettos
The effect of mass immigration on immigrant communities

Even if diversity has downsides, surely the dynamism it brings is necessary to economic survival in the long-term? After all, diversity allows people to learn from different cultures and so for ideas to spread around the world. Think of everything that makes our lives better, from the food we eat to the technology in our houses to fusion music such as rock'n'roll. It's obvious: diversity enriches. G Pascal Zachary wrote in *The Diversity Advantage* that 'hybridity brings innovation and homogeneity brings stagnation' and that 'strangers instinctively question things that natives take for granted. They stimulate new perspectives because, simply, many things strike them as odd or stupid. That's why it's great for any tribe to have a smart stranger injected into it.' While Bhikhu Parekh argued in *Rethinking Multiculturalism:* 'Different artistic, literary, musical, moral and other traditions interrogate, challenge and probe each other's ideas, and often throw up wholly new ideas and sensibilities that none of them could have generated on their own.'

Diversity can certainly drive productivity and innovation in high-skill workplaces. Scott Page, the University of Michigan political scientist and author of *The Difference: How the Power of Diversity Creates Better Groups, Firms, Schools, and Societies,* argued that diverse teams of employees 'tend to be more productive'. And this is certainly the thinking in the corridors of power. John Elliott, Chief Economist at the Home Office, suggested that: 'We can think of migrants contributing to the productivity of native workers directly though spillover effects. One might imagine a migrant surgeon standing next to a domestic surgeon and them learning from each other.' Sometimes the argument for immigration is put in terms of biological diversity, as the alternative to incest; or an eco-metaphor is used, proponents suggesting that without large-scale immigration countries became 'stagnant' like some sort of dying post-Soviet central Asian swamp. In the words of Randolph Bourne, an early 20th-century advocate of diversity: 'We have needed the new peoples... to save us from our own stagnation.'[89]

Historically, at least, none of this is true. The overwhelming majority of new ideas and perspectives have not come from mass immigration, but from natives who brought ideas back from abroad, through small settlements of skilled foreigners, or from literature and other forms of media. Britain's least stagnant period, the late 18th and 19th centuries, a period of unprecedented advancement in culture, politics and healthcare, coincided with almost no significant immigration, despite it also being an age of hugely increased levels of trade. Not only did the country advance in almost every field, it was also able to import new ideas – not to mention many foreign words into the English language – with almost negligible immigration. Neither was it entirely due to empire; the supposed dynamic benefits of diversity are mostly due to trade, education and freedom, not the movement of people. In the 17th century the mono-ethnic Netherlands and England surged ahead of other countries in political and scientific development, while the multi-racial super-states of eastern Europe were bogged down by reaction; the Ottoman Empire retreated into itself, turning away from printing, science and political reform, and in Austria-Hungary and Russia progress was held back by ethnic and religious rivalries and fears. Open borders do not necessarily make for open minds. In fact the arrival of newcomers in large numbers questioning native practices can cause people to become defensive about their traditions, as even people who dislike their own families tend to defend them against strangers; it took a Catholic to start the Reformation, and later Christians to question the truth of the Bible.

In the last four decades Britain has imported millions of immigrants from around the world while almost abandoning the teaching of languages, so that from 1997 to 2007 the proportion of British children learning a GCSE in a foreign language almost halved.[90] My father grew up in rural England and did not meet a black person until he visited the United States, yet speaks eight languages; I was raised within earshot of the Notting Hill Carnival and can just about ask the way to the train station in French. While Enoch Powell, that hate figure of British racism, could, for all his faults, speak Urdu fluently. How many products of the current British education system, and all its equality and diversity classes, can understand any Asian languages, except those of Asian descent? Likewise an appreciation of Turkish architecture, Greek philosophy or German music does not require the importation of large numbers of people. I grew up with people from all around the world, and although their friendship enriched my life, beyond one or two Armenian swear words I'm not sure I learned anything about other cultures merely from being around people with different colour skin. Schoolboys in London comprehensives don't sit around discoursing on the great Hindu religious texts. Some shallow attachment to diversity acts as a substitute for real learning and cultural enrichment

Diversity certainly does carry benefits where professions require certain culturally-specific skills. Throughout history immigrants have often brought new techniques that the natives did not themselves possess. Sometimes this has been through drift and chance, and sometimes the deliberate work of despots. After expelling the Jews, Edward I brought over Italians to run the banks, Lombard Street in the City of London being the only reminder of a group long absorbed into the gene pool (although almost certainly the economy still suffered from the Jews' expulsion). In late medieval England immigrants from the Low Countries were encouraged to establish the wool and beer industries, the Dutch having brewing skills that were unavailable in England. In Russia Peter the Great imported western Europeans to run industries that were unknown in his kingdom, while his successor Catherine brought in German farmers to the Volga region.

The name given to multi-racial Britain, the 'Chicken tikka masala society', after a dish created in Birmingham by the Indian-born millionaire Sir Gulum Noon, reflects the fact that food is perhaps the one area where diversity really has brought dynamism and innovation. Britain has enjoyed a culinary revolution, and now has 10,000 Indian restaurants (of which about 7,000 are actually run by Bangladeshis), part of a curry industry worth over £3 billion a year. Today chefs remain one of the five most immigrant-dominated professions, being a skill in which natives really cannot perform as well as immigrants (restaurants in London's Chinatown have threatened to go on strike over immigration raids with the perfectly sensible point that British-born chefs simply could not cook Chinese food as well[91]). But aside from food, there is very little in the way of innovation that actually comes from immigration. Britain, like the rest of Europe, acquires most of its new ideas from the United States, without any significant movement of peoples. In contrast very few new business practices, technological or medical innovations have recently arrived from Africa, the Middle East or South Asia, the regions of origins for most immigrants. The argument that 'without the oxygen generated by fresh water, it would stagnate', in Zachary's words, does not bear out. Immigrants are only necessary for innovation when bringing specific skills unknown to the country.

Even this argument may be outdated; in the global economy, thanks to new communication techniques, immigration is no longer a necessity for the steady transference of new ideas. Japan is the most culturally absorbent nation on earth, and has almost no immigration. Technology also means that the benefits of diversity can be realised without the costs of large upheavals. Rock'n'roll was an early example of technology-induced fusion, of white Appalachian music and black blues from the Mississippi delta. Rock'n'roll should never have developed in such a segregated society, yet it did because recording technology meant that white musicians were able to listen to black music on vinyl. Technology, not integration, allowed this to develop. (Of course the music itself can be credited with changing social attitudes, which led to greater integration.)

Besides which, the argument that large-scale immigration connects us to different parts of the world is a double-edged sword. Britain's large Indian and Chinese communities may prove useful in forging closer ties with those countries, but in other cases we may not necessarily want them. Pakistan, Afghanistan and

Somalia are the most concentrated centres of terrorism and Islamic fundamentalism in the world; with none of their futures looking especially bright, our links to them through the large and growing immigrant communities in Britain are a security weakness.

Rather than fostering dynamism, diversity might even retard it by removing the necessity that gives birth to invention. Almost alone of the industrialised nations, Japan has accepted that a decline in the birth rate will bring labour shortages, but rather than hiring large numbers of immigrants, they have developed robots to do much of their dirty work. Robots are more expensive than immigrants in the short term, and less effective, but Japan's cheap labour diet has spurred its robotic development far ahead of the West's. And unless *The Terminator* turns out to be true, it's a policy far less likely to cause future social unrest.[92]

'The Diversity Paradox'

There are certainly cultural and educational advantages to immigration, but these are largely felt at the top of the skills range, in university departments and highly-skilled jobs. Just as Italian political economists Alberto Alesina and Eliana La Ferrara argue that diversity is a drain on poor countries, and a benefit to rich countries, it may also be that it's a drag on poor communities and a benefit to rich ones.[93] Outside of this elite the social costs do not justify its small benefits. Page calls this the 'diversity paradox', and argues that, with diversity bringing both benefits and drawbacks, 'there's got to be a limit'. If social solidarity declines too far as a result of immigration, any economic benefits will disappear.

And these drawbacks are often felt most by immigrants themselves, and their children. Migrant groups can become 'market-dominant minorities', in Amy Chua's phrase, but they can also become ghettoised, brought in to perform unskilled, badly-paid and short-term jobs, often becoming a racial underclass by the second generation, the children growing up in low-waged, often workless, households with an abiding sense of humiliation and confusion about identity.

Britain has experience of both phenomena. British Indians tended to come from urban and mercantile classes, and already by

1981 a third of Indian males were classed as professionals, a higher proportion than white Britons. According to a 2002 cabinet office report one in 20 British-Indian men is a doctor, compared to 1 in 200 white men, and today there are seven times as many millionaire Patels as Smiths, even though Smiths outnumber them 10 to 1. The surname comes from Gujarat, an area of western India that has given England some of its most dynamic citizens of recent years.

Sikhs are the most successful immigrant group since the Jews, with higher average incomes than whites, and the highest average rate of home ownership, at 82 per cent. A 2010 study found that Thames Valley Sikhs and Hindus are most likely to be typical 'Middle Britons' in their lifestyle, attitudes and earnings, with the *Daily Mail* describing them as 'the bedrock of Middle Britain'. The little-mentioned Chinese in Britain are also successful, for, like an Athenian wife, the true measure of a minority's success is that it is never talked about. Some 45 per cent of Chinese-British men work in professional or managerial jobs, compared to 25 per cent of whites and Indians; Chinese pupils are 20 percentage points ahead of white British pupils in achieving five passes at grade A*-C, and four times more likely to achieve three or more science A-levels than the general population. Indians are three times as likely. In retrospect the British Government's decision in 1981 to prevent Hong Kongers from moving to Britain seems foolish. Despite this the Chinese population has grown significantly, from 5,000 in 1951 to ten times that number in 1971, most of them from the former colony, to roughly half a million today. This has caused few problems. But rather than illustrating the innate benefits of diversity, Chinese immigration shows that how well the party swings cannot entirely be blamed on the host.

The role of Indian and Chinese immigrants as 'market-dominant minorities' in Britain is similar to Asians in east Africa, the Chinese in south-east Asia and Europeans in Zimbabwe. Such groups have often become crucial to a country's economy, and their expulsion led to economic and social disaster, such as in Amin's Uganda, Nasser's Egypt, where Jews, Italians, Greeks and Armenians were forced out, Mugabe's Zimbabwe, or post-Saddam Iraq, from where most of the country's Christians have fled. Elite minorities are the upside of diversity, yet Britain often shuns them. For example, although a disproportionately educated, middle-class minority, European countries other than Sweden have so far refused to give preferential treatment to Iraqi Christians, despite having a greater claim to being persecuted, because it would be discriminatory. And yet anyone who cites the Huguenots as precedent must be aware that highly-educated immigrants of the same religious background who are being persecuted for their religion are more likely to be successful, well-integrated citizens; 17th-century England would have had a lot more problems had it instead imported 70,000 or even 700,000 ardent French Catholics, some of whom believed that England should be converted to Catholicism by force.

Non-elite immigration

Elite migration is one thing, but mass immigration can lead to the formation of an underclass, so that rather than bringing innovation, immigration creates a different form of stagnation. Pakistanis and Bangladeshis, who had a different demographic profile to Indian migrants, coming largely from rural areas, are twice as likely to be unemployed as the general population, while three-quarters of their children live in households earning less than half the national wage. Meanwhile black Caribbean and Bangladeshi men have unemployment rates of 14 per cent, twice the white rate, and Pakistanis 11 per cent; and only 28 per cent of boys from black Caribbean families achieve 5 or more A*-C grades, 20 points below the white British average, with Pakistani rates lying halfway between. Across Western Europe, Britain included, welfare levels, unemployment levels and various other negative indices of social deprivation are higher among most immigrant communities and their children than natives.

Immigrant communities can also be adversely affected by structures created by different societies. The West Indian islands from which many newcomers came in the 1950s already had a long tradition of fatherlessness, possibly a legacy of slavery, but it was held in check by the region's strong Christian culture, and by economic necessity. They arrived in a country where Christianity was in rapid retreat, and in which fatherlessness was subsidised by the state, housing rules having been changed in the 1970s to give priority to single-parent families. As church attendance dropped off for second-generation Caribbean immigrants, levels of father-lessness rocketed. The creation of a black underclass, seriously aggravated by low employment prospects and racial discrimina-tion, mirrored the problems of the United States, where Daniel Patrick Moynihan's 1965 report, *The Negro Family*, accurately warned that activist government policies would harm those they were supposed to be helping, increasing welfare dependency and other social pathologies. At the same time the US's immigration policy, changed that year, undercut blacks, just as many 19th-century African-American leaders had warned, to such an extent that black male unemployment rose sharply in the decades following.

This has had painful consequences. Journalist Rod Liddle sparked outrage in December 2009 by writing on his *Spectator* blog: 'The overwhelming majority of street crime, knife crime, gun crime, robbery and crimes of sexual violence in London is carried out by young men from the African-Caribbean community. Of course, in return, we have rap music, goat curry and a far more vibrant and diverse understanding of cultures which were once alien to us. For which, many thanks.' Liddle, a Left-wing writer who likes to provoke metropolitan liberals, was spurred by the case of two teenage rappers who tried to murder a pregnant 15-year-old girl one had impregnated for getting in the way of their careers, a case that caused not a fraction of the outrage that his comments did. The Press Complaints Commission ruled against the writer, the first time such a judgment had been cast on a blog, on the grounds that 'overwhelming' was an inaccurate word, although in terms of London proper (the postal area, rather than the county) it was not far off. Rather it was the tone that caused offence, and the fact that he had broken the ultimate taboo. If race is to our society what sex was to the Victorians, then inter-racial crime must be the female orgasm; and one is about as likely to hear black-on-white crime mentioned on Radio 4 as one might have heard the old Home Service discussing the G-spot.[94]

But in June 2010 the *Daily Telegraph* followed up Liddle's claims with a Freedom of Information request and found that, indeed, black men committed 67 per cent of street crimes in the capital, despite comprising just 15 per cent of the male population, and committed a disproportionate amount of crime in every category. So whatever his provocative language, Liddle's essential point was true, that immigration and the policies of multiculturalism had brought levels of violence alien to recent English history, including an almost American-style level of gun-crime.

When the issue is raised at all, the accepted, indeed uncontested, explanation in the media is that crime is caused by poverty, past injustices or racism, or because young men are stereotyped. This is appealing because it suggests that not only is such crime caused by structural faults, but that it can be indoctrinated out. Yet this explanation does not stand up to scrutiny. Bangladeshis are far poorer and commit less crime, while Pakistanis have higher rates of unemployment. Police racism and stereotyping is also an unlikely answer. Criminologist Marian Fitzgerald, who conducted the most thorough study of stop and search, concluded that black people were stopped more because of information from third parties, not profiling.

And the Marxist interpretation of crime ignores the fact that the West Indies has a very high crime rate, and has had one for some time. Britain's murder rate today is between 1.23 per 100,000 people, having peaked in the early 2000s, but still roughly twice what it was in the late 1950s (which does not take into account advances in medical technology and better detection and prevention technology). In Jamaica the homicide rate was 64 per 100,000 in 2009, while the figure for Trinidad and Tobago was 42, and Belize's is 30.8, all of which make America's urban dystopias look like dull Scandinavian suburbs in comparison. Even Barbados, considered a very civilised and genteel island by its many British admirers, has a homicide rate of 7.5. And while crime in Jamaica has massively increased since independence, in the early 1970s its homicide rate was still about 8 per 100,000, almost ten times that of England. It seems unlikely that this does not have a bearing on London crime patterns today.

Advocates for greater diversity often use the word 'fusion' or other terms borrowed from cooking or music, but not all cultural mixtures are positive. Few would say that the 'fusion' of European and Arab anti-Semitism in the late 20th century was an exciting example of cultural hybridity, yet people often assume the merging of cultures is, in itself, a good thing.

Across Europe fashion and popular culture is influenced by immigrants: in France *le look banlieue* is adopted by fashion-conscious teens, and in British inner cities and suburbs particular strands of West Indian social mores have come to influence a new urban subculture, alongside the global dominance of African-American music. From the late 1980s and 1990s some strands of this youth culture became more aggressive, and in the early 1990s the arrival of dancehall reggae (or ragga), a style of music often characterised (or caricatured) by its violence, coincided with the growing prevalence of pseudo-Jamaican accents among London teenagers. The Jafaican (fake Jamaican) dialect's most famous speaker is Tim Westwood, the radio DJ who sounds like an inner-city black youth but in fact grew up in East Anglia and attended a private school, and whose father, William Westwood, was the Bishop of Peterborough. Westwood, despite this, is highly respected in the music industry, even though he certainly influenced the Sacha Baron-Cohen character, Ali G. It should be bizarre; were an Englishman to start speaking in an inexplicable French or German accent he would be regarded as such a figure of contempt that people would probably take the trouble to wind down their car windows to shout abuse at him. Yet Jafaican has become widespread.

Accents and fashions display underlying insecurities and cultural aspirations; the rise of Received Pronunciation reflected a desire by the middle classes to embrace the values, lifestyles and habits of the British elite. In London the adoption of Jafaican, even among the privately-educated, reflects both a lack of confidence in British cultural values and an aspiration towards some form of ghetto authenticity. Middle-aged liberals may celebrate this example of cultural fusion, but people do not always adopt accents out of fondness for another culture, but rather insecurity and fear-driven conformity. London schoolchildren speak with perceived 'black' accents to appear more streetwise and tougher than they are, not out of admiration for Booker T

Washington or Martin Luther King.

But accents, especially affected ones, carry values with them, and likewise the adoption of certain fashions sends a particular cultural signal, in this case suggesting that the wearer and speaker has the aggressive, uncivil value system of the ghetto. Despite the despair expressed by many black teachers, the media hails the vitality and cultural vibrancy of London's hybrid youth culture, with its new and exciting slang which has made the country world leaders in certain musical genres, and this fusion has certainly made England a more vibrant, exciting place. But walking around London at 4 o'clock on a weekday afternoon, George Orwell would find it hard to recognise the gentle nation of which he said that 'in no country inhabited by white men is it easier to shove people off the pavement'.

What Charles Canning would make it of is another matter. Canning was the Postmaster General who in 1854 devised the original London postal areas, which were then subdivided in 1917. Those arbitrary and practical sub-divisions are now a matter of life of death to some, now that the city has the almost absurd phenomenon of 'postcode killings', with teenagers murdered for stepping into the wrong territory. Among the victims of recent years are 14-year-old Paul Erhahon, murdered because of a dispute between people living in E11 (Leytonstone) and E15 (Stratford), and 16-year-old Nassirudeen Osawe of N1 (Islington), stabbed to death by a Hackney (E5) gang. Meanwhile firearm offences in London rose by 89 per cent in the 2000s, while gun-related injuries and death jumped from 865 in 1998/9 to 1,760 a decade later. Police officers now routinely carry Heckler & Koch MP5 submachine guns, capable of firing 800 rounds a minute, and Glock semi-automatic pistols. In January 2010 a Freedom of Information request revealed that CO19 armed officers undertook eight operations in London estates the previous year, but officers in 'community impact assessment documents' had written that they were worried about the 'adverse' impact on community relations as suspects were 'predominantly black'. Community impact document are mandatory forms that police must now fill in to assess how a crime or operation would affect 'community cohesion', yet another layer of bureaucracy that diversity has imposed on the police.

Having to both fight crime and tread the path of community relations, the police now have a bewildering array of diverse criminal street gangs. Among the worst affected is Britain's 250,000-strong Somali community, of whom 48 per cent have no qualifications and barely a quarter of whom are employed, and who have fled a generation-long civil war for an alien environment. Rageh Omaar, the Somali-born television journalist, has talked of the 'crisis of our young men' and a 'sense of denial' within the community. As a *Times* report from 2009 noted: 'The most desta-bilising by-product of the large-scale Somali migration to Britain has been the propensity of a significant number of young Somali men to become involved in crime and to use violence. It is not the done thing for senior police officers to discuss such trends bluntly — the racial overtones are too sensitive — but on the front line the reality has been inescapable.'

The media are psychologically incapable of addressing this issue for fear of inflaming racial tension. The denial has become so ingrained that a broadcasting establishment that values challenging and taboo-breaking art becomes as strict as the Lord Chamberlain when it comes to discussing crime. A play that, for example, portrayed a statistically-accurate picture of interracial violence would never see the light of day, and no scriptwriter would even bother with a synopsis. Instead people seem to prefer the portrayal given in *White Teeth*, Zadie Smith's best-selling novel of multi-cultural Britain. One passage, describing the political rad-icalisation of a young Muslim, encapsulates the attitude of the London media class to inter-racial violence: 'The second reason for Mo's conversion was more personal. Violence. Violence and theft.' Mo's violent attackers were all different, the novel goes on, 'but they all had one thing in common, these people. They were all white.'

That corner shop owners suffer from intimidation and violence is undoubtedly true, but Zadie Smith's fictional school, Glenard Oak, was based on Hampstead Comprehensive in Cricklewood. That a shopkeeper in such a multi-racial area, as it already was in the 1980s, would be attacked only by white people is unlikely. It may well have happened, and such a person might really have existed, but certainly it reflects a world the readers want to believe in, that of a Muslim storeowner driven to extremism by white racism and violence. (No storeowner has ever become a suicide bomber. It is dealing with white liberals in academia, not white yobs in corner shops, which leads young Muslims to radicalisation. Shopkeepers do not have enough leisure time to build up the resentment and self-pity that leads to radicalisation.) Television and radio drama has often focused on the violence and aggression experienced by newly-arrived Asian and black families in white working-class areas. That is an accurate view, but not a panoramic one, and the impression of racial violence embedded in the national consciousness does not reflect the reality.

In its drama output the dominant BBC has created an idealised world of diversity for our living rooms. Television and theatre creatives proclaim a need for greater realism, but in many ways art has become less realistic than before the age of kitchen-sink dramas, and the London that television presents can often resemble some sort of parallel universe for people who actually live in the capital. And diversity is promoted in the media to such an extent that for two decades many people living in cities such as Carlisle or Newcastle might as well have been watching television from another country. Where older viewers do enjoy programmes that more closely resemble the England they grew up with, it is with a sense of guilt. When Brian True-Maye, producer of the ITV series *Midsomer Murders*, suggested there was no racial diversity in the rural-based programme because it was a 'bastion of Englishness', he was forced to step down by the makers.

And where 'diversity' has merely been a transition to ghettoisation, television again distorts. As Rod Liddle has pointed out, *Eastenders* still reflects the East End as it was in about 1981, where in reality Albert Square would be predominantly non-white, and the Queen Vic closed down. The real East Enders now live in Essex. It is propaganda with the best intentions, of course, and one would not wish the media to encourage ethnic hatred, but it perhaps allows us to sidestep difficult issues.

The factual media also has rules about mentioning crime and ethnicity, something encoded in Article 12ii of the newspaper's

Code of Practice: 'Details of an individual's race, colour, religion, sexual orientation, physical or mental illness or disability must be avoided unless genuinely relevant to the story.' And there are good reasons for this since, without it, newspapers might attempt to pander to the prejudice of readers (British newspapers almost certainly would, and in recent years some have tended to use the descriptive term 'Muslim' in headlines even when it was irrelevant to the crime committed). So it is understandable why the media downplays crime statistics. As with every aspect of the diversity experiment, highlighting the problems would risk aggravating it; white flight and general hostility might increase, and in turn minorities might feel targeted and rejected. But it is a problem nonetheless, and I have yet to hear of any ailment that has been cured before it has been diagnosed.

8

Multiculturalism
The liberal response to diversity

Just as Rushdie said, the new empire was built, with the British state adapting to its new colonial population just as it did the old one.

For the problems raised by importing new subject peoples, a solution came in the form of multiculturalism, a policy that can be traced back to Home Secretary Roy Jenkins's hailing, in 1966, of a new era of 'cultural diversity, coupled with equal opportunity in an atmosphere of mutual tolerance'.

Few political ideas of recent years have enjoyed such a meteoritic rise and fall as multiculturalism, so that today many liberals argue that it has been a failure, although what they mean by this term is not always clear. While 'soft multiculturalism' refers simply to cultural interaction, which most of us agree is generally a positive thing, multiculturalism can also refer to the idea that a society filled with diverse cultural, ethnic and racial groups is in itself a good, so that multicultural becomes just another word for multiracial. Most commonly, however, it is used to describe 'hard multiculturalism', the specific government policy that each culture should be valued equally, and that 'white' British culture should not be supreme. Multiculturalism as a policy was, in effect, the application of anti-racist doctrine to run a multi-ethnic society.

On a practical level the policy of dealing with minorities through unelected appointees within that community followed the system employed in previous diverse societies, such as the Ottoman Empire, and in the British Raj in India. But the philosophical idea behind it, that each culture must be equally valuable, was novel, and heavily influenced by the cultural relativism of the early 20th century, pioneered by the likes of German-American anthropologist Franz Boas. It was on a trip to the Arctic to study the Inuit that Boas concluded with these influential words: 'I often ask myself what advantages our "good society" possesses over that of the "savages". The more I see of their customs the more I realise we have no right to look down on them... As a thinking person, for me the most important result of this trip lies in the strengthening of my point of view that the idea of a 'cultured' person is merely relative.' That the Inuit strangled their elderly did not strike this thinking person as being less cultured, presumably.

The common view among European progressives had been that progress was attainable for all, and that there was such a thing as progress. Eighteenth-century French philosopher Denis Diderot suggested that people were less developed because of the climate and environment, and that habits 'are not African or Asiatic or European. They are good or bad.' He believed that 'everywhere a people should be educated, free and virtuous'. Diderot drew a distinction between people and culture – people were potentially equal but cultural forms were not. This made him one of the forefathers of liberalism, yet today many would see that statement as offensively racist, because it accepts that European norms are superior. Boas, in contrast concluded that progress was neither possible nor welcome, because no society was necessarily better than any others, and such ideas gained currency after the Holocaust. In 1971 two noted anthropologists, Catherine and Ronald Berndt, wrote: 'In serious comparative studies, "savage" and "barbarian", with its "barbarous" overtones, are no longer acceptable as labels for categories of mankind... There is something altogether too derogatory about them, too obviously ethnocentric.'

Such ideas were not entirely new. In the 16th century miserablist French philosopher Michel de Montaigne wrote of cannibals in the Caribbean that 'each man calls barbarism whatever is not his own practice; for it seems we have no other test of truth and reason than the example and pattern of the opinions and customs of the country we live in'. What was different in the post-war period was that speculative philosophical musings became a basis for society-wide policy. (Besides which, I doubt he would have welcomed such cannibals living around the corner from the Château de Montaigne.)

This would lead to some suggestions that even now appear absurd, such as anthropologist Bob Scholte's claim that 'Western science is only a culturally specific form of ethnoscience, not a universally valid way of verification or falsification'. While in a 1985 book, *Evolution as Religion*, Mary Midgley said that evolution was a modern original myth.[95] Richard Dawkins even recalled an anthropologist who told him a tribe who believed that the moon was an old calabash tossed into the sky could claim as much scientific truth as those people who believed it was a satellite orbiting the earth: 'They are brought up to see the world in another way. Neither way is more true than the other.' One can only imagine Professor Dawkins' face upon being told this.

The vast majority of people who did not spend their late teens in humanities classes might ignore such debate as academic self-indulgence, the modern equivalent to medieval theologians debating the number of angels who can dance on a pin,[96] but such thinking can have far wider effects on society at large, and it was within this environment that the policy of multiculturalism was allowed to develop.

Immigration before multiculturalism

This would create a very different environment for immigrants in the late 20th century to that of a century earlier. In 1885 a government inquiry into Jewish immigration concluded that 'steps must be taken to cause the foreign poor upon arrival to imbibe notions proper to civilised life in this country'. The Jewish community itself took the steps. Gerry Black's *Jewish London* recalls that: 'Schools... were the main vehicles for integration... The Jews' Free School in Bell Lane led the way... Between 1880 and 1914, one third of all London's Jewish children passed through its doors. Many were foreign-born, and arrived unable to speak the language. The school taught them English from day one, provided them with a refuge and a means of escape from poverty, educated them in both secular and religious studies, anglicised them and sent them out in the world fit to integrate into society... The *Jewish Chronicle* boasted that a young Pole could be placed in the Jews'

Free School with the assurance that at the end of his training he would be turned out a young Englishman'.

The JFS, as it is now known, successfully turned young Poles and Russians into English gentlemen, without their losing their Jewishness, and is today still one of the best state schools in the capital. And although the Jewish community themselves organised and paid for the school, it was symptomatic of a confident host culture which believed that foreigners wishing to live within the realm should become Englishmen, and of a minority who believed the same thing.

The Jewish community of the 1890s could turn children into 'English gentlemen' because there was a clear understanding of what that meant. Chief Rabbi Jonathan Sacks wrote of a *Times* editorial written on Sir Moses Montefiore's hundredth birthday in 1884, which had said that he had shown that 'fervent Judaism and patriotic citizenship are absolutely compatible with one another'. The Chief Rabbi reflected: 'My parents lived those values and taught them to us. They became the first Jews in their families for perhaps a thousand years not to teach their children Yiddish, because they wanted us to be English and to identify with the wider society.'

Indeed immigrants in successful assimilationist cultures are often hyper-patriotic, the Irish and Italians in America being prime examples (even Alf Garnett, the bigoted working-class Tory from the comedy *Till Death Do Us Part*, is supposed to have secret Jewish roots, a running joke in later episodes).

But by the time it came to educating young Pakistanis a century later no one was sure, for the same cultural forces that make mass immigration seem desirable also make integration difficult; assimilating into a void is a hard act for immigrants to pull off.

Ethnic minorities, the new thinking went, should not be forced to adopt a 'white' British identity, but instead should express their own, live by their own values and pursue their own lifestyles, and to say otherwise would be to argue that their culture might be in some way inferior. In conservative eyes, as Rushdie wrote in his essay 'The New Empire within Britain', 'A black man could only become integrated when he started behaving like a white one.' In the words of New Left activist Todd Gitlin: 'The very language of commonality could be perceived by the new movements as a colonialist smothering – an ideology to rationalise white male dominance.' Almost without resistance, multiculturalism meant that the Marxist definition of racism became the only one, so that it was racist to expect the same standards of behaviour.

The high watermark of multiculturalism came with the 2000 *Commission on the Future of Multi-Ethnic Britain*, set up by the Runnymede Trust, a 'race equality think-tank' funded by, among other governmental bodies, the Home Office, the EHRC and the Commission on Integration and Cohesion. The report concluded that Britain was 'both a community of citizens and a community of communities, both a liberal and a multicultural society', and since citizens had 'different needs', equal treatment required 'full account to be taken of their differences'. Equality 'must be defined in a culturally sensitive way and applied in a discriminating but not discriminatory manner'.

In other words – the state should treat people differently. But more tellingly the Parekh report, as it was known, being compiled by Labour peer Bhikhu Parekh, stated that 'Britishness' was an alien concept for many citizens as it had 'systematic, largely unspoken, racial connotations'. Since Britishness is the culture of a country that was almost entirely white until half a century before, to enforce it on newcomers is to enforce white cultural values. Integration must therefore be racist. Multiculturalism, 'celebrating diversity' or however one wishes to describe policies that argued against the need for integration, is essentially the official recognition of self-hatred.

Although multiculturalists do not hate themselves and *their* values, only those of conservatives who still cling to outdated attachments of nationhood and church and other racist, patriarchal institutions. Multiculturalism is fundamentally dishonest, because those who enthused for it most think their beliefs – universal, state-enforced equality, sexual tolerance and gender equality – are empirically right and uniquely derived not from dogma or prejudice but unquestionable moral truths. 'Self-hating liberals' rarely have a low opinion of themselves. So while multiculturalists are happy for minorities to reject British history and British patriotism, they expect them to embrace the values of the sexual revolution, even (sometimes) at the risk of suffering the lethal allegation of racism. These Left-liberal values are represented as universal, almost eternal, yet it is misguided to think they are necessary enduring. If native Britons became a minority in Britain, would their replacements necessary inherit their beliefs? There is nothing about British air that makes people liberal. Indeed the ultra-conservative values that postmodernists unleashed may prove stronger than them.

Post-modernism

It was a dishonest policy because immigrant cultures, rather than being genuinely valued by multiculturalists, merely provide a useful way to undermine conservative cultural mores, of use in recruiting allies against what Tony Blair called 'the forces of conservatism'. As James Bennett wrote in *New Criterion* magazine: 'Postmodernists deliberately embraced mass immigration without assimilation – specifically suppressing assimilation, in fact – in order to break down adherence to a common culture and to subvert prevailing family systems. A population without a common language, common assumptions, or indeed any means of generating a genuine polity is easier to manipulate and turn into the common clay from which a new transnational order can be moulded.

'As few outside of the minority recruited in the universities find such a future attractive, postmodernism has cultivated (or imported) as allies groups that hold or can be taught to hold grievances against the mainstream societies. They include racial, ethnic, religious, and sexual minorities who do not accept one or more shared premise or cultural characteristic of the common culture. Concepts of racial and ethnic authenticity and grievance narratives are used to bind these groups as allies against the majority culture, no matter how divergent the actual practices of the minorities are from the preferences of the postmodernists.'

Central to this majority culture was native religious dominance. Where there was religious plurality local government attempted to raise minority religions to equal status and to accommodate them as much as possible. In one sense multiculturalism was a natural extension of widening ideas of religious tolerance that had been developing for centuries. Blair Worden wrote in *The English Civil Wars* that: 'In a society without a police force or, ordinarily, a standing army, the preservation of order will seem dependent on the coherence, even the uniformity, of ideas and beliefs.' Seventeenth-century Englishmen did not believe that religious tolerance could be extended beyond Anglicanism without society descending into chaos, their eighteenth century descendents beyond Protestantism, and 19th-century Englishmen beyond Christianity. Perhaps a truly multi-cultural society is the next step in evolution, and today's sceptics are as outdated as their fearful forefathers. Yet those expansions of tolerance only tolerated faiths on the understanding that they unquestionably accepted the political settlement of the country, and it was understood that tolerance did not mean equality of cultures. Nineteenth-century Catholics and Jews could vote, own land and be recognised in every way as equal citizens, but Great Britain was still a Protestant country, and everyone knew it. Although this often resulted in prejudice, it became less oppressive with assimilation, greater secularisation and an ever more light-touched, unspoken Anglican dominance, which is where Britain had arrived at by the latter half of the 20th century.

The multiculturalist response was to knock down the whole edifice. From the 1980s schools in areas such as Waltham Forest and Newham in east London began to celebrate Eid and Diwali. Rather than being inclusive, this often had a socially divisive effect, since religious minorities, happy to accept the primacy of Christianity, felt resentment when another minority religion was given preference. If Hinduism is given official recognition, why not Islam? If Islam, why not Buddhism or Baha'ism? Why not paganism, which has now been given a certain amount of official status, with prisoners allowed dispensation for particular feasts. Britain's religious framework eventually begins to resemble the late Austro-Hungarian Empire, where orders in the Imperial Army had to be given in 16 languages, and this brings large social and financial costs. In May 2004 the CRE published guidelines for businesses on ways it should provide prayer rooms and give religious holidays to non-Christians; business leaders said the cost of implementing it could be £100 million a year.

As with 'political correctness', multiculturalism is often best known by the absurd decisions it inspires, in this case tabloid articles about local councils being overly sensitive to religious minorities. Many newspaper stories about 'offended Muslims' are exaggerated or entirely made up, and in many more cases action was taken not by Muslims but by offended white liberals using Islam to promote their agenda. Most Muslims prefer to live in a broadly Christian country than an atheistic one, and find objections to Christmas and other festivals baffling. Anjum Anwar, chairman of Lancashire Forum of Faiths, said downplaying Christianity 'provoke[s] antagonism towards Muslims and others by foisting on them an anti-Christian agenda they do not hold'. When Tower Hamlets banned the serving of hot cross buns because 'We are moving away from a religious theme for Easter', the Muslim Council of Britain called the decision 'very, very bizarre' and said such actions caused a backlash.

Multiculturalism was an extension of imperialism, with separate communities subject not to the rules of the land but to those of their group. This had been the system in the Ottoman Empire, where different ethnic and religious communities had separate laws, and the logical conclusion of multiculturalism was similar. Often this development was spurred by the introduction of human rights laws, as when Rastafarians have been spared prison for possessing cannabis. But cultural relativism has had some catastrophic effects. In Australia Aborigines were often treated according to their own customs rather than 'whitefella law', and as a result children were raped and murdered because social services were reluctant to intervene. In Britain some 15 Asian women and girls are murdered every year in honour killings. At the trial of Abdalla Yones, an Iraqi Kurdish refugee who killed his daughter Heshu for having a relationship with a Lebanese Christian, the judge said he would take cultural customs into consideration, leaving Kurdish feminists in the gallery to look on in despair. In another case twenty-year-old Tasleem Begum was murdered by her brother-in-law, who ran her over and reversed over her body three times, and then told the court the great shame she had brought on the family had altered the balance of his mind.

The plea was accepted and the judge gave him just six and a half years for manslaughter. Begum, raised in Bradford, had been forced into a marriage at the age of 16 to a much older man in Pakistan, but had fallen in love with another. Multiculturalism led the authorities to regard something as different, rather than wrong, and in doing so they allowed British citizens to suffer torture, murder and mutilation.

On a broader level the acceptance of cultural equality makes it harder to understand what the accepted norms of a society are, and for those living at the fringes of society this is especially tragic. White doctors have even been unable to recognise insanity, with one Asian doctor recalling 'a severely unwell Nigerian woman whose delusions and hallucinations about witchcraft were accepted by her doctors as a cultural norm', and a Sikh woman who had become sexually and financially reckless in the early stages of manic depression. 'Her husband's attempts to get her help were dismissed as the cultural response of an Asian male unable to deal with financial independence,' a doctor noted.[97]

The 1975 Bullock Report into education, *A Language for Life*, heralded the start of multiculturalism in the classroom. It recommended that 'No child should be expected to cast off the language and culture of the home as he crosses the school threshold, and the curriculum should reflect those aspects of his life', while 'All teachers need to be aware of the way books and pictures shape children's attitudes to one another and to society, and of the ethnocentric bias of many books in use in schools'. Furthermore, teachers were expected to have an understanding of Creole dialect 'and a positive and sympathetic attitude towards it'. It also argued that 'there should be further research into the teaching of their own language to children of immigrant communities and into the various aspects of bilingualism in schools,' and 'every school with pupils whose original language is not English should adopt a positive attitude to their bilingualism and wherever possible help maintain and deepen their knowledge of their mother-tongue'. Some of the proposals were even implemented in all-white schools.

And in the 1985 *Education for All* report, which investigated the 'educational needs and attainments of pupils of West Indian origin', Lord Swann and his team called for a multiculturalist curriculum to address racism in schools. On top of the extra demands placed on teachers – how many white people can speak Creole? – many educationalists have argued that multiculturalism in the classroom, and the pressure for teachers to help minority pupils raise their 'self-image', led to a decline in literacy and academic performance. According to Sandra Stotsky, author of *Losing Our Language,* multicultural textbooks have been less rigorous and demanding than those they replaced, and led to a lowering of general standards to accommodate minority pupils. Besides which, speaking to children in Creole will not help their opportunities in British society, which would be maximised by learning standard English.

This also had serious implications for social cohesion. When, in 1984, a headmaster in Bradford published an article criticising the policy of multiculturalism, he became the victim of a hate campaign of extreme ferocity. Ray Honeyford had been headmaster of Drummond Middle School for four years but had become increasingly disturbed by the effect of education policy on minority children. Honeyford, the son of an unskilled labourer injured in the trenches and one of 11 children who grew up in a house in Manchester without an indoor toilet or book, came to believe that multicultural policies were retarding social mobility.

In the article, which appeared in a small periodical, *The Salisbury Review,* he argued that the debasement of language used by anti-racism bureaucrats had made it difficult to talk honestly or clearly about racial and cultural matters, such as the way that some Muslim women were taught, quoting Orwell to the effect that politicised language 'is designed to make lies sound truthful' and 'to give an impression of solidity to pure wind'. He compared the current system of multiculturalism with the example of Jews in the 19th century, who were responsible for the upkeep of their own traditions, and who did not rely on the patronage of the state. He explained that immigrants often sent their children back to Pakistan or Bangladesh for years at a time, to stop them from becoming too British, and that the authorities turned a blind eye. In contrast any white parent who kept their child away from school would be punished. He wrote: 'I am left with the ethically indefensible task of complying with a school attendance policy which is determined not, as the law requires, on the basis of individual parental responsibility, but by the parent's country of origin – a blatant and officially sanctioned policy of racial discrimination.' Indeed 'positive' discrimination, the term usually given to policies that set a lower bar for non-whites, was an intrinsic part of multi-cultural thinking.

Honeyford argued that the children of Pakistani immigrants could only acquire a British identity if their education stressed the primacy of its language, culture, history and traditions. More provocatively, the headmaster questioned whether educational differences between groups were purely down to discrimination, arguing that the relative success of Indians was a result of their cultural values, while implying that the failure of others was not explained by prejudice. To suggest that differences in average group outcomes was not the result of white racism was, and still is, against anti-racist orthodoxy. One pressure group branded him a 'blatant racist' and said he should be sacked if he did not accept 'massive in-service training courses to purge [him] of [his] racist ideology and outlook', while a press release by the Bradford Drummond Parents' Support Group stated: 'one wonders whether Mr Honeyford will be the next person to be advocating bird shots [sic] fired at the black children at the school'.[98]

After the local newspaper drew attention to the article, a campaign gathered steam, led by anti-racist activists. Honeyford received several death threats, the police hooked up an alarm to his house at one point, and for months he entered the school under police protection from a small but militant group of pickets. A few small children even joined in the chants of 'racist, racist'. After several months the Bradford Education ordered Honeyford to attend a 'kind of public trial in a local college on the charge of disloyalty', in Theodore Dalrymple's words, but acquitted him. There were never any complaints about his teaching and the school was heavily oversubscribed with local Muslims, but Honeyford was forced to resign, and never taught again. After his departure the school was given an Urdu name and the last few whites left.

The Honeyford affair showed that all debate over race and

immigration had been shut down, and that the merest suspicion of 'racism' turned off all rational facilities. A race allegation could be as damning as a rape allegation. As with all systems built on self-deceit, multicultural Britain had to punish anyone who questioned the illusion, for fear it would crumble. In 1986 a Bristol teacher who had lent his support to Honeyford was even told to leave after colleagues said they 'no longer wished to work with him'.

A generation later and Honeyford has been vindicated – but too late.

Riots and the birth of the Multiculturalism Industry

State-funded multiculturalism accelerated in the 1980s due to a combination of factors: a multi-ethnic society in which the prevailing culture had no self-confidence; largely unaccountable local government with large amounts of money; and the worst riots in 20th century British history.

By the early 1980s Brixton in south London had become notorious either for crime or police racism, depending on one's view, and relations between the authorities and the black community were as bad as in some US cities, inflamed by the police's use of Sus laws, which allowed officers to stop and search on suspicion. Tension increased in early April 1981 when police stopped 1,000 people in four days and arrested 118, causing Lambeth Council leader Ted Knight to condemn police for behaving like 'an invading army'; in contrast many white people in south London felt that Brixton was an alien place to them, and one where they did not feel safe. The arrest of a man on April 10 proved the catalyst for widespread violence; within 36 hours 5,000 rioters had burned down 30 buildings and damaged 120 more, while over 100 cars and vans, including 56 police vehicles, were burned, and 300 policemen and 65 civilians were seriously injured. That year there were also riots in Liverpool, Birmingham and Bristol.

Multiculturalism as official state policy was motivated by a fear that Britain's inner cities would be threatened by permanent racial violence. Sir George Young was made Britain's first 'minister for race relations', and said that the Government's policy was to 'back the good guys, the sensible, moderate, responsible leaders of ethnic groups. If they are seen to deliver, to get financial support from central government for urban projects, then that reinforces their standing and credibility in the community. If they don't deliver, people will turn to the militants.' The government's aim, according to the *Sunday Times's* profile of Young, was 'the creation in Britain of a small but prosperous black middle class'. Here was a Conservative Government believing it could simply 'create' a middle class through state intervention. What they did create was a moderately prosperous group of political activists dependent on the state, and financially incentivised to see racism in every criticism of multicultural policy.

Put in charge of the inquiry into the riots, Lord Scarman found no evidence that the riots had been the result of 'institutional racism', but instead 'complex political, social and economic factors'. But without 'urgent action', he said, racial disadvantage could become an 'endemic, ineradicable disease threatening the very survival of our society'. This sidestepped the fact that racial disadvantage, by which he meant differences in average outcomes between different groups, is a feature of every racially-diverse society in history: there has never been one without it.

Despite stock photos of the decade showing Yuppies wielding brick-sized mobile phones, the 1980s were in some ways the glory years of Britain's Far-Left. In the late 1970s many radicals had left small Trotskyite organisations to join the Labour Party, many of whom would end up going into government in 1997. They looked to local government as the path to power, often using this mundane world as a way of funding radical politics. Among these were the 'Socialist Republic of South Yorkshire', led by David Blunkett, who would later become 'the most authoritarian home secretary in living memory' in Shami Chakrabarti's phrase, and the Greater London Council, led by future London mayor Ken Livingstone, who had taken power in a palace coup in 1981.

Local democracy in Britain has many flaws, but perhaps the most problematic is that only 25 per cent of council income comes directly from local taxpayers, which encourages apathy among voters and wastefulness by councils. People do not notice (or care) when money goes towards sectional interests, since most council funds come from Whitehall. In the early 1980s councils had large budgets, little accountability (turn-outs at British local elections are notoriously low, and until recently there were no directly elected local politicians) and growing numbers of minority voters. It was a disastrous combination.

Following the Brixton riots, the House of Commons home affairs committee encouraged local authorities to 'make as much direct contact as possible with ethnic minorities'. This they did, sort of. Between 1981 and 1986 the GLC pioneered 'a new strategy of making minority communities feel part of British society', organising consultations, drawing up equal opportunities policies, establishing race relations units, and dolling out buckets of cash. This was not democracy in action. On average fewer than 40 people attended each consultation organised by the GLC's Ethnic Minorities Unit (EMU), which was distributing £6.2 million a year to hundreds of groups at the time of the GLC's abolition[99] (at a time when the GLC kept a giant, constantly updated counter on the roof of County Hall of the capital's unemployment figures, visible from the House of Commons across the river). Meanwhile Birmingham City Council adopted multiculturalism as official policy after the 1985 Handsworth riots. It created nine umbrella groups, based on ethnicity and religion, which were supposed to represent the needs of their community in telling the council how to develop policy and allocate taxpayers' money.

Behind multiculturalism was a broad Left view that it would be a progressive coalition of minorities, both racial and sexual, to balance white male conservative dominance – the Rainbow Alliance.[100] Although Trotskyites hold radical views on sexual morality, religion and other social mores that would not go down a storm in Pakistan, it was a marriage of convenience in other ways, too. While the individualistic capitalism of belle époque Europe espoused by Conservatives was fairly alien to some newcomers, many immigrants felt extreme discomfort at taking welfare from the British state. Often they were persuaded to do so by political radicals who emphasised that any largesse was in compensation for imperialism. In this way multiculturalism may have actually kept old wounds festering. But behind the theory, multiculturalism often merely reflected the political realities of demography. In Britain's case empowering minorities meant delivering votes for political parties, in return for increased spending on their community, and the Labour Party in particular actively targeted clan elders who could carry votes. Multiculturalism made it easier for some communities to do better from state handouts than others, as Pakistani immigrants brought with them the biradari village system, with its mutual ties of obligation and sense of loyalty to the powerful figures in the community. This led to a sense of grievance among West Indians, who had no clan to offer politicians, and were less adept at working the system.

Neo-Colonialism

Treating minorities almost like colonial subjects, multiculturalism mimicked the old imperial structures, with 'community leaders' replacing the maharajahs the ruling whites dealt with, and with whom they would raise their concerns. It also resembled the corporatist structure of many European countries, where groups such as churches and unions meet directly with government officials. In Germany, Austria, Spain or the Republic of Ireland the church, usually the Catholic but also established Lutheran and Calvinist churches, runs some social services, as religious groups have always done. In England Anglican schools have long been funded by the state, and were joined by Catholic and Jewish schools in 1944. But these developed in societies where there was little danger of religious power aggravating sectarianism.

In Birmingham the council's multiculturalism policy was blamed for the Lozells race riots of October 2005, which began with a rumour that a black girl had been gang-raped in an Asian-owned shop selling Afro products (it had evolved from two men raping a 32-year-old to 25 men raping a 14-year-old). A night of violence ensued in which an innocent young man was murdered on his way home. The riots illustrated how racism and racial tension in Britain was not, as Salman Rushdie and others might have us believe, a problem of white people, but a problem of human nature. Inter-racial conflict not involving whites is also increasingly common in the United States, especially in California, where Latinos have been accused of ethnic cleansing by blacks. Lozells also had twice the national average of mixed-race children, which showed how intermixing does not insulate against tribal conflict (some parts of Bosnia had intermarriage rates as high as 50 per cent at the start of the Yugoslav war).

Councils such as Birmingham allocated money on ethnic or religious lines, creating an incentive for organisations to claim money on behalf of ethnic groups and so for people to identify with those groups. In a state that valued the equality of groups, representatives of underachieving minorities could always demand taxpayer's money, and this led to resentment and division. Following the northern race riots of 2001, a House of Commons report concluded that government funds in the north had accelerated racial division, and 'focusing resources on predominantly white council estates or Asian areas of run-down private housing could cause serious resentment in the area that did not receive funding'. This played a part in segregation.

Social housing also helps to aggravate segregation by ethnicity rather than financial status, as in the 'grand ensembles' of France, Sweden's 'Million Program' and in Britain, where a housing policy based on need helped to provoke racial resentment by favouring groups with larger families. When in 2006 the Institute of Community Studies (now the Young Foundation) followed up a social study in Bethnal Green they had conducted 50 years previously, they found that the social housing policy introduced in the 1970s had broken up the social structure of the white working class and replaced them with Bengalis.

The paradox is that multiculturalism, by recognising separateness, is also an argument for monoethnicity. Multiculturalism is often a means of protection, and is a necessity in Northern Ireland, where there is a cross-community coalition, or in Lebanon, where different groups own certain government positions; otherwise minorities would always be excluded. But protection sometimes necessitates separation, politically and even physically. When in the late 1970s militant Bangladeshi squatters protested against discrimination in housing (a 1982 report found that Bengalis comprised just 0.3 per cent of tenants on the best estates), the

GLC offered to consider Bengali-only housing estates. Although the press dubbed it the "Ghetto Plan" and the protestors rejected it, one of its leaders later came to change her mind.[101] What the GLC proposed might seem appalling, but they were only offering a more naked version of multiculturalism. Immigrant communities certainly do prefer to live together, and even in the absence of government action will do so perhaps indefinitely; after Tower Hamlets changed its housing allocation rules in 1984, 90 per cent of offers to Asians of council housing on "white" estates were refused, even though the housing quality was often better.

Advocates of multiculturalism argue that immigrants prefer to stick together because of racism and the fear of racial violence, as well as the bonds of community. This is perfectly reasonable, but if this is case, why not the same for natives too? If multicultural-ism is right because minorities feel better among themselves, why have mass immigration at all, since it must obviously make everyone miserable? (And if diversity 'enriches' and strengthens, why integrate, since that will only reduce diversity?) All the arguments for multiculturalism – that people feel safer, more comfortable among people of the same group, and that they need their own cultural identity – are arguments against immigration, since English people must also feel the same. If people categorised as "white Britons" are not afforded that indulgence because they are a majority, do they attain it when they become a minority?

Even the Bullock Report (inadvertently) expressed the contra-diction by stating: 'It is particularly important that children from families of overseas origin should see people of their own communities in the role of teacher and helper.' In more recent years, with the chronic lack of black male role models, some anti-racists have even proposed all-black schools because they would create a sense of community, one where people felt at ease and were able to learn in the context of their own culture. All true, no doubt, but registering high on the irony-meter.[102]

Anti-racism is itself contradictory. Many former activists now lament that it moved from tackling racism to expressing cultural differences between groups. But the anti-racist movement has always consisted of a large number of ethnic minority political leaders who, while opposing racism in its crudest form, were essentially ethno-centrists themselves, standing up for the rights of their people against white oppression. Any 'anti-racist' group with the name 'black' or 'Asian' in it is essentially a contradiction, if they define racism in the modern sense.

Not only does multiculturalism nullify the arguments for mass immigration, it can even sound like racism. When Lebanese cultural critic Amin Maalouf wrote: 'Why should we take the diversity of human cultures less seriously than the diversity of animal or plant species?' he unconsciously echoed 18th-century philosopher Joseph de Maistre, spiritual godfather to the European Far-Right, who said that there were no 'men', only Frenchmen, Italians, Russians or Persians. It also resembled Herder, for whom each people were a self-contained entity: 'Every nation has its own inner centre of happiness, as every sphere has its own centre of gravity'. Herder even questioned whether 'one such single ideal can act as an arbiter, praising or condemning other nations or periods, their customs and laws', making him both the godfather of ethnic nationalism and multiculturalism. But, why not? They're basically the same thing. 'Diversity' is merely the reinvention of racism but with Europeans barred from the party, as if they are ethnoholics who, given a sniff of nationalism, will end up disgracing themselves once again by having too much and starting a war.

This contradiction rests on the Marxist idea that racism is the monopoly of the dominant (white) population, yet racism is clearly evident in every group in every society. What might be called 'cultural recognition' by a minority would be seen as racism in Europeans; after all, as Kenan Malik has pointed out in his critiques of multiculturalism[103], no councils funds a 'white community centres', even in areas where they do constitute a minority. Inevitably the Far-Right has come to use the language of diversity and multiculturalism to promote racial exclusion. They are, after all, in favour of diversity, the preservation of different racial groups rather than the integration of humanity. The use of 'diversity' in this context horrifies multiculturalists, but this is diversity in a truer and older sense; indeed polygenism, the 19th-century racialist theory of human origins, was called 'the doctrine of diversity'.

Multiculturalism created a more tribal society and, free to express their own identities, many people did. One academic study observed that the 'model of engagement through Umbrella Groups tended to result in competition between BME communities for resources. Rather than prioritising needs and cross-community working, the different Umbrella Groups generally attempted to maximise their own interests.' Ethnic pressure groups trying to maximise the interests of their own ethnic group – who would have predicted that?

Capitalism by its very nature drives not just technical progress but progressive politics, especially integration. In his Philosophical Letters 18th-century philosopher Voltaire noted in the London Stock Exchange that 'the Jew, the Mahometan, and the Christian deal with one another as if they were of the same religion, and reserve the name of infidel for those who go bankrupt'.

The American state's traditional indifference to people's lives forces immigrants to integrate; the European social model has had the opposite effect, insulating newcomers against the pressures to become Europeans. State-funded translation services epitomise this: while the cost of the London 999 service employing linguists fluent in 150 tongues is justified in that it saves lives, less can be said about the £50 million spent annually by local and central government on translation services.[104] The costs involved are relatively small, but like the appearance of street signs in minority languages, or in the case of Bengali in the Museum of Childhood, at a national museum, it sends an anti-integrationist signal.

What's more, multiculturalism increases separation not just between natives and immigrants, but between minorities, especially when it was inevitably seen that one group was favoured over another. When the BNP were forced to open membership to non-white members they found a willing recruit in Rajinder Singh, an elderly Sikh who was motivated by a fear of Islam, enough to overcome their obvious racism. One of the leading figure in the English Defence League is another Sikh, Guramit Singh. Although these two are considered eccentrics, there is a common belief among Sikhs that Muslims receive preferential treatment. As

Bhupinder Singh of the Sikh Information website told the *Guardian*: 'We have issues sometimes; with turbans and with bangles. But at the end of the day, I just don't think any community should be allowed to change Britain. It's fine as it is'.[105]

But Britain is changing. One result of multiculturalism, and years of state-financed incentives for people to see themselves as separate 'communities', is that people rarely use the term Pakistani anymore – now they say 'Muslim'. This may have been accelerated by the policy of engaging through 'community leaders' that encouraged a Muslim identity; it may be a natural product of a multi-faith society. Asian anti-racist organisations in the 1970s, such as the Asian Youth Movement, were secular and largely socialist, but from the early 1980s political organisations were increasingly linked to the mosque. And multiculturalism meant that British taxpayers helped to pay for semi-secularised communities to become increasingly sectarian.

Like London and Birmingham, Bradford Council also adopted a multicultural policy from 1981. It published an equal opportunities statement, created race relations units and established a 12-point race relations plan declaring that every section of the 'multiracial, multicultural city' had 'an equal right to maintain its own identity, culture, language, religion and customs'. The first aim of its race relations initiative was to 'bring about social justice' by ensuring 'Equality of esteem between different cultures'. That year the council began funding the British Council of Mosques to create 'new channel of communication'. But there were significant differences between the policy in London, where division resulted from race, and involved many different groups wanting 'equality', and in Bradford, where leaders saw multiculturalism as a way to prevent assimilation, to stop their sons becoming negatively Westernised into drugs and gangs.

Yasmin Alibhai-Brown, a liberal Muslim columnist who writes Left-wing articles about race for the *Independent* and Right-wing pieces about Western decadence in the *Daily Mail*, wrote that, appalled by our excessively consumerist and permissive society (as are many non-Muslims), Muslim families feel overly protective towards their children. She quoted a corner shop owner who 'spoke for many' when he said: 'When I first came to England, it was a nice country – polite, respectful. People knew good behaviour. My older children had English friends, no problem. Now these girls, nearly naked in the roads, drinking and swearing, sex everywhere. I can't let my young daughters be like that. So I send them to Muslim schools. I don't want to, but it is bad out there.'

Growing attachment to Islam came about partly as a reaction to changing morals in English society. But what the elders feared was not so much Westernisation but deracination, and the post-Christian, post-sexual revolution Britain. And the state was willing to help. Bradford Council funded BCM's social projects, including two centres for the elderly, a variety of advice workers, a service for women in hospital and clinics, and a series of Muslim youth and community centres. And, according to Kenan Malik 'For what the pattern of mosque building in Bradford reveals is that it was not the piety of first-generation Muslims that led to the Islamisation of the town. It was, rather, the power, influence and money that accrued to religious leaders in the 1980s as a result of Bradford City Council's multicultural policies. Multiculturalism helped paint Bradford Muslim green.'

9

British Values
After multiculturalism

The *Onion's* spoof headline about the Axis alliance, 'Japanese sign pact with white supremacists in well-thought out scheme', could equally have applied to the liberal alliance with religious minorities. Ultra-conservative immigrants were allies in the culture war against native conservatives, and like many victorious allies, the two fell out badly in victory.

And after the fall out over a multiculturalism that claimed no culture was better than any other, what next? Many argue that the best way to integrate minorities is by promoting British values for everyone. But what are those values? It is a problem that many European countries have struggled with.

In the Netherlands immigration rules were toughened after the murder of Theo Van Gogh in 2005; imported spouses would have to be 21, and the partner already in Holland would have to fulfil a minimum income requirement. Germany and Denmark also raised the required age and brought in civic examinations and language tests. On top of this non-Western applicants for residency would be assessed on their understanding of Dutch life and culture, which included being shown images of gay men expressing affection and bare-breasted women on beach. This was in line with the Europe-wide attitude expressed by German politician Wolfgang Schauble, who said of public sexuality that 'Someone who doesn't want to see these kinds of things shouldn't move to a country where they're reality'. But most natives do not want to see them either; British public surveys show that over half of both Muslims and non-Muslims are offended by public drunkenness, while Muslims and non-Muslims alike are offended by public sexuality.[106] Yet where whites and minorities do share common values, they are at odds with metropolitan ones. The secular-Left response to Islam is to tear down the native Christian culture, rather like a man setting fire to his own house to get rid of an unwanted visitor. Yet is de-Christianisation going to make integration easier? Most Muslims, when polled, express favourable views towards Christianity, and respect for Christian institutions, but the 'European values' politicians talk about are often alien both to European natives and to Muslims.

When protesters against the visit of Pope Benedict XVI to Britain accused the Pontiff of opposing 'British values', they were primarily talking of the right to contraception, abortion and gay marriage, yet all of these are novelties, and to millions of Britons they are questionable ones. In contrast conservatives who admire Islam's strong family values, modesty and respect for the elderly compare it with British society's increasing consumerism, sexualisation and child abandonment. Anyone who compares the behaviour of people buying curry on a Friday night in a typical British city with those serving it might have slightly mixed feelings about imposing 'British values'. If a culture is defined by its decadence, is integration a triumph or a failure? When Muslim girls catch chlamydia at school and Muslim boys are being treated for cirrhosis of the liver in their 20s will we celebrate the victory of Britishness?

Sometimes it is hard to see who better reflects British culture. When a Muslim group in January 2005 persuaded the Advertising Standards Agency to ban an underwear ad near a mosque, many natives would have agreed with them (and these ads were far less racy than many seen on billboards). Many people in Britain feel uncomfortable about the over-sexualisation of public life, in advertising, television and other forms of media, which they view as a form of aggression, and yet there are no bodies, including religious groups, which have the power to speak up for them. As was shown in Balsall Heath and Lumb Lane, Islam is sometimes the only authority strong enough to fill a moral vacuum. As Saul Bellow wrote in *The Closing of the American Mind*: 'When public morality becomes a ghost town, it's a place into which anyone can ride and declare himself sheriff.' This is indeed what happened in a country that threw off the shackles of religiously-inspired moral regulation and immigration controls at the same time.

Critics might counter that we do not have a clear, fixed notion of what being British means, and that that's a sign of maturity and liberation. Today a school teaching the children of Russian immigrants to become 'English gentlemen', as it was understood in 1900, would be laughed at and condemned, and its teachers would be blacklisted, and yet who has gained from this decon-struction – the comfortable, well-educated graduates who deride such outdated ideas, or the children who do not know what to aspire to or what norms to live by? Scorn for 'British values' is easy when one is cushioned by education, wealth and social exclusivity, and living off the social capital of generations. Further down the social ladder, and in the chaos of communities where dozens of languages are spoken and where various social pathologies are rife, such norms are more necessary. Cultural values are forms of social pressure, as well as instructions; and while PhD students do not need external discipline, fourth years in inner-city schools certainly do. Where immigrants do have money and therefore choice, such as the Russian or Arab multimillionaires of west London, they opt overwhelmingly to embrace the most obvious facet of Christian, conservative British values – the public school.

The problem is that outside of these sub-cultures much of British society feels uncomfortable with this boarding school idea of England, and has steadily abandoned it. Yet this surely makes the process of integration harder, by making the rules of integration less clear. And the more relaxed a club or institution is about behaviour, the stricter its membership rules have to be, or the more expensive and exclusive. Likewise the more open an organisation, the more rigid its rules and norms tend to be; otherwise chaos and disorder soon rule. In the words of the Canadian novelist Yann Martel the nation is either a 'great hotel' or 'the collective accumulated wisdom of a shared past'. Multiculturalists take the former view, yet an open immigration policy and a society with unclear values is not a combination that will last very long.

National Identity

In 1955 a Colonial Office report stated that: 'A large coloured community as a noticeable feature of our social life would weaken... the concept of England or Britain to which people of British stock throughout the Commonwealth are attached.' After 7/7 it became clear that segregation was intensifying and that multiculturalism had been an abject failure. Yet in one sense national identity has only been weakened at the intellectual level. At a popular level people in England are aware of what Englishness means and what it stands for. But the intellectual abandonment of English identity and patriotism has left it proletarianised, characterised by football fans and the St George's Cross. This, in turn, further stigmatises such attachments.

Some thinkers believe that we can overcome the problems of diversity by forging a new British identity that could appeal to all cultures. France and the United States provide the two most obvious models, but can a traditionally ethno-centric national identity (albeit an understated one) be replaced with an allegiance to a British constitution based on universal values?

Labour began seriously looking into British identity at the turn of the century. In 2002 Tony Blair appointed Michael Willis as the 'minister of patriotism', to explore national identity. The Home Office panel proposed a citizen programme for immigrants, which would inform new arrivals of the country's values. And yet this is a paradox. As Professor Robert Colls of Leicester University wrote: 'The British government proposes a "statement of values" setting out what binds us together. But if the values do bind us, why do we need a statement? And if they don't bind us, in what sense are they our values?' National identities, he pointed out, 'happen when nations see themselves as one, regardless of all that divides them, which can include the state'.

National identity is a historical relationship that binds an extended family (even if it is one that adopts) with a shared history, not a set of values. David Cameron, in a speech in Munich in February 2011 in which he condemned multiculturalism, said that 'a genuinely liberal country... believes in certain values and actively promotes them. Freedom of speech, freedom of worship, democracy, the rule of law, equal rights regardless of race, sex or sexuality. It says to its citizens, this is what defines us as a society: to belong here is to believe in these things.' One might ask – since when? To belong here does not mean necessarily believing in anything, except for an attachment to this country, its history and its laws, through ancestry or adoption. Christian hotel owners who refuse to give same-sex couples double beds fall outside of Cameron's citizenship; for that matter so does the entire Church of England. Are Anglicans opposed to 'British values'?

The universalist idea of the nation being a collection of people with 'similar values' or interests is itself less liberal than the traditional nation-state. Clubs made up of people sharing similar interests are voluntary associations where membership depends on like-minded views. But most people do not choose their nations any more than they choose their families, and where they do, as in the United States, the society has to exert strong pressure to integrate. England's self-image as a land of eccentrics may be rather exaggerated, but not entirely so; that being English meant not having to conform along political, cultural and religious lines was a strength derived from its traditional homogeneity. The bond of the nation, irrational though it was, was strong enough to make people submit to the will of the common good without the need for authoritarianism. Vastly diverse countries, in contrast, must force that submission on the people, whether through legislation, illiberal policing or other areas of greater state intervention. Once one takes out the historical relationship that binds a nation and its citizens, and views it as a 'great hotel', it becomes easier for some unscrupulous proprietor to start imposing his own vision on the residents.

Contrary to what is often claimed, 'universal' ideas about right and wrong and respect for the law are not values on which a nation can be built, precisely because ideas are not always universal, something illustrated by the question of religious offence. People will only respect a system of law framed around their ethical values or one they feel belongs to them; they may fear the law, but that is an altogether different thing. A state without a nation, a patch of land inhabited by people with nothing in common except that they share the same geographic co-ordinates, may function up to a point, but some level of coercion would be needed to keep this society together. Indeed that is what diversity is bringing.

After 7/7 the Government began to think about a 'British equivalent of the US Fourth of July'. The Fabian Society suggested July 5, the anniversary of the NHS, using this product of the nation-state to symbolise and unite a post-national state. Many of the ideas about national identity mimic American civic patriotism, which is superficially attractive. In fact much of what we associate with Americanism dates to that country's first great period of mass immigration, and was created following the assassination of President William McKinley by a Polish-American radical (who was, like many British Islamist terrorists, native-born and well-educated). In James Bennett's words: 'A consensus quickly developed that what was needed was not only more robust cultural assimilation, but also a civic creed of "Americanism" proactively promoted among all Americans, natives and immigrants.' The Pledge of Allegiance, the flag salute in schools and the religious hymns about the American way of life all date back to this period. Yet the differences are significant: America was a relatively young country, assimilating immigrants from the same continent, the vast majority following the same religion (if different strains), and it still took a 40-year immigration pause to integrate them. The US was everything Europe isn't – dynamic, culturally confident, highly fertile, thinly populated and economically expanding. It at least had the right ingredients and utensils for a melting pot.

France also has a republican tradition that helps assimilation, but this is a product of its revolution (itself still a divisive issue). For historical reasons Britain never developed such republican institutions, and any attempt to create them now might be seen by white conservatives as proof that their country was slipping away from them. To alter institutions so obviously in the name of uniting a disparate society would rob this new identity of legitimacy in the eyes of many. It would be what the Weimar Republic was to Germans in 1919, and its symbols one more source of resentment. Even a written constitution would be highly contentious, especially as it would inevitably be written in the uninspiring gobbledygook of the day, something along the lines of: 'We hold these truths to be self-evident, that all people are created equal, that they are endowed by with certain unalienable

Human Rights, that among these are Life, Liberty and the pursuit of Happiness, regardless of race, sexual orientation, religion, belief or non-belief, gender assignment etc etc.' France's secularism developed in a monocultural, almost uniformly Catholic country whose citizens felt free to attack Catholicism, without the presence of outsiders who might make them feel culturally defensive (the same thing happened in Turkey under Atatürk). French-style secularism in Britain today would almost certainly be resented even by agnostics who saw attacks on religious tradition as a sop to Muslims (sops that Muslims did not even want). Even small matters, such as the replacing of Christian symbols at Christmas (themselves often 19th-century inventions and created to sell tat), can become a source of division.

The process of forging a new Britishness has begun with citizenship tests and ceremonies that, in the words of the BBC's Mark Easton, aimed to create 'a sense of identity that overarches creed, culture or ethnic background… built around the ideas of shared values' such as 'tolerance of diversity and cultural difference'. The early signs are not promising. When Home Secretary David Blunkett announced in 2005 that foreigners seeking Indefinite Leave to Remain, or naturalisation, were to be set a written test about 'Britishness', there was much amused press speculation about what newcomers would be asked, something along the lines of: 'What is the correct phrase when starting a fight in a public house?' or 'Who has larger breasts – Jordan or Jodie Marsh?' Yet the real thing is far more farcical than a Right-wing hack's worst nightmare.

The Government presented the test as a means to creating a British melting pot based on, but obviously morally superior to, the American model. Blunkett's successor John Reid peers out from the pages of the official handbook, *A Journey to Citizenship*, telling newcomers that the exams 'have encouraged people who have decided to make their lives in Britain to learn more about our culture and institutions'. That they have certainly done. In total no fewer than 29 of the 408 potential test questions are about claiming state benefits, and another 65 concern other rights such as free healthcare, education and working hour regulations. Foreign arrivals might be bemused by the idea that British culture should be defined by welfare, as if Shakespeare's Globe was less culturally significant than the nearby London Bridge JobCentrePlus. But indeed the major advantage to having Indefinite Leave to Remain rather than just Limited Leave is being able to claim Jobseeker's Allowance, housing benefits and the full buffet of the European welfare state.

And what kind of Britishness are they embracing? As well as questions about quangos, single-parent families, drug use and smoking laws, there are 9 on the EU, and a further 16 questions about women's rights and the history of female suffrage. There is a reasonable argument that, since many immigrants come from countries where a 'women's right to choose' means opting whether to be beheaded or stoned to death for adultery, newcomers should be informed about the one area of life where liberals feel unembarrassed moral superiority over immigrants. And one could even justify the 20 questions about the history of immigration, on top of another 11 about the racial and religious diversity of Britain. Yet there are just four questions about *all the rest of British history put together* – and the test organisers managed to get two of the answers wrong, claiming as false the statement 'The Church of England is a Catholic church and has existed since the 1530s' (the C of E is 'Catholic and Reformed', just not Roman Catholic) and that 'the monarch of the UK is not allowed to marry anyone who is not Protestant' (only Roman Catholics are barred). There is not a single question about Alfred the Great, Magna Carta, the creation of Parliament, the King James Bible, the Civil War, Habeas Corpus, the Glorious Revolution or the Great Reform Act.

A deconstructed national identity makes it easier for leaders to mould a new country around their ideas, and Labour certainly used mass immigration – and the related national identity crisis – as a way of changing Britishness, something that was never the intention of those who first welcomed immigrants in the 1950s and 60s. In 2002 the Government introduced Citizenship classes 'to teach children about national identity and break down the barriers between different faiths and cultures', both a symptom of a nation in crisis and a means to further proselytise the faith of multiculturalism, even if that word has been rebranded as 'diversity'. The curriculum from the website of the Department for Children, Schools and Families, entitled *Britain: A Diverse Society?* asks children to 'Build on the class display of individual identities and the local community. Does it reflect the cultural diversity of Britain? Why is it important to recognise and celebrate all identities?' and 'Debate issues relating to diversity, e.g. the rights and responsibilities of different communities, what it means to be British, attitudes towards refugees.'

In 2010 a report, *Citizenship Established?*, found that discussions designed to tackle immigration led some pupils to 'assert ideas tantamount to racism'. Ofsted, which visited 91 secondary schools as part of the study, called for a rise in the number of specially-trained citizenship teachers. Some might argue that imparting the principles of citizenship would be better achieved by teaching History and English, but these subjects offer fewer opportunities for promoting a multicultural vision of Britain. What those classes are teaching is not citizenship but a Marxist interpretation of race, something which is bound to make pupils assert 'ideas tantamount to racism', since any questioning of the official orthodoxy on racism is proof of racism.

A New Multicultural History

Creating a new identity requires creating a new history, too, and one of the assumptions that the education National Curriculum proclaims is that all students should be prepared for 'life in a multicultural society'. Trevor Philips has even decreed that British schoolchildren should learn 'race relations and multiculturalism with every subject they study – from Spanish to science',[107] a common practice of totalitarian states where the values of the ruling party are imbued in every aspect of education. Even church schools, accused of 'indoctrinating' pupils, try to at least keep religion confined to Religious Studies.

Just as Benedict Anderson thought that 'imagined communities' were invented, so they can be reinvented, and advocates of 'the nation of immigrants' theory are doing just that, creating a multicultural British back-story with a very small number of individuals. An entire pseudo-national history has been built on Mary Seacole, a magnificent but historically not very significant

Jamaican-born Victorian nurse; her multicultural brand has been attached to numerous awards, university departments and hospitals in the past decade, while a statue opposite Parliament is being planned.

Rather than being used to bring unity under a historical British identity that would be 'too white' for many in the teaching establishment, history is also used to address minority grievances. Many educators promote the teaching of trans-Atlantic slavery or the Crusades as a way of making minorities feel more included, but how this is supposed to bring a class together, or forge a common national identity, is anyone's guess. Black History Month is suggested as an antidote to low self-esteem among black men, and a supposed link between slavery and black-on-black street violence (although low self-esteem is linked to suicide, not homicide). Meanwhile the annual Islamic Awareness Week, which follows Black History Month in November (like Christianity, multiculturalism has a busy calendar of worship), recently focused on the subject 'Past and Present: 1000 years of Islam in Britain', which told of 'the Islam and Britain you never knew'. It went on: 'Today's Britain would be very different without Islam!' Does it matter that this statement is not true? That before the 1960s Islam had an insignificant influence on Britain?

Sometimes well-meaning educators can unwittingly veer off into parody, as when the BBC schools website declared that the 'Vikings arrived, bringing a distinctive new influence to the cultural pot'. Rape, pillage, slaughter. Many a time a monk in Northumbria or Mercia must have pondered the great vibrancy that the Vikings had brought to the area, before moving to Wessex for the 'better quality of life'.

If multiculturalism is a faith, then Spitalfields, just to the east of the City of London, is its holy land. The district is often cited as an example of Britain's rich tapestry because it is one of the very few areas in the country that does have a significant history of immigration, with waves of French, Irish, Russian Jews and Bengalis. It even has a Museum of Immigration and Diversity, a Grade II listed building erected in 1719 by Huguenot silk merchant Peter Abraham Ogier, which became a synagogue in 1869 until falling into disrepair in the 1960s. Across the river

Southwark Council portrayed the history of the south bank in a mural: 'Southwark is a highly cosmopolitan area with a rich mixture of communities going back centuries. German, Dutch and Flemish craftspeople excluded by the City of London settled in Southwark… immigrants from Ireland took up manual jobs… the labour shortage was eased by workers and their families invited from the Caribbean and West Africa… communities from China, Cyprus, Vietnam, Somalia, Ethiopia, Bosnia and Croatia… just under a third of our population is from an ethnic minority and over a hundred languages are spoken by our children.' As Michael Collins recalled in *The Likes of Us*, one bemused local looked at the mural and commented: 'You wouldn't think us English had ever lived here if you look at this.'

Many British street names have been altered to reflect the change in culture and demographics. There is a Samsara Road in Bromsgrove, a Masjid Lane in Tower Hamlets, which uses the Arabic term for mosque, while in Lewisham there is a Khadija Walk, after the Prophet Mohammed's first wife, the first person after him to convert to Islam. In Oldham there are roads named after Sir Muhammad Iqbal and Muhammad Ali Jinnah, founders of Pakistan. There is also a Jinnah Road in Redditch, and a Jinnah Court in Bradford, which also has a Qureshi View and a Kinara Close.

Like any faith, it has its martyrs too. Tower Hamlets council named a Whitechapel park in honour of Altab Ali, a 25-year-old Bangladeshi who was murdered in 1978 during a period when racist attacks were common in the area (although the gang was reportedly mixed-race). The killing was commemorated by renaming St Mary's Park, just off Whitechapel High Street, and the site of the original medieval chapel from which the area gets it name. Yet the borough has never thought it suitable to name anything after William Booth, William Beveridge, Sylvia Pankhurst, Marie Lloyd, Samuel Pepys, Dr Thomas Bernard or any of the other notable people who were born, raised or lived there. Blair Peach, a New Zealand-born anti-racism activist who died at the hands of the police in 1979, has a school in Ealing named after him. In comparison almost no policemen or soldiers killed in the line of duty, nor even that many prime ministers, have had such an honour.

Tower Hamlets Council, like those of Luton and Leicester, has recently taken to lining its streets with banners advertising the unity of its residents, as the whole of London did in the aftermath of the 7/7 bombings, and perhaps it is only a matter of time before some borough takes to proclaiming 'diversity is strength' on public billboards.

But all the attempts at defining or redefining British identity will be redundant if the country itself disappears. One of the by-products of diversity is a decline in Britishness in favour of more explicit identities; according to the most recent survey, 51 per cent of ethnic minority members consider themselves British first, but only 29 per cent of whites now do, as opposed to 52 per cent who consider themselves primarily English (something only 11 per cent of non-whites identify as).[108] It may be that as Sir Bernard Crick, designer of Britain's 'citizenship curriculum' put it, 'to the immigrant, Britishness is essentially a legal and political structure… When the immigrant says I am British, he is not saying he wants to be English or Scottish or Welsh.' Englishness is more explicitly racial, and people from minority groups who call themselves British often still use 'English' as interchangeable with 'white'. Indeed the rise of English identity may be a reaction to the de-racialising of Britishness. After all, if everyone else has their specific identity, why can't the white British do the same?

Minorities tend to favour super-national states, because it allows for hyphenated identities, and because they are more vulnerable to persecution in smaller break-offs, and yet because Scotland has had very little immigration in recent years, this vastly different experience of life in the two nations may be helping them to diverge. Although the Scottish National Party is keen to court 'new Scots', the SNP does not campaign for Scottish independence as such, rather for Scotland to be a part of a European super-state (a Right-of-centre anti-EU Scottish separatist party would probably find little support among minorities, least of all Catholics). And the mother of all super-states, the European Union, is very popular among immigrants and minorities, 85 per cent in some polls favouring it. The EU itself is at the forefront of the campaign against 'Islamophobia', knowing it can rely on religious minorities, especially one whose hyper-identity stretches across borders, to support super-national states. Yet Islam, or perhaps a fear of it, is paradoxically the one thing that unites Europeans, the only potential external threat big enough to make the various countries forget their differences. Belgian historian Henri Pirenne, author of *Mohammed and Charlemagne*, wrote that the Muslim invasions of the first millennium helped to form the consciousness of Europe. And opposition to Islam today is increasingly creating a pan-European identity stronger than that imposed by Brussels. Indeed the one politician with a continent-wide following is Geert Wilders.

One question remains largely unasked about all this change – did the immigrants who chose to make Britain their home want it? Perhaps not, and certainly few were asked. British Airway's flag-decoration farce of 1996, when the airline dropped the Union Jack logo from its tailfins, serves as a metaphor. At the height of the multiculturalism craze BA Chief Executive Bob Ayling said that 'perhaps we need to lose some of our old-fashioned Britishness and take on board some of the new British traits'. These were Britain's new 'friendly, diverse and open-to-all cultural image', and among the new images that graced the fleet were symbols of the Ndebele tribe in Zimbabwe and a type of sari, as well as various animals and trees. The company hoped that the £60m makeover would connect with the 60 per cent of passengers who were not British. The public, British and non-British alike, hated it, and the company soon repainted the tail fins. As a BA spokesman later said. 'It is not just Britons who like our Britishness.'

So what do foreigners think of the new, diverse Britain, tolerant and open but also rude, unequal, vulgar and violent? Anglophiles sometimes look at the country transformed by multiculturalism and find that, whatever its faults, they rather preferred the old one.

10

The War on Racism
The expansion of the state

Diversity was always viewed as a 'liberal' idea, yet as a society becomes more diverse it become less liberal. Because the idea that all ethnic division can be eased out through a mixture of interaction and propaganda is optimistic, as it fails, the logical next stop is to force it by law. Therefore a diverse society requires a great deal more state intervention to maintain the peace and minimise conflict, often with laws that would have struck previous generations as decidedly illiberal.

Years before 'diversity' became a political catchphrase in the west, Singapore had pioneered a system that would later become called multiculturalism. In the city-state, which has a Chinese majority and Malay and Indian minorities, the government may arbitrarily arrest anyone accused of criticising other ethnic groups, and any speech, website or demonstration which offends any community is immediately shut down. The Singaporeans value multiculturalism, but they believe that it cannot co-exist with free speech; Europeans are learning the same lesson. And so in Britain unelected state bodies have been allowed to direct laws dictating what businesses can and cannot do, the state has embarked on social engineering projects with the aim of creating 'equality', and the scope of free speech has been curtailed.

As with many features of the multicultural society, the race relations industry originally began with a totally different aim to that which it later adopted. The Institute of Race Relations (IRR) was established as an independent educational charity in 1958 to 'carry out research, publish and collect resources on race relations throughout the world'. Its first head was a former colonial provincial governor in India, and it had a distinctly imperial feel. In 1972, however, there was a 'radical transformation of the organisation from a policy-oriented, establishment, academic institution into an anti-racist "thinktank".' In its own words: 'The IRR began to concentrate on responding to the needs of Black people and making direct analyses of institutionalised racism in Britain and the rest of Europe... Today, the IRR is at the cutting edge of the research and analysis that inform the struggle for racial justice in Britain, Europe and internationally.' Their investigations cover racism in the media, 'police racism, exclusions from school, deaths in custody, the plight of asylum seekers, anti-Muslim racism, the impact of anti-terrorist legislation and attacks on multiculturalism'. The group also monitors the 'integration debate' in the media, all of this funded by state bodies, including the Heritage Lottery Fund, the Big Lottery and the European Programme on Integration and Migration.

The Commission for Racial Equality was established by the 1976 Race Relations Act with the aim of encouraging greater integration, using 'its legal powers to help eradicate racial discrimination and harassment' and 'to raise public awareness of racial discrimination and injustice, and to win support for efforts to create a fairer and more equal society', among other things, before, in 2004, being amalgamated with various other bodies to form the Equality and Human Rights Commission. That some blatant racism existed at the time is undeniable, but the problem with such organisations is that as many of their stated goals – such as ending racism – are essentially as impossible as, for example, ending jealousy or bitterness, their scope for expansion is infinite. Even when pressure groups such as Stonewall achieve their stated aim – in their case abolishing the Conservative Government's Section 28, which banned local authorities from promoting homosexuality – they rarely then return to their farm like Cincinnatus. The essence of the problem is in the name – did the CRE aim to create equality before the law, or was their aim to create equality of outcomes between different races? Inevitably it and its successor organisation have chosen the latter route.

New Labour created a quangocracy of unprecedented size, and within that a race equality industry that employs a number of university-educated people of all colours. Just as Queen Victoria preferred Indian maharajas to the English poor, today's aristocrats of the state love multicultural 'community leaders', a caste of minority diversity-advocates ready to speak up for their community, whether their community asked for it or not. When in 2009 the EHRC produced a Muslim Women Power List, what was supposed to be a celebration of success in reality showed just how many of Britain's leading female Muslims were not successful businesswomen or scientists but members of the race industry. Among those listed were a Professor of Politics and Women's Studies, a member of a taxpayer-funded Muslim women's pressure group and Baroness Pola Uddin, 'Chair of the Government's Task Force for championing minority women'.

The EHRC in turn funds several hundred organisations (286 in 2008), groups such as the Bath & North East Somerset Racial Equality Council, Black & Minority Ethnic Carers Support Service, Gypsy/Travel Education & Information Project North East (GTEIP), MOSAIC Black & Mixed Parentage Family Group, North Yorkshire Black and Minority Ethnic Strategy Board, and the Pakistan Community Association and Multicultural Advice Centre. On top of this there are hundreds of independent organisations that speak for various communities, seek money from local authorities, and claim racism as their default line of attack, as predictable as a first-level opponent in a boxing video game.

Then there are the charities. The dividing line between charity and pressure group is sometimes not clear cut; many charities are explicitly political, wielding considerable influence on Government policy. In some cases the taxpayer funds a pressure group to lobby the Government to spend more money on funding for pressure groups, often appearing on taxpayer-funded television and radio and presented as disinterested critics. Meanwhile the jobs they advertise help to fund newspapers, both national and local, which use their editorial power to support this quangocracy and label critics as racists. Among other things many anti-racist charities campaign for looser immigration controls, further increasing the diversity that is their bread and butter; even when polls of ethnic minorities show they oppose further immigration and see greater diversity as threatening their position. Many campaigning charities are partly funded by the state, so their employees argue, to act as a counter-balance to the interests of big business; yet immigration appears to be the one area where both government and big business are funding the same side.

There are also various immigrant-advocacy NGOs, many of which evolved out of religious charitable organisations and which embraced universalism as their new faith. There are at least a dozen pro-refugee activist bodies funded by the British state, all of which carry greater moral standing than any overtly state-run body. The same goes for think-tanks; between 2008 and 2009 the broadly pro-immigration IPPR received money from at least two dozen government bodies, including five departments of state, the EHRC, the Government Equalities Office and half a dozen local councils; in contrast MigrationWatch UK, the only non-partisan body that opposes mass immigration, has never received a penny from any state body.

The race industry still thrives in local politics. London under its first mayor, Ken Livingstone, might have taken off where he left it under the GLC, but even under Conservative Boris Johnson the city's strategy, 'Equal Life Chances for All', promises a commitment to 'eliminating institutional discrimination', which includes 'unwitting prejudice'. It also states that Mayoral appointees will 'reflect the diversity of London'. As Councillor Harry Phibbs asked on the leading blog ConservativeHome: 'What is the 'right level of representation' for ethnic groups in the workforce? What is 'unwitting prejudice' and is this a fair basis for race discrimination cases? Does 'responsible procurement' create a burden for businesses who have to produce race equality assessments etc?' Even Conservatives have come to publicly accept the language of equality and diversity.

Having arisen to counter white racism, the race relations industry now has the secondary, expensive task of monitoring communal relations weakened by immigration. Britain's Department for Communities and Local Government is responsible for 'community cohesion', among its other roles, but this, inevitably, filters through to every area of the country's enormous state apparatus. After it was announced that one in 25 school pupils in Bristol were Somali, up from one in 500 in 2002, and that Somalis were now a majority in two schools, the taxpayer-funded Institute of Community Cohesion said that 'There needs to be a systematic, high profile, council-wide commitment to addressing community cohesion in general and the challenges raised by the growing diversity in schools in particular. Without this the situation is likely to deteriorate.' More resources, presumably? A director of Support Against Racist Incidents (SARI), another partly-taxpayer-funded charity, said: 'We all need to respond and implement the recommendations to help communities learn to live with respect and build cohesion for the future.' Who would pay for all this, both financially and socially? And what benefits does Britain obtain in return?

All the suggested remedies to multiculturalism have one thing in common – they necessitate a further expansion of the state. ECHR chief Trevor Phillips suggested increased support for English-language instruction and investing in 'community centres' and other places that allow for 'meaningful interaction across ethnic lines'. State-funded monoculturalism? Phillips said: 'We need to respect people's ethnicity but also give them, at some point in the week, an opportunity to meet and want to be with people with whom they have something in common that isn't defined by their ethnicity.' But who will pay for these institutions that will, almost by definition, be attended by people least likely to need them?

Elsewhere diversity will require further legislation. Philippe Legrain suggested that: 'Reaping the full benefits of diversity requires vigorous anti-discrimination laws, encouragement of social mobility, and tolerance of differences – all of which are desirable anyway.' But a society that needs 'vigorous' laws for the smooth interaction of its citizenship has already failed. It cannot function by legislation alone. Diego Gambetta, a social scientist who specialises in the area of trust, says: 'Societies which rely heavily on the use of force are likely to be less efficient, more costly, and more unpleasant than those where trust is maintained by other means.' Legislations and lawyers are a symptom of a failing society; any proposal which comes with an increase in either should be treated with scepticism.

And perhaps the most intrusive consequence of diversity is the need it creates for more legislation. Anti-discrimination laws originated in the United States, to counter anti-black laws enacted after the American Civil War. Britain had no such laws; however, as the American experience showed, with a multi-racial society came some quite unpleasant behaviour towards minorities. British anti-discrimination law has its origins in the Constantine v Imperial Hotels Ltd ruling, which came after a scandalous incident involving the popular professional cricketer Learie Constantine. In 1943 the West Indies international had travelled to London with his family to play in an England v Dominions match and made a reservation at the Imperial Hotel in Russell Square. When they arrived some US servicemen complained and the hotel told them that they could only stay one night. Constantine took them to court. Although racial discrimination was not illegal, he argued that they breached the common law principle that innkeepers must not refuse accommodation without just cause. He won, and racial discrimination was fully outlawed by the Race Relations Act of 1965.

Today there are a total of 116 anti-discrimination laws, covering not just race but sex, sexuality, religion, disability and four other protected characteristics.

Indirect Discrimination

The great masterpiece of social engineering legislation was Harriet Harman's 2010 Equality Bill, described by Trevor Phillips as a move from 'purely anti-discrimination law' to 'pro-fairness law'. Phillips told the Human Rights Lawyers Association in June 2007 that the Equality and Human Rights Commission would be 'a change maker for the whole of society'. And in a speech to the Employment Lawyers' Association he spoke of 'outcomes, rather than processes, focusing on results and narrowing equality gaps' and of 'putting the fear of God into employers and the like' through the effective use of legal powers. It's a telling phrase; if diversity is such a blessing for employers, as they are always told, why do we need highly-paid state officials to put 'the fear of God' into anyone who does not wish to receive it?

Among Phillips's methods to increase 'fairness' was a plan to change the definition of 'indirect discrimination', a term so legally vague that, faced with a legal threat backed by the EHRC, many firms will simply give in.

Equality provisions introduced under Labour already outlawed indirect discrimination, which 'occurs when a provision, criterion or practice, applied equally to everyone, puts people from a particular racial group (based on race or ethnic or national origin) at a disadvantage',[109] because they cannot comply with it, an example being employers who insist on a UK qualification, or who ask that staff work in the evening (which discriminates against women, as primary carers of children). This is unlawful unless it can be shown that 'the provision, criterion or practice is a proportionate means of achieving a legitimate aim'. It is, of course, very difficult for a provision or criterion to affect every group at the same rate, and though defenders of this system point to 'legitimate aim' as proof that employers who aren't guilty of 'indirect discrimination' won't be harmed, ambiguous laws can create terror in innocent people; small businesses cannot afford the expensive lawyers necessary to fight cases often brought with the blessing and support of government anti-racism agencies, or to prove that their organisations have a 'legitimate aim' in behaving in a way that might indirectly discriminate. The irony is that were such legislation around in the 1950s and 1960s the recruitment of London Underground staff from the West Indies and textile workers from Pakistan might have been illegal.

And after 2010 the burden of proof in race discrimination cases involving education and training was shifted, so that once a complainant could show that he or she had suffered a disadvantage, it was up to the employer to prove that it was not because of discrimination. As David Green noted in the *Daily Telegraph*, 'the essence of freedom is to know when the law could be used against you, but the new anti-discrimination law will make it impossible to know in advance when you have done wrong... For centuries our laws have prevented governments from harassing people by bringing arbitrary charges against them. On the occasions when charges are brought, the burden of proof lies with the authorities'.[110]

This is not only burdensome for employers, it is also unfairly so for small employers, who cannot afford the legal fees required to navigate the diversity maze. Indeed Jonah Goldberg, author of *Liberal Fascism*, argues that diversity programmes actually help big business because they cost their smaller rivals more, while allowing them to buy relatively cheap credibility.

Not many people now argue that the Race Relations Acts of 1965 and 1968, which outlawed racial discrimination in workplaces, were a mistake. They came in response to many employers refusing to take on black workers, which contributed to already high levels of unemployment among immigrants. But there are now few areas of life in which diversity has not become a set goal of institutions, whether it is government departments or private firms, and the 2000 Race Relations Act now places a positive duty on 43,000 public authorities 'to promote good relations between persons of different racial groups'. This poses a serious question about personal freedom, and to what extent, if it is assumed that diversity is a 'good', the state should force it upon everyone.

But many people have a vested interest in this system. In *Deutschland Schafft Ab*, 'Germany Abolishes Itself', Bundesbank governor Thilo Sarrazin noted that 'a host of integration specialists, Islam scholars, sociologists, political scientists, and activists, and a raft of naive politicians work hand in hand, and tirelessly, on belittlement, self-deception and denial'. Immigration created and empowered a class of so-called *Gutmenschen* in government and academia, a caste of people for whom diversity is truly 'enriching'.

In turn the public sector diversity industry gives employment to many others in the private sector, all repeating the same mantra. One business in Stafford sells educational posters which 'promote and celebrate the diversity of society in which we live' and claims to be 'a one stop shop for all equality and diversity needs, whether it is racial, cultural, religious, linguistic, ageist, gender, sexual orientation or disability equality. Whether it is in education, government departments, hospitals, public services or business.' Equality and diversity 'needs'? As they explain: 'Making equality and diversity central to employment and service delivery is not an optional extra. European and UK law is explicit in the importance of these issues. Every public sector organisation requires equality to be mainstreamed within all aspects of service delivery and public duty. Organisations of the future are going to find the implications more and more important if they are going to reflect the diversity of their staff and clientele.' So either 'celebrate' diversity, or the Government will put you out of business.

Some MPs have gone further by suggesting that all job applications should have to be blank to strike out 'unwitting' prejudice, and government employees have even gone undercover to show that white employers were more likely to choose white applicants.[111] But while it may be the case that white people (perhaps unconsciously) favour whites, the same is almost certainly true for blacks, Asians, Catholics, Mormons, Armenians and people from the same universities or towns. To what extent can the state regulate every area of our lives, even our personal preferences? Should the government seek to maintain peace and public order or change human nature? The latter policy does not have a promising record.

In 2010 the Equality and Human Rights Commission produced a report, 'How Fair is Britain?', in which it stated, among other things, that: 'People from some ethnic groups are more likely to be in higher skilled, professional occupations than others' and that 'Chinese and Indian men are nearly twice as likely as white British men to be in professional jobs'. But what has this to do with fairness? Chinese and Indian men are more likely to be professionals because they are more likely to have professional qualifications, and have passed their exams; because more have presumably worked hard at school, and had parents who made their children work. The anti-racist doctrine that there must be equality of outcomes sometimes has tragic consequences. In 2005 the Government demanded in its action plan, 'Delivering race equality in mental health care', that health authorities must reduce 'disproportionate' admissions of black patients to psychiatric wards, even though these do reflect relative rates of mental ill health. Dr Swaran Singh concluded: 'Following this logic, an ill young black male could be denied admission if a ward required elderly white females to restore ethnic balance.'

With the scope for the state's obsession with equality expanded, the report looked at relative differences between religious communities, sexes, social classes and sexual orientations – every 'protected characteristic' listed under the Equality Act. Yet as a basis for massive government intervention to equalise society, it is a recipe for permanent conflict. As the *Telegraph* reported, the EHRC 'says more should be done to ensure that Muslims in particular are helped to find jobs'. How is this fair to individuals who lose out on jobs solely because of their ethnic background?

It is impossible to ensure that every category of person is given equal representation in every field and industry, and achieves the same success. But this has not stopped governments from trying to artificially engineer equality and diversity. Modern racial quotas began in the United States following the Civil Rights Act, and were used in state industries where blacks were blatantly excluded (although quotas were first used in the early 20th century to limit the number of high-achieving Jews in top schools, universities and professions). There were police departments serving hundreds of thousands of blacks that did not include a single black employee, which was not just morally wrong but counter-productive. But this evolved into the idea that all races and groups should be equally represented in every area of life, an impossible goal. Racial quotas are as yet illegal in the UK, although the use of internships for ethnic minorities is widespread. Labour has also introduced an informal quota for its own representatives in the form of an all-black shortlist in the Brent South constituency,[112] where they chose a former 'national race and equality officer' for the GMB union. But quotas are very much on the agenda still, and if America's example is anything to go, where 'disparate impact'[113] cases have crippled many public sector services, we will see ever more pressure to introduce them into every area of the public sector. And yet the question remains – would any equality and diversity officials fly in a plane if the safety technician were hired on account of their race rather than suitability?

Equality and Diversity is now imbedded in British law, with 'general duties to promote equality' making it a legal requirement 'to promote equality in the areas of disability, gender and race'. Policy-makers from Parliament down to local government must asses all new (and eventually, all existing) policies for their impact on equality, not just of race but of sex, sexuality and a host of other protected characteristics. It can be applied to everything from the building of new schools to the closure of bus routes.

Every one of the countless tentacles of the state, whether at national, local or quasi-government level, now has an 'equality and diversity' statement, and every arm of Government must meet Race Equality Guidelines.

The irony is that diversity would be less problematic if people were willing to accept the inequalities that followed. Enthusiasts often use the analogy of biodiversity or other terms associated with nature, linking diversity with healthiness and ruggedness in contrast to monoculturalism, 'stale, inbred, infertile', in G Pascal Zachary's words. Yet biodiversity exists because of the cruelty of nature. Diversity cannot be defended on socialist or social democratic grounds, because it depends on creative destruction. Diversity by its very nature brings inequality, and just as Communism singularly failed to produce equality of outcomes between individuals, so its 21st-century successor has and will fail to produce equality of outcomes between groups. The problem is that, like with its ideological cousin, this Utopian goal involves huge state growth and restrictions on liberty in pursuit of that goal.

Hate Crime

Hate crime legislation also originated in the US, and in Britain began with the Crime and Disorder Act 1998, which created offences of racially aggravated assault, criminal damage and harassment. The range is now vast, and some of what passes as a 'hate crime' would once have been considered simple rudeness rather than a legal matter; hardly surprising, then, that there are 50,000 'racist incidents' in schools every year that have to be logged. Hate crime legislation accelerated with the appalling murder of black teenager Stephen Lawrence in Eltham, south-east London, which lead to some of the most illiberal laws in modern British history.

The eighteen-year-old was killed on April 22, 1993 by a gang heard to shout 'What, what, nigger?' by Lawrence's friend Duwayne Brooks. The first police investigation came to nothing because the police could not find enough evidence to satisfy the Crown Prosecution Service, and forensic evidence proved negative. A second investigation took place in April 1994 but also failed. The family then took their complaints to the Police Complaints Authority, which led to an internal investigation by Kent Police. They found that there was not 'any evidence to support allegations of racist conduct by police officers'. Then in June 1997 new Home Secretary Jack Straw announced that there would be a new inquiry into the Police's handling of the investigation, at a cost of £3 million. It began in March 1998, with a formal hearing in Elephant and Castle, south London.

The inquiry departed, in the words of sociologist Norman Dennis, from practices 'which have traditionally been regarded as essential in English law. Rules of evidence were modified and witnesses were harassed, both by the members of the inquiry team and by the crowd in the public gallery. Representatives of the Metropolitan Police were asked to "confess" to charges of racism, even if only in their private thoughts. They were even asked to testify to the existence of the racist thoughts of other people. It is part neither of the English judicial process nor of English public inquiries to put people on trial for their thoughts. The proceedings bore some resemblance to the Stalinist show trials of the 1930s.'

The Macpherson inquiry ruled out from the earliest days having to meet the requirement of evidence of racism, as in evidence that blacks would have been treated worse than whites in the same situation. And though there was no actual evidence of this, the report found the Metropolitan Police and British society in general guilty of some indescribable, vague 'institutional' racism. The police had been ineffective in dealing with a perceived racist crime, therefore that ineffectiveness was due to police racism. It was down to policemen's 'unwitting' thoughts and conduct, which put charges of racism outside the boundaries of proof or rebuttal. The 'proof' was circular and self-reinforcing, so to question whether the murder of Stephen Lawrence was a purely racist crime was, in itself, evidence of racism.

The Macpherson inquiry was clearly influenced by the recent Truth and Reconciliation Commission in South Africa, and certainly created a subliminal parallel between apartheid South Africa and racist Britain. One of Sir William's three advisors, Dr Richard Stone, told Metropolitan Police commissioner Sir Paul

Condon: 'It seems to me, Sir Paul, that the door is open. It is like when Winnie Mandela was challenged in the Truth Commission in South Africa by Desmond Tutu to acknowledge that she had done wrong... I say to you now, just say, 'Yes, I acknowledge institutional racism in the police'... Could you do that today?' (Mandela had been convicted of kidnapping and assaulting a 14-year-old who was murdered in her home by her thugs.) One of the pieces of 'evidence' that one Acting Inspector was being racist in not approaching the Lawrences in hospital was that he had never taken a race awareness course. As Dennis wrote: 'On this "evidence" (whose natural home is in some utopia from the wilder shores of totalitarian social work) if someone has not take the appropriate course on "child abuse awareness" he is incestuous; if he has not taken the appropriate course on "sexual preference awareness" he is a proven homophobe; if he has not taken a racial-awareness course he is a racist.'

At the inquiry Dr Robin Oakley described a form of undetected racism in the police 'usually covert rather than overt, unintended so far as motivation is concerned, acted out unconsciously by individuals, and an expression of collective rather than purely individual sentiment'. Kent police's 'failure to find racism was due to the fact, then, that they were looking in an archaic police way for what is ordinarily called "evidence" that identifiable individuals had been doing overt racist things.' According to Dr Oakley, they should have been looking for 'collective sentiments' that individuals were not expressing, and for racism that the "racists" were not conscious of.

Macpherson put the question of racist motive, intention, and conduct more or less outside the boundaries of empirical verification or rebuttal, for in the words of Karl Popper: 'The essential difference between scientific and other versions of reality is that science allows observable data to disprove its own statements.' Macpherson's definition of racism is unfalsifiable, as it is impossible to prove that someone is not being racist. He recommended that 'Any incident (not any "crime") that involves interaction with any person from the minority of "colour, ethnic origin or culture", is racist if anyone at all, whether from the minority or from the majority, says he or she thinks it is.' He also recommended that any racist incident that is a crime, and any racist incident that has nothing to do with a crime, must be 'investigated with equal commitment' by the police. More chilling, the report also recommended a change in the law so that where there is a prosecutable offence which involves 'racist language', then prosecution should be allowed for the use of such language 'other than in a public place'. Conservative journalist and future London Mayor Boris Johnson pointed out that: 'Not even under the law of Ceausescuâ's Romania could you be prosecuted for what you said in your own kitchen.'[114]

The Queen's Counsel at the Macpherson inquiry said that 'anyone who murders for racist motives... should escape is doubly repellent'. So was the murder of Stephen Lawrence twice as repellent as an intra-racial murder? Hate crime legislation, which now includes a raft of offences such as 'transphobia', are justified on the grounds that such crimes create terror across a community, because of their motive. But almost any inter-racial crime could be perceived as racially motivated, even if a primary motive is established; the only way to fairly deal with suspected hate crime is to treat all inter-racial crimes as racially-motivated and so 'doubly repellent'. Yet the justification that inter-racial murder must be severely and disproportionately punished because of fears it could set off a tinderbox only serves to illustrate the essential fragility of multi-ethnic societies. Indeed there is an ancient precedent for this principle, in the England of Alfred the Great, when the country was divided between Anglo-Saxons and Danes. In 886 the *wergild* (the amount of blood money payable to the family of a man killed) for an inter-ethnic murder was set at eight half-marks of gold, far higher than the normal wergild for the highest social rank, an early recognition that inter-communal violence was potentially explosive.[115]

Hate crime legislation is paradoxical because, like racism, it pays far more due to race than really exists. Racism is spectral, and whereas very few people are entirely free of racial prejudice in one form or another, very few are entirely racist, in that they solely or even predominantly judge someone by the colour of their skin. Most people have prejudices of some sort, but they rarely hate people unlike them, and most violence is intra-racial; indeed the majority of murders are committed by acquaintances, not strangers of a different colour. Far more men hate their friends and family than hate other races, if crime statistics are anything to go by.

And punishments doled out for 'hate crimes' can be wildly disproportionate to the offence. A man who posted six racist messages on a website dedicated to Anthony Walker, a black teenager murdered in Liverpool in 2005, was sentenced to 2 years and 8 months in jail. Neil Martin had suggested that Walker's parents should leave on a 'banana boat' and that whites should celebrate his murder. Utterly despicable, but his sentence for publishing 'material likely to stir up racial hatred' is in stark contrast to the far lighter sentences regularly handed out for burglary, robbery or grievous bodily harm. In Teeside that same month Kenneth Yorke was able to inflict a violent nine-hour rape on a woman he had dragged off the street, having just received a suspended sentence three months earlier for grievous bodily harm, despite eighty-three previous offences for crime and dishonesty. In 2012 a man in Swansea was jailed for almost two months for a 'racially aggravated public order offence' after posting messages on Twitter following the collapse of Bolton Wanderers player Fabrice Muamba at an FA Cup quarter-final, an extraordinarily harsh sentence for the unpleasant, but very minor, offence of internet trolling.

Anti Racist Doctrine

After the decline and fall of the Soviet Union Britain's Trotskyite Left was scattered into various tribes, many taking on environmentalist causes, some getting anti-religion, and others going into anti-racist politics, which became the class struggle by other means. Anti-racism inherited from the radical tradition the mindset of Maximilien Robespierre, who declared that you are either entirely free or entirely a slave: 'If you do not do all for liberty, you have done not a thing.' You are either anti-racist or racist, and anyone who tries to question anti-racism must be racist. To believe in this idea one does not need to rationally question whether it makes sense or works, but simply to believe it is right.

In the words of one critic of multiculturalism, it 'belongs to a family of antinomian beliefs with a long religious history behind them' where 'a doctrine of the purity of the heart was advanced as transcending mere rules of right and wrong. And the result has always been to constitute an elite of the pure in heart who would, of course, need the power to reform society so that it fully shared this ideal purity.'[116]

Just as Puritans saw sin in everyone, and to Bolsheviks counter-revolutionary tendencies were all around, so anti-racists can spot impure thoughts towards non-whites, even among the consciously innocent. By the time of Macpherson this ideology had gained a stranglehold on the state. In 1991 the central Council for Education and Training in Social Work (CCETSW) set out the implementation of its new Diploma in Social Work. The first tenet was 'the self-evident truth' that 'racism is endemic in the values, attitudes and structures of British society'. Its Training Manual developed the 'Rules of social work', among which were that 'steps need to be taken to promote permeation of all aspects of the curriculum by an anti-racist analysis'. All 'racist materials' had to be withdrawn from the syllabus and CCETSW would decide what was racist. In the Rules there is no freedom of speech for opinions that can be constructed as 'racist' or favourable to 'racism'. Meanwhile 'anti-racist practice requires the adoption of explicit values', and the first value is that individual problems have roots in 'political structures' and 'not in individual or cultural pathology'. A second value is that racial oppression and discrimination are everywhere to be found in British society even when invisible.

The doctrine of anti-racism also permeates through education, both in the US and Britain. Among the many anti-racist programmes, children at one school in Otley, Leeds, work on the 'Stephen Lawrence Education Standard', an initiative set up by the local education board, in which 'monitoring pupils' commitment to equality and diversity' and 'mandatory anti-racist training for staff and governors, a written equality policy, and individual checks on successes and setbacks for minority pupils' are part of the programme. Over 300 education authorities sent staff to the project's launch. Yet if one does not believe that the state can enforce equality of outcomes, nor eliminate prejudice – and the overwhelming evidence from history and science suggests it cannot – then such lessons are, at best, a waste of time, and at worst counter-productive.

Such programmes are obviously not enough for Trevor Phillips, who also blames prejudice for the relative success and failure of different groups in schools. In a speech to employment lawyers in 2007 he said that 'it defies belief that our teaching profession is so prejudiced, but also so subtle in its exercise of prejudice, as to preserve the educational failure of black boys and Pakistani and Bangladeshi pupils whilst allowing those of Indian and Chinese heritage to exceed the achievements of white pupils. Bluntly, we will never eradicate inequality just by finding all the discriminators and taking them to court.' Phillips's job, and that of many other state-employed *Gutmenschen*, depends on the belief that certain groups are held back not by individual behavior or cultural traits but by racism. Deftly avoiding the obvious question why only some groups are affected, he suggests it is 'subtle' racism that, for some inexplicable reason, is only directed against some groups.

Besides which, anti-racist activism has a dubious success record on countering prejudice, which is broken down by reality, not by politics. The creation of an Irish race-relations lobby in the 1980s made absolutely no difference to the output of feeble jokes about thick paddies, which were long ingrained (and even up until the decade of my birth newspaper cartoons still depicted the aboriginal Gaels as mono-browed Cro-Magnons whose social development had halted at some period in the late Stone Age when alcohol was discovered). But Irish jokes did start to die out during the late 1990s as the Irish economy enjoyed a spectacular rise, with Ireland's per capita income overtaking Britain's for the first time in history at the end of the century. As a result Irish migration to Britain changed, mass working-class immigration being replaced with a far smaller elite movement of educated professionals. By the start of this century Irish immigrants earned more than natives, making any joke look outdated and nonsensical, far more of a humour-killer than offensiveness, since popular jokes tend to reflect often-harsh realities.

It is usually conservatives who are accused of 'moral panic', yet that is what followed the Macpherson report. In *The Likes of Us*, Michael Collins compared it to the tabloids' obsession with child molesters: 'Any day you expected a name-and-shame campaign listing convicted racists, like the roll-call of paedophiles compiled by the *News of the World.*' Where hysteria leads, authoritarianism usually follows, especially where the target is not actions but feelings. Macpherson had recommended the abolition of the double jeopardy rule if there was 'viable evidence'; double jeopardy, the rule by which an individual cannot be tried for the same crime twice, had been part of English Common Law since the 11th century, and is a vital protection against persecution by the state; at least it was until its abolition in 2003. Historians of England during the demographic revolution may marvel at how easily it gave up its freedoms.

Meanwhile the nation's racist-hunters have invented new areas to weed out sin. As well as the 'institutional racism' of the Metropolitan Police, there is also unwitting racism, subconscious racism, potential racism and dog-whistle racism, in which politicians who speak out about issues of legitimate concern are deemed racist because the causes of those concerns are disproportionately linked to one group. Discussing crime means a politician must be attacking blacks, mentioning terrorism is anti-Muslim, so that it becomes impossible to discuss any problem if it can be interpreted racially. In a strangely Freudian way it is the accuser who is making an association that the dog-whistle racist was not necessarily thinking; if an ardent moralist denounced a painting because he – and only he – could sense its arousing homoerotic undertones, one might suspect that all was not well in his marriage. Besides which, people wouldn't need to 'whistle' about certain issues, at frequencies presumably only anti-racist activists and dolphins can pick up, if they were allowed to discuss them in human language.

One group of anti-racists even organised a petition to stop the Metropolitan Police from asking music promoters what style of music would be played at events because it was 'potentially racist', as it was aimed at bashment, R&B and garage, 'types of music that are popular with people from ethnic minority communities and that seems extraordinary in today's modern, diverse multicultural London,' as the letter to the *Guardian* put it. Yet events playing garage (or certain types of reggae) do attract a far higher rate of violence than those playing other genres of music, and the police are wise to know what crowd they are dealing with; just as they are to know whether a sporting event is hosting a Village XI v Old Boys or West Ham United v Millwall. On the morning that Radio 4's *Today* programme ran a feature about the petition, police were investigating the murder of a man who had been decapitated outside the Ministry of Sound nightclub. It would be racist to ask what type of music was playing that night.

George Orwell wrote in *1984*: 'The B vocabulary consisted of words which had been deliberately constructed for political purposes: words, that is to say, which were intended to impose a desirable mental attitude upon the person using them.' The aim was to create a person who was 'naturally orthodox', in Newspeak a 'goodthinker'.

'Political correctness' is a phrase much overused by journalists, sometimes with the words 'gone mad' after it, and the popular press has often focused on its euphemistic language. But PC is not primarily about the funny terms, which can be absurd but arose partly from a noble attempt to be kind (even a black-hearted conservative can see that making the only minority or gay or disabled person feel welcome is not a Stalinist thing to do, but a compassionate one). It is really about closing down debate, seeking – as Orwell foresaw – to make contrary ideas utterly unsayable. From Enoch Powell to historian David Starkey, who in 2011 told *Newsnight* that the London riots were a product of a black subculture, proponents of diversity have silenced opposition not with debate but with the claim that what they say is offensive or dangerous. Overuse of 'hate' terms – racist, sexist, homophobe, Islamophobe – is corrosive to reasonable debate, because they suggest that the hater is corrupted by some prejudice which makes their views, whatever the logic of their argument, inadmissible. In Peter Brimelow's famous phrase: 'A racist is a conservative winning an argument with a liberal.' And if debate is closed down in politics and in academia, it is only a matter of time before it becomes not simply unspeakable but illegal.

It is human nature that once a subject becomes sacred all rational debate is extinguished, and this has been the case wherever the sacred values of race have become a part of discourse. As journalist Anthony Browne noted: 'It is a pattern in the US, Britain and elsewhere in Europe, that once ethnic minorities reach a certain critical mass in a country, then the politics of race defines the politics of every other issue: the imperative to combat racism overwhelms any other consideration, whether it is the environment, the working class, law and order, or even disease control.'[117]

The authorities have even begun to search for criminal thinking in children. SureStart, the Labour Government's flagship programme for improving state childcare, has guidelines which state: 'Children reflect the attitudes and values of all around them, including racial attitudes and values. While eliminating racial discrimination and promoting equality of opportunity are important in ensuring race equality, they are insufficient in themselves to counter any prevailing racist attitudes and behaviour. In order to offset the process whereby children may learn to be racially prejudiced at an early age, specific and positive action needs to be taken on a regular basis to ensure [children] value aspects of other people's lives (such as their skin colour, physical features, culture, language or religion) equally rather than seeing them as less worthy than theirs or ranking them in a racial hierarchy.'

In July 2008 the National Children's Bureau released a 366-page guide *Young Children and Racial Justice* counseling adults on recognising racist behavior in young children, even those who 'react negatively to a culinary tradition other than their own by saying 'yuck'.[118] Even nursery staff must be alert for racist remarks among toddlers, the Government-sponsored agency report said.

By the end of the 2000s Orwell's predictions seemed more eerily true than ever, not so much the more obviously Soviet elements, such as the poverty and the state brutality, but rather the mental straitjacketing. In particular his predictions of thought-crime and Newspeak have turned out to be prescient, which is why the Left-wing writer has become a hero not just to libertarians but also to the anti-immigration Right. Orwell could not have foreseen how race would come to obsess western thinking, but it is from the Far-Left's view of this subject that thoughtcrime has become a reality. The Macpherson inquiry and various other aspects of anti-racist thinking would have shocked Orwell, precisely because he was so right; as the saying goes, *Nineteen Eighty-Four* was a warning, not an instructions manual.

11

The New Blasphemy Laws
Regulating religion

The first decade of the 21st century saw some of the biggest peacetime assaults on British freedom in over 300 years, authoritarian laws passed by former student radicals, the same people who would once have shouted 'Fascist' at Enoch Powell and now removed ancient freedoms in the name of diversity. Sixties-era liberalism, for all its attachment to ideas about personal freedom and choice, is hostile to individual responsibility when it creates inequality, and believes that the state is necessary to regulate large areas of life. And one of the attractions of diversity is that it requires the state to be involved in many areas where it has traditionally been absent, because non-diverse organisations that do not bridge across racial and religious lines (and many do not) can be viewed as at best discriminatory and at worst a threat to community relations. A diverse, multi-racial society is less self-policing, more prone to communal strife, and for this reason vulnerable to Singapore-style authoritarianism.

The brunt of this illiberalism is borne by Muslims themselves, which may be a necessary way of monitoring the small but significant number of extremists, but puts a largely blameless section of the population under suspicion.

Following 9/11 many former protectors of all things ethnic now turned against a religion they saw as threatening European values, although some have upped their attacks on Christianity as well by way of compensation. Indeed the first decade of the 21st century saw a steep rise in anti-religious sentiment, with New Atheist writers such as Richard Dawkins, Christopher Hitchens, Daniel Dennett and Sam Harris (known as 'the Four Horsemen') expressing the increasing popular view that 'religion poisons everything', in Hitchens's words. New Atheism's popularity was partly a reaction to the growing strength of political Evangelical Christianity in the United States, and opposition to the churches' traditional views on homosexuality, but a displaced fear of Islam certainly played a part.

Discomfort with religion has led to increasing calls for greater French-style *laicite*, in particular in the area of faith schools, but while this is often framed in terms of opposition to all religious conservatism, countering Muslim separatism is clearly the most urgent motive. Writing in *The Independent* Christina Patterson suggested that 'a properly civilised society would accept that while lovely little C of E schools were once an excellent place for children to learn about the religion that shaped their culture, art and laws, you can't have them without having the madrassa run by the mad mullah next door, and therefore, sadly, you can't have either'. Church schools are a good thing, but diversity requires state-enforced uniformity. A Catholic or Anglican might ask why they should have to sacrifice their schools, among the most successful in the country, because of another religion – this was not part of the terms and conditions of mass immigration.

Some Muslim schools do, indeed, acquire their money and ethos from highly dubious sources. A *Dispatches* documentary broadcast on Channel 4 in February 2011 showed children at a school in Birmingham being taught that Hindus drink cow's urine, while the Saudis inject large amounts of money into European schools to promote their ultra-conservative brand of Islam, one of which was found to be teaching children in Britain that the Jews were descended from pigs and dogs. Many Muslim schools do not, however; indeed many Muslim communities, such as the Ahmadiyya in south-west London, are specifically anti-jihad and do not produce 'mad mullahs'.

Already Christian charities have suffered, as the proliferation of radical Islam has meant the authorities having to redefine their tra-ditionally relaxed relationship with the various Christian institu-tions that are woven into the social fabric, further raising the transaction costs within society. It had always been assumed that religious organisations working in advancing religion, education and the relief of poverty were acting 'charitably', that is for the public benefit. This presumption had evolved over centuries, and had been protected and regulated (lightly) through Parliament. The regulation was light because Parliament had a long and extensive relationship with Christian institutions. In response to the growth of religious charities with which Parliament did not have an extensive relationship, the Charities Act 2006 removed from the various local and national institutions of the Church of England (and other Christian churches) the presumption of acting charitably, meaning that all 13,000 Parochial Church Councils, many of the Finance Committees of the 43 Anglican Dioceses, the Archbishops' Council, the Church Commissioners and the countless number of charitable organisations in whole or in part related to the Church must now satisfy the Charity Commission that they are of public benefit. To cope with all this extra work the Charity Commission established a Faith and Social Cohesion Unit.

The French have applied *laïcite* to that most physically obvious sign of Islamic separateness, women's clothing, in response to a huge increase in the number of women adopting Middle Eastern dress that covers them from head to toe. So much have these fashions transformed the appearance of many European neighbourhoods, that in the 21st century women's religious fashion became a political issue in British life for the first time in many centuries.

In 2006 former Home Secretary Jack Straw made headlines by calling the veil a 'visible statement of separation and difference' and revealing that he asked women who came to his surgery to remove their facial coverings (in front of another female). The veil debate highlights the high transaction costs of a society that incorporates both a post-war view of human rights, in which a human right is violated if anyone's pursuit of personal happiness is interfered with, and one that accepts competing cultures. When 14-year-old Luton schoolgirl Shabina Begum won the right to cover her face at school using human rights laws, she called it 'a victory for all Muslims who wish to preserve their identity and values despite prejudice and bigotry'. Yet the girl was Bangladeshi-British, not Arabic, and in many cases these are not young women following traditional customs, but British people who have chosen to adopt cultural norms at odds with British tradition, partly in reaction to over-sexualisation. That incident came soon after a

Dewsbury schoolteacher was fired for refusing to remove her hijab, and a hairdresser was forced to pay out for 'indirect discrimination' for not hiring a woman who would not remove her headscarf.

The increasing popularity of the veil has led many states to reach for the statute books. In 2004 France and five German regions banned the wearing of headscarves in public schools. The proposal had first been raised in France back in 1985, and it was not so alien to the republic, where state-enforced secularism had been the norm since the early 20th century. France deflected the charge of Islamophobia by also banning 'large crosses' in schools, whatever that means (certain rappers have been known to wear comedy-sized crucifixes, but not French Catholics). In 2011 France and Belgium then banned the wearing of the veil in public. In Britain burqa laws have been proposed by a Tory MP but got no further; aside from practical matters, such as not being allowed into banks, or airport searches, it has not been considered the state's business what people wear since the late medieval or early modern period.

But although there is as yet little appetite for state intervention, the face covering does represent a social problem, or at least a visible symptom of one. When people talk about the problems of diversity they usually use the word 'culture' and culture, at its most basic level, is about the ground rules of communication and behaviour. Without these even the most basic kind of rubbing along becomes problematic. Ultimately any state that has to legislate for the clothing of its immigrant communities has to wonder if its immigration policy has failed.

Thoughtcrime

Today there are estimated to be some 2,000 active British jihadists in 200 networks under surveillance,[119] of which 1,000 are deemed potential bombers. The 150-strong British brigade in Iraq[120] was just under half the size of the total number of Muslims in the British Army. Government officials also say that 'dozens' of Somalis in Britain have returned to their homeland to join the militant group al-Shabaab.

A thousand potential bombers is considerably more than the Provisional IRA at full strength, and while the risks of any individual dying in a terror attack in Britain are exceptionally small, a terrorist presence entails huge costs, not least the restrictions on freedom required to keep us safe. They are, alas, necessary, for the potential impact on inter-communal relations becomes more volatile as society becomes more diverse. And so the Government responded to the terrorist threat with the most authoritarian measures seen in peacetime. Among these were the ban on burning flags (and Korans), a ban on taking photographs of landmarks, and the introduction of 28 days without trial. Labour used the threat of terrorism to campaign for ID cards, while the Terrorism Act 2006 also criminalised the 'glorification' of terrorism, a measure that resulted, in 2008, in 'Lyrical Terrorist' Samina Malik receiving a nine-month suspended sentence for writing some bad poetry. Among the lines were:

> Let us make Jihad
> Move to the front line
> To chop chop head of kuffar swine
> It's not as messy or as hard as some may think
> It's all about the flow of the wrist

Admittedly this is not likely to appear in any anthology of great English romantic poetry, but it is hardly a crime. There have also been several borderline cases where young British Muslims have been sent to jail for spending time on jihadi sites, but have arguably not gone beyond the fantasising stage, and to an extent Muslims are entitled to feel aggrieved. Home Secretary Charles Clarke even suggested that claiming 'terrorists go straight to paradise when they die' could be illegal, an offence that would have been inconceivable a generation ago. Britain has had an Irish terrorism problem since the 1860s but never have the authorities felt the need to jail anyone for singing *Kevin Barry* or *The Old Alarm Clock* at pub closing time. Irishmen in Britain have always been free to voice their support for political violence, so long as they did not aide it.

Throughout the 1990s and 2000s the range of views deemed

as acceptable shrunk, while the calls for 'hate speech' to be stamped out with legal measures have grown, at the expense of long-held freedom. The taking of offence has become justification enough for outrage, censorship or even prosecution, whether or not such offence-taking was justified. Offence crime is not just confined to race hate; as long as someone is offended, a crime has been committed, so that people uttering conservative views on homosexuality that until a generation ago were almost universal are now breaking the law. Yet these have been, so far, unevenly applied; although several Evangelical Christian street preachers have been arrested for quoting biblical condemnation of homosexual acts, and elderly Christians interrogated for 'potentially homophobic attitudes',[121] the authorities have been less keen to arrest the many Islamic preachers who have called for the execution of gays.

Anyone accused of stirring up hate, as the authorities view it, can be harassed in the Singapore style. This was illustrated starkly in February 2009 when Dutch MP Geert Wilders was banned from entering Britain on the grounds that he represented a threat to public order. He had been invited to the House of Lords to show a film, *Fitna*, (Arabic for 'disagreement and division among people') which claimed that the Koran inspired acts of violence. A factor in the Government's decision was a fear of French-style riots, as it was believed that several thousand protestors would head to Westminster.

To cope with religious diversity the state has introduced laws protecting religion from insult just as England's archaic blasphemy law was finally abolished in 2008 (partly, it was argued, to encourage Islamic countries to abolish their far harsher laws). Historically blasphemy is a crime against God, and by extension, the social order. England's law protected only Anglicanism, the religion of the state; after all, a blasphemy law that protects two religions is nonsensical, since two religions cannot both be right. This view was expressed by Lord Chief Justice Sir Matthew Hale, trying John Taylor in 1676 for the crime of calling Jesus Christ a 'bastard and whoremaker' and religion 'a cheat'. Justice Hale said that 'such kind of wicked and blasphemous words were not only an offence against God and religion but a crime against the laws,

States and Government; and therefore punishable in this court;
that to say religion is a cheat, is to dissolve all those obligations
whereby civil societies are preserved and Christianity being parcel
of the laws of England, therefore to reproach the Christian
religion is to speak in subversion of the law.'

But Britain's blasphemy laws were far from strict; indeed they
were less oppressive than the diversity-era blasphemy laws,
suggesting that not only is English liberalism in decline, but that
multiculturalism is akin to a new state religion. The last person to
be imprisoned for the crime was a Bradford trouser-salesman with
the ironic name John William Gott, who in 1921 was given nine
months with hard labour for publishing an anti-Christian
pamphlet called *Rib Ticklers*, which among other things compared
Jesus' journey into Jerusalem on a donkey with the actions of a
circus clown. It was his second conviction that year, the previous
one being for an 'obscene' pamphlet about birth control, and it
followed a 15-year-long struggle for socialism and secularism
(although he spent much of his time campaigning against other
tiny secularist groups in obscure internecine feuds that would put
religious believers to shame). And while Mary Whitehouse won
her case against *Gay News* in 1977 for publishing a poem that
suggested that Jesus had several gay experiences, it was at the cost
of making the blasphemy law a laughing stock. But rather than
arguing that no religion should be protected, in a sign of things to
come Lord Scarman said blasphemy laws should extend to other
religions and protect them from 'scurrility, ridicule and contempt'.
The 1985 Law Commission report rejected this idea, but two
judges out of five added a note of dissent, arguing that it was 'the
duty of our citizens, in our society of different races and people
of different faiths and of no faith, not purposely to insult or
outrage the religious feelings of others'.

The issue of religious criticism is far more complex in a diverse
society, where religion is so closely linked with identity. Criticism
of a religion, no matter how justified, can become criticism of a
religious community and a race, however voluntary religion is in
theory. And in one of New Labour's various authoritarian spasms
Home Secretary David Blunkett proposed making it a crime to
'stir up religious hatred' under the Religious and Racial Hatred Bill,

a proposal that would have effectively banned ridicule of religion, including jokes, if people were sufficiently offended.

The Law Against Incitement to Religious Hatred failed to criminalise criticism of Islam; it was left to the undemocratic House of Lords to insist on protection for 'discussion, criticism or expressions of antipathy, dislike, ridicule, insult or abuse of particular religions or the beliefs or practises of their adherents', an amendment which the Commons failed to overturn by just one vote. Yet there are now more than 35 Acts of Parliament, 52 Statutory Instruments, 13 Codes of Practice, 3 Codes of Guidance and 16 European Commission Directives that deal with discrimination, animosities and hatred. Together, various Public Order Acts and related laws make it illegal to hate anyone because of their race, colour, ethnic origin, nationality, national origin, religion, lack of religion, sex, sexual orientation, gender identity, disability or age. As Jon Gower Davies wrote in *A New Inquisition: Religious Persecution in Britain Today*: 'The law has been invited to insert its punitive, plodding and primitive self into areas of life from which we have long been accustomed to assume not simply its absence, but the positive existence of a freely-negotiated civic culture.'

And in the absence of a freely-negotiated civic culture, citizens are vulnerable to action by the authorities. In 2009 Ben and Sharon Vogelenzang, hotel owners from Liverpool, were accused of a 'religiously aggravated hate crime' after a conversation with a female Muslim guest, Ericka Tazi, and pursued by the police and the Crown Prosecution Service (CPS). Following allegations that they had said women were 'oppressed' by Islam and that Mohammed was a 'warlord', the police, advised by the CPS, charged the couple with a religiously-aggravated public order offence. Over several months six police officers, led by a detective chief inspector, assembled a case against the Vogelenzangs. When the full story came to court, it transpired that a Muslim doctor had also been eating breakfast in the hotel and found nothing objectionable about their conduct (he asked for his name to be kept confidential for, among other things, fear of retaliation). The case was dismissed by a judge who, in a twist that should have had British patriots choking on their roast beef and boiled bread, cited

European law granting freedom of religion.

The damage was already done. While the Vogelenzangs were still innocent until proven guilty, the local NHS authority, which accounted for 80 per cent of the couple's business, cancelled all of its bookings with the hotel. This is the danger for private citizens accused of 'hate'; even if they win, the stigma will stick, and if they happen to live in one of the many Sovietised regions of Britain where a boycott by the public sector is fatal (and located beside a hospital, they were especially vulnerable), they must prove themselves sufficiently orthodox on equality and diversity doctrine to satisfy the local bureaucrats too, and the obligation of local state institutions to promote equality and diversity. So while it used to be custom that people in England did not discuss religion and politics in public, now it is the law.

The Vogelenzangs were the latest victims of the anti-racism doctrine that had spread throughout the state. The Crown Prosecution Service, which had encouraged the case, is another body captured by the ideology, giving official encouragement to a 'staff network' called the National Black Crown Prosecution Association (NBCPA), which it gives £80,000 a year, and whose members are allowed over 300 days off a year to perform NBCPA duties. The NBCPA's main objective is to advance the careers of ethnic minorities within the CPS but it also takes an interest in the impact of CPS decisions on minorities. The existence of such bodies, given official approval from the very top, scares officials into making decisions that will not damage their careers. As in the USSR, where being considered politically unsound could ruin a public servant's prospects, so in Britain no one wants to be considered insufficiently zealous about equality and diversity.

And so we are much less free to criticise religion now than we were half a century ago and further. As Gower Davies put it: 'The British people might be forgiven for thinking that their basic religious-cultural inheritance, the culture under which we have grown up, is not just out of control but under some insidious attack. This British culture validates a public seeking for religious truth, not a trial: and it is more or less at ease with jokes and ribaldries, and ill at ease with censorship of them or with threats made at their authors. Being forbidden to express opinion, whether by actual punishment or the threat of it, or by the experience of being threatened, results, as the Psalmist has it, in a society in which 'we bless with our mouth, but inwardly we curse'.[122]

Critics are threatened on the one hand by the diversity-blasphemy laws and on the other by the secondary, de facto blasphemy law protecting Islam, which makes it doubly protected in a way that Christianity has not been for centuries.

Taking a far more modern and multicultural approach than Mary Whitehouse, in 1999 Sheikh Omar Bakri Muhammad, popularly known as the Tottenham Ayatollah, declared a fatwa against Terence McNally, whose play *Corpus Christi* had depicted Jesus as a homosexual. The Syrian-born sharia judge declared that the Church of England, by failing to take action, 'had neglected the honour of the Virgin Mary and Jesus'. In a moment of woolly liberalism the sheikh said that if McNally converted to Islam and repented 'he would still be executed, but his family would be cared for by the Islamic state carrying out the sentence and he could be buried in a Muslim graveyard'. What liberal fantasy world do these sharia judges live in? They'll be sending him on safari next.

Censorship

In response to the threat of violence from religious fanatics the art world has taken to self-censorship. In June 2007 the Royal Court cancelled a version of *Lysistrata* set in a Muslim heaven for fear of causing offence. The previous year Whitechapel Art Gallery removed a life-sized nude doll by surrealist artist Hans Bellmere so 'not to shock the population' of the Muslim area. Tim Marlow of White Cube art gallery has said that self-censorship is common, but few would admit it. While comedy writers Dick Clement and Ian La Frenais 'sadly abandoned' the idea of a comedy series about Bin Laden settling down with his family in an ordinary English suburb, which sounds eerily like the famously disastrous BSB comedy *Heil Honey I'm Home,* because 'of the chances of causing grave offence'. And yet, more than art, comedy is a necessary safety valve for society's various conflicts, and a healthy one too.

It is understandable. Those who mock religion often pay with their lives, most famously Theo Van Gogh, the Dutch filmmaker murdered in November 2004. Anyone concerned about the future should be aware of how quickly the acceptable boundaries can shift. In 2005 the Tate Gallery refused to exhibit John Latham's conceptual piece *God is Great*, originally made in 1991, which featured a six-foot high plate of glass with a Talmud, Bible and Koran. It said it would not be 'appropriate' following the London bombings, which angered not just Latham, but the Muslim Council of Britain, which said it had not been consulted and 'sometimes presumptions are incorrectly made about what is unacceptable to Muslims and this can be counter-productive'. But a lot changed from 1991 to 2005; the Muslim population of Britain more than doubled and became more radicalised and assertive, and as it doubles once again, by 2025, how likely is it that Londoners will ever be able to see his work? Latham was in the Avant-garde of 1960s art, where freedom to criticise and mock religion went without saying; 50 years later London is a very different place.

Liberals comfort themselves by suggesting that, since they would not wish to exercise the freedom to offend, they should willingly give it up. But it is one thing to avoid offence out of kindness and generosity, from a position of strength; quite another out of fear and weakness.

That weakness was illustrated starkly in 2005, following worldwide protests that followed the publication of cartoons depicting the Prophet Mohammed. The rage was fairly contrived, and the saga rich in irony. It began because a member of the Danish Left Socialists, Kare Bluitgen, wished to produce a children's book of the Koran and the life of Mohammed to present a positive image of Islam to young Danes. She could not find any artists willing to illustrate the book, for some inexplicable reason, which lead a small provincial newspaper, *Jyllands-Posten*, to suggest a competition, partly to make a statement about freedom.

The cartoons initially attracted no attention. The affair was whipped up by Ahmad Abu Laban, an asylum seeker who arrived in Denmark in 1984, having been expelled by the United Arab Emirates and Egypt. Head of the Islamic Society of Denmark, an organisation closely linked to the Muslim Brotherhood, he had come to Denmark because his son was disabled, and repaid

Denmark's hospitality by touring the Middle East calling for action against the Danes, presenting a dossier of the offending cartoons (which included some fakes not from the newspaper).

The Islamic world erupted, with violent protests outside Danish embassies across the Middle East, moving onto Norwegian targets when a paper in Norway reprinted the pictures, leading to several hundred deaths. The Danish Prime Minister and Foreign Minister blamed the cartoonists, while European and world leaders went out of their way to condemn these grossly offensive comics. The Foreign Office declared in a message to the Organisation for Islamic Cooperation: 'The whole international community stands with them in their staunch rejection of those who distort the noble faith of Islam. We join them in celebrating the values of Islamic civilisation. Their values are our values.' Rather than supporting a fellow European democracy with an impeccable record of freedom, ethical government and humane treatment of refugees, Europe bowed before the leaders of the most intolerant states on earth. The EU expressed 'regret', while Foreign Secretary Jack Straw said freedom of speech is fine, but not if it led to 'open season'. Several continental newspapers republished the pictures in solidarity, but not a single major British publication did. Indeed newspapers warned about Islamophobia while they were themselves too scared of Muslims – they were literally Islamophobic – to publish the cartoons. Only two college magazines printed the pictures, and both editors were sacked, one of them going into hiding.

UN Secretary-General Kofi Anan even said that 'the offensive caricatures of the Prophet Mohammed were first published in a European country which has recently acquired a significant Muslim population, and is not yet sure how to adjust to it'. But was it not up to Muslims to adjust to them, not vice versa? Once again the European Left went into cognitive dissonance mode. Social scientist Jytte Klausen pointed out that three years previously, 'Jyllands-Posten refused to publish cartoons portraying Jesus, on the ground that they would offend readers'. But a conservative newspaper is perfectly within its rights to not offend Christianity, for fear of upsetting its readers. The Daily Telegraph would not mock Christ, just as it would not attack foxhunters, and nor would the *Guardian* ridicule social workers or teachers. There is a difference between doing something out of genuine affection (and business self-interest) and out of fear. It is telling that Jack Straw said it was 'disrespectful' for European papers to republish, while Kofi Annan and Louise Arbour, the UN High Commissioner for Human Rights, also used the word 'respect' after the cartoon affair, since respect can also mean fear (in Latin *adore* means both). Does Europe respect Islam, or fear it?

In February 2006 Norway's Minister of Labour and Social Inclusion called a press conference, which featured the largest collection of imams in the country's history, and issued an abject apology to Mohammed Hamdan, head of Norway's Islamic Council. Hamdan, accepting on behalf of 46 organisations, asked that all threats against the editor of the Norwegian publication and his family be withdrawn. That year Norway passed a law making offensive statements about religion punishable by a fine and imprisonment.

It was not the only one. Following the affair Ireland introduced blasphemy laws for the first time, with the Defamation Act making the publication or utterance of blasphemous matter a crime punishable by a €25,000 (£22,500) fine. Ireland never had blasphemy laws when it was a borderline Catholic theocracy, but it did under multiculturalism. In response secularist campaigners set up an Exhibition of Blasphemous Art at the Irish Museum of Contemporary Art (Imoca) in Dublin on Good Friday, 2010, against a law that they said 'prevents intellectual debate'. The artists tested this theory with works such as 'F— Christmas', 'Bible Gun' and 'Resur-erection', which all satirised religious figures such as Jesus Christ and the Virgin Mary, although one particular 7th century figure was strangely absent. Not a single one mocked Islam, for the simple reason that long before the artists would be spending their lives under armed guard, the entire state machinery would have been forcing them to back down to spare Ireland a repeat of Denmark's ordeal.[123]

Like female genital mutilation and honour killings in Europe, these blasphemy laws are not a product of religion (or at least Christianity) but a combination of mass immigration and moral uncertainty. It is easier to blame these problems on religion in general, when in reality there is only one religion that threatens freedom in Europe, which is why the people behind the exhibition (quite understandably) did not mock its founder. Attacking Christianity is not going to change this threat. In fact, and to paraphrase Napoleon, a less-than-fanatical believer who understood society's need for faith, a nation that does not respect its own religion will soon learn to respect someone else's.

12

The Revolt of the Elites
Globalism in one country

The working classes failed the revolutionaries. Rather than rejecting bourgeois patriotism, as they were supposed to do, they fought and died in their millions in the First World War, and the Second, and when the 1960s generation called for revolution the workers were more interested in mortgages, holidays and washing machines. So the Left found new groups to act as the vanguard of international revolution.

According to the popular Marxist theory of nationalism, patriotism presents the workers with the false consciousness of an artificially-constructed national identity, distracting them from their true interests of internationalism and pan-worker solidarity. Nationalism has indeed been used by unscrupulous and venal men to distract the poor from material problems at home, and it always will be; today Middle Eastern dictators who have reduced their countries to ruin can always blame America and Israel for their troubles, while in the former Yugoslavia pathological nationalism was promoted by gangster-demagogues who financially profited from the bloodshed, while happily setting aside ethnic divisions in the criminal trades that flourished in war.

But the experience of recent decades has turned the conventional theory on its head. National loyalty is a two-way relationship, not just about keeping the worker loyal but keeping the boss loyal too, the noble man obliged to give employment to the artisan. Freed of patriotism, today it is the middle classes who have overthrown the workers, or rather replaced them with more compliant ones. And at the very top the new elites, the global footloose force called "international capital" in the words of the *Economist*, have few ties of loyalty to any place. American social critic Christopher Lasch called this 'the revolt of the elites' and warned that 'the chief threat' to the social order 'seems to come from those at the top of the social hierarchy'. So while patriotism may have been required, according to Marxist theory, to keep the working class working and fighting, now they are needed for neither, and their patriotism has been ghettoised. When the globe-trotting elite espouse open borders they often describe it in terms of air travel, a world of vibrant, diverse, cross-cultural pollination, similar to the business class lounges they are used to. For the rest of society universalism has also become all too like their experience of flying, marked by heightened security, reduced freedom, CCTV, armed police and overcrowding.

And globalism in one country, a product of radical Left-wing universalism and middle-class economic self-interest, has left the native poor with no function in society. And perversely it is the poor who have become scapegoats for the failings in the post-racial utopia.

One of the subjects often featured in Black History Month is the 1865 Morant Bay rebellion in Jamaica, in which almost a thousand people died in protests against a poll tax that prevented the black majority from voting. Governor John Eyre put down the uprising with horrific brutality, with rebels executed without proper trial, and even pregnant women flogged. It was not Britain's finest hour. And yet when a banquet was held in Governor Eyre's honour in Southampton by grateful members of the British Empire, a much larger 'Jamaica Committee' of mostly working-class men held a counter-rally across the city, the largest popular meeting in Southampton's history.

The English working classes had shown considerable self-sacrifice for the brotherhood of man over the previous four years. The American Civil War, that which begun in 1861, caused severe hardship for workers in north-west England, and yet during the 'Lancashire Cotton Famine' they declared their overwhelming support for the aims of the North in ending slavery, against their economic interests. On New Year's Eve, 1862, cotton workers held a meeting at the Free Trade Hall in Manchester in which they resolved that, despite their hardship, they would support the Union in its campaign against slavery. They sent a letter to

President Abraham Lincoln in the name of the 'Working People of Manchester', in which they stated that: '… the vast progress which you have made in the short space of twenty months fills us with hope that every stain on your freedom will shortly be removed, and that the erasure of that foul blot on civilisation and Christianity – chattel slavery – during your presidency, will cause the name of Abraham Lincoln to be honoured and revered by posterity'.

The following month the president sent an address to the cotton workers of Lancashire, thanking them for their support. 'I know and deeply deplore the sufferings which the working people of Manchester and in all Europe are called to endure in this crisis,' he said: 'Through the action of disloyal citizens, the working people of Europe have been subjected to a severe trial for the purpose of forcing their sanction to that attempt. Under the circumstances I cannot but regard your decisive utterances on the question as an instance of sublime Christian heroism which has not been surpassed in any age or in any country. It is indeed an energetic and re-inspiring assurance of the inherent truth and of the ultimate and universal triumph of justice, humanity and freedom.'

The African-American abolitionist, Frederick Douglass, inspired working men in England for years to come, with Thomas Burt, the leader of the Northumbrian miners at the end of the 19th century, paying tribute to the influence Douglass had had on his life and that of others workers.[124] Indeed the British poor had good reason to empathise with their fellow downtrodden of the world, often working and living in conditions that were a step up from slavery, but not much more. No wonder, then, that white guilt was rare among working-class men and women during the days of the *Empire Windrush*. But it was this sense of brotherhood, and of workers of the world having common cause, as well as a common humanity, that led the workers' leadership's 20th century successors to support the cause of mass immigration and the later rationale of diversity. And yet who has won from the creation of a new empire within Britain, the descendants of the factory workers or those of the factory owners?

*

Diversity and the Working Class

Diversity has indeed had profound effects on working-class life. By mid-2009 52 public houses were closing in Britain every week, and while the ban on smoking two years earlier aggravated the problem, as did cheap supermarket alcohol, one factor is that working-class English people have deserted large swathes of urban England. Yet the sight of sad little derelict pubs in urban England, which like the churches of old Byzantium are now museum pieces, is an image that some members of the people's party find strangely un-poignant. Between London and Leeds many old football stadiums, cathedrals of working class life, are in areas of white flight, their fan base having left. Many clubs have moved to identikit out-of-town grounds situated near shopping centres and motorways, leading some to lament that these new grounds left clubs cut off from their roots. Maybe, but perhaps the clubs have only followed their supporters as they left the inner cities to new immigrants; the outer suburb is now the home of English working class life.

Football, now as expensive as opera and with many players earning more in a week than a fan would make in four years, reflects the best and worst aspects of new English life – open-minded to the world and its talent, exciting and glamorous, yet disconnected from its roots, massively unequal, and the behavior of fans kept civilised only by CCTV, heavy policing and high costs. And since most players come from a different country, let alone a different town, even Michel Platini, the FIFA president and former France captain (and the son of an immigrant), was moved to ask what relationship a Liverpool team made up entirely of foreigners had to the working-class people of Liverpool.

Just as globalism has, despite tremendous benefits, left many people around the world deskilled and disenfranchised, so too has the policy of globalism in one country. It was left to Dagenham Labour MP Jon Cruddas to reflect in 2005 that 'immigration has been used as an informal reserve army of cheap labour. People see this at their workplace, feel it in their pocket and see it in their community – and therefore perceive it as a critical component of their own relative impoverishment. Objectively, the social wage of many of my constituents is in decline. House prices rise inexorably, and public service improvements fail to match local population expansion. At work, their conditions, in real terms, are in decline through the unregulated use of cheap migrant labour.' The strange thing is that this was Labour Party policy.

As Karl Marx wrote in 1847: 'The main purpose of the bourgeois in relation to the worker is, of course, to have the commodity labour as cheaply as possible, which is only possible when the supply of this commodity is as large as possible in relation to the demand for it.' Not only does this reduce wages through an increased labour supply, but ethnically diverse workforces are less willing and able to join together to demand better wages and conditions (just as in ancient societies slaves from the same ethnic group were kept apart to minimise rebellion). And when they strike against vastly cheaper foreign labour being brought in, they are called racist, while big business's demands for looser immigration rules are given a sympathetic hearing in the liberal media; at least when 19th century industrialists purposely depressed wages or moved colonial subjects to foreign lands to work the fields they did not claim the moral high ground while doing so. As George Walden put it in *Time to Emigrate?:* 'Why go to the trouble of travelling vast distances to exploit people, in the heat and the dust, when we can import them in their millions and exploit them here? What a lot of our profiteers are really after is a new generation of home-grown coolies and punkah-wallahs.' Importation of immigrants to serve London's rich was carried out in the name of Left-wing ideals, and no doubt many supporters hold those ideals genuinely. But, helping the rich and harming the poor, they are not ideals that would be recognisable to Left-wingers of a couple of generations before. And today when people talk admiringly of immigrant workers who put in extended hours while native workmen leave at five, few seem willing to make the argument that British workers should enjoy leisure and family time without being viewed as idle, competing against people working Victorian hours.

In the last two decades of the 20th century Labour evolved from being a traditional socialist to a socially and economically liberal party, with policies aimed at middle-class progressives. For a generation hugely influenced by the New Left and neo-liberalism, diversity became the perfect policy, giving Labour's new supporters a chance to show their moral credentials, while bringing down the cost of services and allowing them to indulge in some old-fashioned Fabian snobbery.

Working-class firebrands of both Left and Right wonder why New Labour abandoned their traditional support in favour of radical campus politics that did nothing for the poor, but as well as offering an alternative politics, it also suited their lifestyles and wallets. It costs nothing to believe in anti-racism, cultural relativism and diversity, and in many ways it's actually profitable. Many wealthy Britons prefer their wine to be brought to them by Poles, their houses cleaned by Brazilians and their children looked after by Romanians. Not only are people from these countries more grateful and obsequious than the natives, but one does not need to feel so embarrassed about the inequalities of life, one's background, accent and intellectual pretences, or the concept of service.

The Left's adoption of new social movements has left their old one, the poor, figures of ridicule and contempt. Michael Collins wrote: 'Historically, the right harboured desires to keep the white working class below stairs... Now, middle-class progressives who had traditionally come out fighting these underdogs' corner, or reporting their condition as missionaries or journalists, were keen to silence them, or bury them without an obituary.' And 'to their pallbearers in the press they were racist, xenophobic, thick, illiterate, parochial. They survived on the distant memory of winning one world cup and two world wars, and were still tuning in to the ailing soap that is the House of Windsor. All they represent and hold dear was reportedly redundant in modern, mul-ticultural Britain.' As middle-class whites have sought out diversity as a status symbol, they have become increasingly contemptuous of the poor. 'The contemporary take on Disraeli's two nations' involved 'the urban, edgy, multicultural city dwellers and their burden - the culturally impoverished, hickish whites everywhere else... And the issues here were not those of putting Beaujolais in the fridge, calling a napkin a serviette, and using the wrong knife. These days, it was the lack of modern etiquette on race that was keeping the white working class below stairs... In this instance, multiculturalism was the faith, and racism, rather than drink, the demon in need of exorcism.'

Left-wing writers sometimes express a view of the poor that would have been unimaginable without large-scale immigration, their apparent racism losing them any sympathy. Liberal commentators, often in rural or wealthy parts of the country, talk about unhappy people stuck in high-immigrant areas in a very similar way to that which some Tories look upon those in areas of high unemployment – that they should simply relocate – ignoring that people are reluctant or unable to move.

Yasmin Alibhai-Brown, a liberal Muslim of African-Asian extraction, is the chief critic of the English working-class, a group of 'beer-swilling blokes' in working men's clubs overwhelmed by self pity, 'the always-wretched and complaining classes', in her words. Attacking what she sees as political pandering to working-class whites, she wrote: 'What they believe – however stupid or vicious – must be awesome. Oh, and they are never to be called racist, not even the scum who drop shit and firebombs through letter boxes of asylum-seekers on estates.' Alibhai-Brown's feelings are perhaps understandable. Many Asians came from impeccably cultured middle-class families but found themselves at the bottom of their new society, rubbing shoulders with poor whites who had lower education levels and yet claimed some ill-deserved racial superiority.

But many in the middle-classes share her feelings, viewing English working-class culture as inherently brutal, violent and drink soaked, lazy, rude and anti-education. Television is filled with such negative portrayals, while historians now focus on the early modern period as proof that it was always so. But while British society until the mid-19th century was violent and bawdy by today's standards, by the 1950s working-class life was peaceful and marked by high levels of education and political involvement, comparatively with other countries and Britain today. The English working classes are not the brutes that the media paints them as, although they have become more brutish in recent years.

After the murder of Stephen Lawrence in Eltham disgust for

the 'white working class' reached a new level. Recalling a *Guardian* description of Eltham, one south London writer commented: 'If you came to this passage cold, unaware of the climate and the newspaper in which it appeared, you could mistake it for the musings of a portly upper-class old-school Tory who had stumbled with a sense of foreboding on a phenomenon called "the teenager".' One might look at the increasing demonology of that Noughties creation, 'the white working class', and ask whether it could have occurred without immigration. Another *Guardian* writer complained about Greenwich's housing policy, that 'because of the local authority's "sons and daughters" tenancy policy, the area has remained almost exclusively white working class'. But the reason for such a policy is that it is good for social cohesion. Were a *Guardian* writer talking about the community spirit of Kurdish villagers or Honduran peasants fighting the effects of globalisation, such closeness would be laudable and he would surely admire their struggle to maintain their social networks. Why liberals do not feel such sympathy for the great-grandchildren of London matchstick girls is something that does not go unnoticed in such parts of the south-east, where 'Left-wing' is a pejorative term (just as, oddly, 'Right-wing' is among the middle classes).

Liberal commentators are happy to characterise the poor as holding bigoted views, yet overlook the inconvenient fact that far, far worse attitudes are found among minority communities; many white fathers would be unhappy for their daughters to marry non-whites, a theme that often appears in drama, but how many actually kill them for it?

The Left's answers to the problems of mass immigration still tend to be economic – if people had jobs and better homes they would not feel resentment and racial animosity. Certainly economic problems aggravate racial tension, and people who are personally unhappy for whatever reason are more likely to look for political explanations for their failures. Depressed wages and housing shortages, which are themselves partly consequences of immigration, are factors in white working-class rage; but the material explanation ignores the fact that what people feel unhappy about is not primarily economic in nature, but social. The conventional explanation as to why people vote BNP is always put in purely economic terms, yet working-class voters have an array of hard-Left parties to choose from, all promising increased social welfare, and none of which require soul-searching, guilt or stigma. They vote BNP because of immigration and its economic *and* social effects.

Diversity's advocates argue that more should be spent on tackling poverty and social exclusion for all people – but if society could solve those problems by abolishing poverty with a chequebook, it would. Huge amounts, in fact, were spent on poor whites in the Labour years, through an expanded welfare programme that did little to reduce unemployment or long-term inequality or poverty. No government or system can guarantee a job for everyone nor ensure that people will never fall on hard times; and it is the institutions of nation, church, family and extended community that give the vulnerable an anchor and cushion during lean years. The increased popularity of extreme Right-wing politics across Europe is in response to a perceived threat to these same institutions that so many on the Left view as artificial and created by the powerful to control the poor, and inherently racist or patriarchal. If people were wealthy, educated and gainfully-employed there would be no need to worry about these issues, but as a safety procedure it is not advisable to build a multicultural society which only functions when people are wealthy and content. If the Northern Ireland Troubles had only involved the comfortable middle classes it would have got no worse than a series of rather bad-tempered letters to the *Belfast Telegraph*.

And poverty and inequality can only be seriously reduced in societies with social capital, exactly what diverse countries are lacking. Socialism, which works best where there are high levels of trust, works less well in multi-ethnic countries, because people do not behave in a socialist manner. You cannot buy social capital, the capital most needed for even modest social reform, and Britain no longer has the level of solidarity needed to seriously tackle poverty. When Labour politicians in BNP targets suggest we simply build more social housing, aside from the obvious question 'where?' on our overcrowded half-island, there is the added problem that British people today are not prepared to pay for more social housing; they may tolerate diverse, different people living beside them, but they're not going to pay their rent for them.

This has not stopped politicians trying to solve the problem by adding poor whites to the list of officially disadvantaged groups, and talking about the 'white working class' almost in ethnic terms; and in 2009 the Department of Communities spent £12 million on 130 'traditional communities', the new jargon for poor white areas, to convince them that they are not losing out on jobs and houses to immigrants. But you cannot simply solve people's problems by turning them in a category of victims.

Rise of Ethnic Nationalism

As Britain has 'embraced' diversity, the issue has festered. A *Newsnight* poll from 2008 found that 58 per cent of the white working class felt that 'nobody speaks out for people like me in Britain today'. Under New Labour the share of adults who considered 'immigration and race relations' as the most important issue facing Britain increased from below 5 per cent to over 40 per cent. For most of 2006 and 2007 immigration was the number one issue of concern to the British public, while an Ipsos MORI poll found that 49 per cent of people agreed that immigrants should be encouraged to return to their country of origin, and 29 per cent said it was likely that racial tension 'will result in violence'.

Contrary to the accepted doctrine that diversity enriches, beyond a certain point it divides – more immigration means more racial hostility. According to the contact theory pre-mass immigration should have been a Fascist hellhole, yet this is not necessarily true. One of the first social studies on this subject, in 1951, asked people: 'Providing, of course, that there is plenty of work about, do you think that coloured colonials should be allowed to go on coming to this country?' The British public favoured it by 46 per cent to 38 per cent, making them more pro-immigration than the British public in polls that followed mass immigration later that decade. The previous year at Lords 30 West Indians ran onto the pitch to celebrate their victory, and local supporters jeered the police when they tried to escort them off. As one West Indian recalled: 'the English people boo him [the policeman], they said "leave him alone! Let him enjoy himself, they won the match, let him enjoy himself".'

America's great periods of ethnic nationalism, 1840-1860, and 1910-1925, coincided with mass immigration; by the end of that second era the KKK had six million members, but the country's closed-door immigration policy from 1925 helped to eliminate the need for nativist organisations. Just as polls showed feelings towards foreigners in the US steadily improved in the long gap between the end of mass immigration in the 1920s and its modern return in 1965, so race relations improved in Britain following the tightening of immigration laws under Edward Heath and Margaret Thatcher, and throughout the 1980s and 1990s social attitudes towards people of other races became more positive. In Britain extreme Right-wing organisations have come and gone with mass immigration, the National Front in response to the first great wave in the 1960s and the BNP under New Labour. Ipsos-Mori polls show that the percentage who strongly agreed to the statement 'there are too many immigrants in Britain' had gone down from 37 per cent in 1989 to 24 per cent in 1994 and 22 per cent in 1999 but had risen to 41 per cent by the end of 2007. A survey for Populus in 2011 found that 60 per cent of people believed that 'immigration had been a bad thing for Britain', and only 12 per cent thought it had improved their neighbourhoods. Some 43 per cent of Asians and 51 per cent of mixed-race people agreed with the former proposition, even though they were themselves products of previous immigration.

Despite overwhelming support for strict immigration controls, even modest reductions are still officially suspect unless expressed in explicitly economic terms. This is the problem with the diversity illusion; once you rule out the possibility that diversity is not a good in itself, and remove the moral justification for limits based on ethnicity, it is difficult to stop. And the Labour Party that won power in 1997 was in thrall to the illusion, dominated by anti-racism activists who believed that immigration restrictions were inherently racist.

It is not as if Labour politicians were unaware that their most socially radical policy was against the wishes of supporters.

Former Sparsbrook MP and Labour deputy leader Roy Hattersley wrote in the *Guardian* in 2009: 'For most of my 33 years in Westminster, I was able to resist Sparsbrook's demands about the great issues of national policy – otherwise, my first decade would have been spent opposing all Commonwealth immigration and my last calling for withdrawal from the European Union.' That will not be a problem anymore, for as of 2009 Sparsbrook was 79.3 per cent non-white, and at council level was represented by Respect, a predominantly Muslim party that campaigns on a platform of opposition to the war in Iraq and 'support for the Palestinian people'. Hattersley, meanwhile, lives in the multicultural melting pot that is rural Derbyshire. Later that year the former MP would write in the *Daily Mail*: 'I am an English patriot… Modesty is an English virtue and it is modest, reticent, peaceful England that I love.' He then went on to say: 'G. K. Chesterton wrote about 'the people of England who have not spoken yet'. They were silent not because they had nothing to say, but because they regarded reticence as a virtue.'

But across Europe mainstream parties have changed their immigration policies on account of popular opposition and the fear of extremism. Gordon Brown marked the beginning of a change in Labour's rhetoric in his first conference speech as Prime Minister in 2007 when he promised 'British jobs for British workers', and soon after, Phil Woolas, the Immigration Minister, said that 'a limit to the population' was simply 'common sense'. In 2009 Alan Johnson became the first Labour Home Secretary to admit the Government had made mistakes in its handling of immigration. Keen to hang onto their core, white working-class vote, Labour's 2010 Election Broadcast used nostalgia to appeal to old tribal loyalties, a melancholy reminder that Labour and the Left once stood up for the workers.

In the days when England was ruled by a monarch the elite replaced difficult rulers with more pliable foreign replacements; as a democracy we have done the same with our working class. Jokes about the Royal Family's foreign origins are old and tired, but we certainly have not had a truly British monarch for many centuries. Yet when Prince William ascends to the throne he will be more ethnically British than the population as a whole, something that could not be said of any king since Edmund II, who reigned briefly in 1016 before being stabbed to death by the culturally-enriching Vikings.

13

A Tribal Society
Democracy, islamophobia and the new sectarianism

At the same time as the *Satanic Verses* controversy was raging an ultimately even more significant event was taking place. In March 1989 an Englishman called Tim Berners-Lee wrote a proposal to describe an information management system, and the following November he published a formal proposal to build a 'Hypertext project' called the 'WorldWideWeb'. His invention was as revolutionary as Gutenberg's, and just as printing had profound effects on the politics of Europe, the most significant being the Protestant Reformation, so has the web. They are still being assessed: one is the spread of radical Islam, another the hardening of public opinion over immigration (if this all sounds too pessimistic, there are more ways in which the net brings humanity together, not least in the potential for crowd-sourcing or momentous events such as the Chilean miners' rescue).

Blogs have certainly shifted the debate. Where journalists have been afraid to criticise the policies of multiculturalism and diversity, amateur bloggers, almost always anonymous, are able to ignore the taboos. Many are clearly mad or unpleasant, but many are not, and people reading them realise that there are perfectly pleasant, decent, educated people out there who are in no sense hateful or Fascist but dislike the radical demographic change being forced on them. 'Ugly populism' may be 'fast food for the disillusioned', in the words of Alibhai-Brown's description of Right-wing bloggers, but what she called the 'undisputed benefits of immigration' is also the nouveau cuisine of the rich. Any economic benefit is short-term, with long-term and permanent social effects, and these benefits are mostly felt by the well-off. To the rich, immigration means Tongan cleaners, Polish handymen and Thai chefs; to the poor queuing, crime and lower wages.

Public opinion certainly turned against immigration during the first decade of the new millennium. Even Lord Jenkins, architect of the permissive society, mused in his old age that 'in retrospect we might have been more cautious about allowing the creation in the 1950s of substantial Muslim communities here'.

Journalists have been warning about a backlash against immigrants since the Windrush arrived, although in one respect, of course, it would not be a backlash, because mass immigration has only ever been accepted begrudgingly, the entire experiment feeling to many people like one long telling off. When Alibhai-Brown warned that people were 'losing their enthusiasm' for 'the undisputed benefits' of immigration, it's hard to see what enthusiasm she was talking about. Most people accepted it, saw the benefits in their friends, but rarely enthused about it.

If views on immigration and diversity have hardened, it might not be a backlash as such, merely that a critical mass of the public's tolerance threshold has been reached. Not many people seriously objected to immigration when the non-white population was 1 per cent; not that many more when it was 3 per cent; but it is now over 10 per cent and projected to reach 20 per cent in the near future, and many might wonder at what point they are allowed to express reservations. Veterans of the Far-Right sometimes claim that the media is now reflecting their views, and that they were right all along, but it may just be that changes have drifted so far in one direction that the warnings of the other extreme can be taken seriously; in the same way that pro-censorship campaigners may be correct about hardcore rape-porn on children's mobile phones, but were not necessarily right about warning in the 1960s about the perils of allowing the word 'bum' to be used on stage. Most people are happy about racial or religious diversity in their areas, schools or workplaces, but only up to a certain point.

As the benefits of diversity have come to look increasingly fragile, so advocates have grown more aggressive towards those who voice doubts. The original opponents of mass immigration in the 1960s and 1970s tended to come from the political fringes, many of them former Fascists, and their electoral appeal was limited. Yet as diversity has increased beyond a stage which the median European found bearable, and as the failures of religious integration have become apparent, new opponents have emerged from the centre-Right and even centre-Left. Across Europe, parties largely untouched by the taint of neo-Fascism but often still described (sometimes inexplicably) as 'Far-Right' have gained large and permanent footholds in politics.

'Libertarian Islamophobes'

The founding father of mainstream European opposition to multiculturalism, Pim Fortuyn, was a flamboyantly gay, Marxist sociology professor who came to view Islam as an 'extraordinary threat' to the Netherlands, not least because he saw first-hand the intolerance of many immigrants towards his sexuality. Fortuyn won 36 per cent of the vote in one regional election and was widely predicted to become prime minister, but his relatively moderate platform of assimilation led to the most extraordinary hostility from the uniformly multiculturalist media, many comparing him to Hitler. His assassin, a simple-minded Left-wing activist called Volkert van der Graaf, said that he killed Fortuyn because he considered him 'a danger to society' as he was using Muslims as 'scapegoats'.

Many critics pointing out the cracks in the system have faced abuse, intimidation and even violence, for like a public limited company that has overstretched itself, those who have put their trust in the system believe that anyone pointing out its faults is causing its downfall. Fortuyn's spiritual heir, Freedom Party leader Geert Wilders, was on trial from 2009 to 2011 on charges of inciting hatred and discrimination for calling Islam a 'Fascist religion', comparing the Koran to *Mein Kampf,* and for calling Moroccan youths violent. For almost four centuries, and barring foreign occupations, the Netherlands has had a tradition of free speech more liberal than anywhere else on earth; without it the 17th-century philosopher Benedict Spinoza could not have articulated atheist views that helped to undermine the strength of the established churches in Europe. It is odd that in the country of Spinoza a politician is put on trial for offending a religion in the 21st century, and yet the Dutch, like the English, seem to think that religious freedom is a necessary sacrifice if it threatens diversity.

On top of the legal threat Wilders is in such personal danger that he is moved to a different location every night, he can only meet his wife once a week because of security concerns, and his life has become 'a situation that I wouldn't wish on my worst enemy'. A historical Dutchman who lived such an existence to denounce Christianity would be lauded; a living one who criticises a more conservative religion is labeled 'extreme' and 'Islamophobic', as if it is a 'phobia' to fear a religion whose followers have repeatedly tried to kill you.

Although called an extremist by the media, his Freedom Party comes from the classical liberal tradition, but it is opposed to mass immigration, especially from Muslim countries. That Wilders, an economically liberal, pro-gay, philo-Semite is labelled 'Far-Right' illustrates how such definitions have shifted. Wilders' ordeal at the hands of both violent Islamists and the Dutch establishment is proof of diversity's failure; freedom to eat two dozen different cuisines in an evening is small comfort if it comes at the expense of freedom of speech and freedom from fear.

Fortuyn's rise signaled a growing realisation among some European liberals that continued immigration, predominantly from the Muslim world, is a threat to liberalism. One of the most striking signs of this is that, according to American writer Bruce Bawer, one of the most eloquent of a new generation of gay conservatives, Dutch gays now support conservative parties over Left-wing ones by a nearly two-to-one margin. There may be good reasons for European gays to be worried, for if the United States is anything to go by, diversity may bring cultural conservatism. It was thanks to increased numbers of African-Americans and Hispanics turning out on the same day to elect Barack Obama that Proposition 8, the Californian law banning gay marriage, was passed, with a majority of whites opposed; and British Muslims are far more conservative than black Americans. While this would please some native social conservatives, it seems unlikely that Right-wing parties this side of the Atlantic will go down the same path of some US Republicans in uniting traditionalists of all creeds; Europe is far less religious, and European conservatives are more likely to see Islam (as long as the Muslim population grows at its current rate) as a threat than gay marriage. In contrast

Wilders, a 'libertarian Islamophobe' in the words of the BBC, is part of a trend in European politics towards socially liberal ethnic nationalists, with most of the new anti-immigration parties in Europe adopting softer policies on issues such as the role of women and homosexuality. In Demark the Danish People's Party is described by one of its most prominent foes as 'having nothing Fascist at all about it, nothing anti-democratic or violent [but] xenophobic, intolerant and anti-Muslim'.[125] The Swiss People's Party has also led the campaign against Islamisation on an economically liberal platform. Even the National Front in France, under new leader Marine Le Pen, has appeared to move away from her father Jean-Marie's traditional Far-Right stance, denouncing anti-Semitism and embracing gay rights.

Elsewhere the vacuum left by mainstream conservatism has been filled by neo-Fascists such as Austria's Freedom Party and the British National Party. The BNP was until 1999 led by John Tyndall, whose avowed neo-Nazism ensured the party's electoral appeal was tiny. His replacement, Nick Griffin, is a shrewder politician, although with a similar political past and with some baggage of his own. As Griffin explained at a lecture to the Ku Klux Klan (he was obviously not shrewd enough not to be recorded addressing the KKK), his party would only move forward if it dropped some of the language of extremism and began talking about 'identity' as a euphemism for race (and in fact adopting much of the language of multiculturalism).

The BNP's website, which offered readers a mixture of outrageous immigration statistics, colourful Islamic radicals, Home Office incompetence, and crime and immigrant benefit fraud, was the most popular British political party site for a while, although following one of the group's various feuds it has suffered numerous technical problems. And thanks largely to their high-profile leader, the BNP won two seats in the European elections of 2009. Although the EU has yet to give Britain a sensible drinking culture, strong family relations or any of the other positive aspects of continental Europe, we are now finally 'truly European' at least in having neo-Fascist representatives in parliament. Despite this, the party retains enough extremist characteristics to ensure it is unlikely to make a breakthrough, including severe in-fighting and an array of strange personalities.[126] But what gains the party made came, in Griffin's own admission, by focusing on Islam.

In the 1980s Griffin and his cohorts in the National Front and the BNP were admirers of Islam and Islamism; some were attracted by the political philosophy of Libya's extravagantly-dressed lunatic dictator Colonel Gaddafi, whose economic mumbo-jumbo, which he called 'the third way', was not entirely distant from the Far-Right's views on economics; besides which, ultra-conservative religious fanatics who hated women, Jews and America's mongrelising capitalism couldn't be all bad. But after 9/11 they changed tact, focusing on Islam, which became a semi-respectable way to oppose diversity.

For forty years conservatives lost the arguments over immigration, despite overwhelming public support. They lost because they lost the intellectual justification for group solidarity and restricted altruism against post-war radical universalism, to the extent that normal human feelings were redefined as forms of mental illness. But Islam allowed conservatives to make arguments using language that liberals would permit.

Diversity therefore led to the re-emergence of sectarianism, long extinct in England except for a tiny corner of Lancashire. It flared up in Luton, a Bedfordshire town with a large Muslim population, where Islamists had been recruiting for the Taliban as far as back as 2001, often openly in the town centre. In 2009 a small protest by a fringe Islamist group at a parade for the Royal Anglian Regiment led to the formation of the United Peoples of Luton, which adopted the name the English Defence League as it rapidly expanded across the country. Largely comprising football supporters, EDL members often sport the St George's Cross of the England team, itself a Crusader flag, and have additionally adopted explicitly Christian imagery. The group's leader, Stephen Lennon, says they are a 'Christian' group and that increasing numbers of its members identify as Christians[127] and their motto, *In hoc signo vinces,* 'From this sign I conquer', is taken from the battle standard of Constantine the Great, the first Christian emperor of Rome. Although its marches have been marked by racist chanting, and racist violence, the EDL itself officially rejects racism, and it is arguably not so much racist as sectarian, a strange by-product of mass immigration. One of its slogans, 'black and white unite', which resembles an anti-racist slogan from the 1970s, reflects the fact that in many areas black and white youths are well-integrated but equally hostile to local Muslim youths.

Mass immigration brings enormous social costs, most of which are borne by the working classes. But although many of the more intelligent people behind some 'counter-jihad' groups are genuinely horrified by certain Islamic attitudes to women, homosexuality or Jews, most people do not go on EDL marches for those reasons. Most people oppose large-scale immigration from countries such as Pakistan, Bangladesh and Somalia not because of Islam but because the newcomers are alien to them and their arrival disrupts their neighbourhood and life.

These are understandable human feelings, but people are unable to articulate them without committing a thought crime. So instead the problems of mass immigration are blamed on Islam, including the problems associated with immigrants themselves, even when they are more to do with dislocation and diversity than religion. Europe was shocked in March 2012 by the horrific attack on a Jewish school in Toulouse by a fanatical Muslim, yet before becoming an Islamist, Mohammed Merah had a long, long record of juvenile crime, with 15 convictions behind him. He discovered religion while in prison, just like many British Islamists. These were not ordinary young men corrupted by the Prophet Mohammed, for Islamism is political; it attracts angry, extreme, violent young men from the immigrant underclass who find others willing to justify their thirst for violence, by using holy texts. Merah's justification – 'you killed my brothers, I kill you' – are not words of faith but naked tribalism.

Conservatism's recent obsession with Islam is partly a reaction to multiculturalism, which holds that all religions are basically the same, which is untrue; the current moral order that emerged from the West, the world of the Enlightenment, the UN and human rights, stems from Christianity. No other religion could have produced it – not Islam, Hinduism or Buddhism, because none have Christianity's concept of the individual, for Christianity is essentially a union of Hellenic and Hebrew civilisations.

Islam, in contrast, lacks not just Western concepts of the individual but also Christianity's historic separation of the state and religion. There is also no doubt that Islam has a very ambiguous attitude to violence in its name.

The religion needs reform, but it is not incapable of it, and huge numbers of Muslims happily set aside the more unpalatable passages of their holy texts, just as Jews and Christians do. For middle-class British Muslims the popular idea that they practice some sort of political-religious death cult strike them as bizarre, so removed from the actual practice of their religion.

Indeed many of the 'Islamic' customs which people object to have little or nothing to do with Islam. Honour killings have been a custom in many Christian cultures, but Christians no longer practice this barbarity for the same reason that British Hindus don't – because they are urban, sophisticated, wealthy and educated. Many Pakistanis from rural Mirpur are not. But it's rather impolite to criticise a national culture; easier just to say 'Islam'. West Africans have brought over child abuse based on ideas about witchcraft, but because they're Christians this attracts less attention in the media.

Islamophobia is a dubious term because it is used to describe both legitimate criticism of a religion, and anti-Muslim hostility. But that's not to say that sectarianism does not exist; the irony is that it has become acceptable partly because conservatives have been unable to articulate decent and legitimate opposition to mass immigration in the first place. But by blaming the problems of mass immigration on Islam itself conservatives are falling into the same utopian thinking as liberals. The problem is not Islam, but the movement of peoples across the world, and the conflict this produces. The problem with mass immigration is not Islam, but mass immigration, which creates the ghettos where sectarianism thrives.

The huge movements of recent years have made Islam and Christianity an anchor of identity to people in Europe. The EDL are essentially a Christianist group, but the sentiments behind sectarianism and nationalism are the same. One cannot blame sectarianism on religion any more than one can blame nationalism on language – it just exists, and it is aggravated by the relentless movement of people in a globalised world.

The same patterns of sectarianism found in Ireland may emerge in some northern English towns where the demographic distribution of white Christians and Asian Muslims is starting to resemble Ulster's fragile balance. While Islam is a hyper-identity for immigrants, Christianity has become one for the natives in response. The Census of 2001 showed that in those parts of England where there are now a large number of Muslim immigrants, there was a jump in the number of whites who described themselves as Christians, despite church attendances continuing to slump.[128] Most likely people were starting to identify as such in opposition to Islam, because for sectarianism to flourish religious faith is not even necessary, for it can become fused onto majority ethnic identity when the minority grows large enough. Although superficially about religious identity, the Northern Ireland Troubles of 1969-1994 was an ethnic conflict between the indigenous Gaelic Irish and the descendants of 17th century British settlers, people once generally called 'Scots-Irish' but now known as Ulster Protestants. Because the Irish lost their language but not their religion under English rule, faith became a marker of ethnicity, so to practise a religion came to mean belonging to an ethnic group, making conversion very difficult. It was not about 'religion'; the UVF did not attack Catholic pubs over the doctrine of transubstantiation, and the IRA didn't massacre Protestant workers because they objected to married clergy.

So even if, as universalists hope, Muslims lose their faith, that is not a guarantee that the problems of religion will not still dominate 21st century Britain. As Eric Kaufmann noted in *Shall the Religious Inherit the Earth?*, there is a difference between affiliation, belief and attendance. People do not necessarily have to believe in God to affiliate with a religion; only 5 per cent of English natives attend church, but six in ten still identify as Christians.

Muslims may come from various nationalities and backgrounds, but Islam still functions as a hyper-identity. And it is a strong one, partly because many of the countries British Muslims come from have weak national identities, Pakistan being a prime example (one of the reasons that Islamism seems to have less appeal to Turks). Alain Finkielkraut calls religion 'an anchor of identity', and Islam, like Christianity, is a universal anchor that provides comfort and belonging to people stuck between nations. The increasingly fragmented nature of the media, dominated by the internet and multiple television channels, may also play a role in assimilating people, not from Pakistanis into Britons, but into Muslims, helping to forge a European pan-Muslim identity.

And Islamic identity is perhaps even stronger in the West, where Muslims are dislocated and feel torn between two countries that, they feel, reject them. Polls suggest that a third of British Muslims claim a stronger connection with Muslims in other countries than fellow Britons, but this figure is much higher among the young. A Channel 4 survey found that 90 per cent of British Muslims are 'strongly attached' to Islam, even though half never attended mosque, and fewer than one in ten attended every day.

And the increased hostility towards Muslims post-9/11, and the excessive use of 'Muslim' in the popular press almost as a term of abuse, has only helped to cement this identity. In the words of Kaufmann: 'when non-white religious people encounter the disdain of white secular natives, religion and ethnicity reinforce each other, insulating religion from the assimilating power of secularism'.

Religion also acts as a stopper on the one force most capable of reducing conflict in a diverse society, being what sociologist Ernest Gellner called a 'counter-entropic' trait – one that prevents marriage and assimilation. In Britain Sikhs, Muslims and Hindus all have low mixed marriage rates, below 10 per cent in each case, and only 0.3 per cent of Muslims marry Hindus or Sikhs, far lower than the percentage (5 per cent) who marry Christians. Just 1 per cent of British Bangladeshi and Pakistanis have white partners, compared to 20 per cent of African-Caribbeans. And neither is there any sign that the religious faith that prevents assimilation is on the decline, British-born Muslims showing a greater attachment to Islam than immigrants. Even though only a quarter of European Muslims attend mosque on a weekly basis, the young are just as likely as the old; among second-generation Bangladeshis and Pakistanis 80 per cent practise their religion, while in the last census only 0.5 per cent of Pakistanis and Bangladeshis said they had no religion, against 11.3 per cent of black Caribbeans and over 20 per cent of whites. British Muslims are not losing their faith, and there is no indication that secularisation will come to the rescue of inter-religious tension.

Eurabian nightmares

Islamic scholar Bernard Lewis famously predicted: 'Europe will have a Muslim majority by the end of the twenty-first century at the very latest'. Plenty of Muslim leaders have said the same thing, among them Colonel Gaddafi, who once boasted that 'the fifty million Muslims of Europe will turn it into a Muslim continent within a few decades'. This is certainly an alarming idea, but 'Eurabia', the prospect of a Muslim demographic takeover of Europe, is popular because it does not contradict current demographic trends. In Britain the Muslim population increased from 82,000 in 1961 to 500,000 in 1980 to over 2 million in the mid-2000s. In just four years in that decade it rose by 500,000, so that in September 2009 the highly respected, non-partisan Pew Forum on Religion and Public Life announced that the Muslim population of Britain was now 2,869,000, a 74 per cent increase over a decade.

As a result the number of British Pakistanis living in ghettos, defined as areas where two-thirds of residents belonged to one ethnic group, tripled during the 1990s. Bradford and Leicester have comparable levels of ghettoisation to Miami and Chicago, something that Englishmen only 20 years ago would have found an astonishing prospect. Theodore Dalrymple noted that 'not since I lived and worked briefly in South Africa under the apartheid regime have I seen a city as racially segregated as Bradford', a sentiment echoed in 2011 by South African-born London headmaster David Levin,[129] who noted that one East End school was now 97 per cent Bangladeshi.

The Cable Report after the Oldham riots talked of 'parallel lives' between the white and Asian population, and while a 2006 study of demography was hailed by London mayor Ken Livingstone as proof that Britain had become less segregated as the number of mixed neighbourhoods had risen from 864 to

1,070 during the 1990s, this was an extremely selective interpretation. As the ethnic population massively increased many areas
appeared to become more diverse, but were also in the process of
transformation. Even white flight looks like integration in its early
stages.

As a basic rule, Samuel Huntingdon stated: 'The more concentrated immigrants become, the slower and less complete their
assimilation.' Trevor Phillips has already warned that racial
segregation in Britain is approaching that of the United States, to
the point 'where things are so divided that there is no turning
back'. Yet while European mainstream liberal opinion reaches the
peak of sanctimoniousness when it comes to America's racial
divisions, the United States is racially divided precisely because it is
more diverse. As Europe starts to develop a similar make-up there
is no reason why its racial politics, prejudices and settlement
patterns will not resemble the USA's, or other highly diverse
societies. What makes the British so special that they can avoid
this? As George Bernard Shaw wrote in *Heartbreak House*: 'Do you
think the laws of God will be suspended in favour of England
because you were born in it?'

The world has changed dramatically since mass immigration
began, and modern technology has changed the nature of
diversity, hampering integration in a way that was not imaginable
when the experiment began. Immigrants have always maintained
some connection with the old country; in 1923 there were 67
Polish language weekly newspapers, 18 monthlies and 19 dailies in
the United States, the largest of which had a circulation of over
100,000, while sociologist Dennis Wrong suggests that today non-
European immigrants are 'probably less unfamiliar with the major
features of the society than were, say, South Italian or Slavic
peasants in the late nineteenth or early twentieth centuries'. That
may be true, but while Slavic peasants were soon forced to become
familiar with American society, today there is little reason for
immigrants to ever lose contact with home. In the Low Countries
the phenomenon of the 'dish city' illustrates how Moroccans and
Turks are able to stay in contact by watching satellite television
from their home country. Pakistanis across Europe send their

children back 'home' for long periods, with 14,365 passenger seats per day just between Manchester and Islamabad. Unlike with previous migrations, ancestral identities are no longer extinguished by lack of contact with the mother country. One can live in Germany and not just live among Turks, but read Turkish websites and watch Turkish television, talk to Turkish relatives on Skype, and to all intents and purposes live in overseas Turkish territory.

In 2006 Rear Admiral Chris Parry warned of 'reverse colonisation', made possible by the internet, cheap foreign travel and free international phone calls which, he said, allowed new migrants to stay connected with their homelands rather than assimilate into the host country's culture. Parry, head of the Ministry of Defence unit tasked with identifying future threats to Britain's security, said Western civilisation was facing its biggest danger since the fall of the Roman Empire, and warned that within a decade African pirates would attack beaches in the Mediterranean. 'Globalisation makes assimilation seem redundant and old-fashioned,' he warned: 'The process acts as a sort of reverse colonisation, where groups of people are self-contained, going back and forth between their countries, exploiting sophisticated networks and using instant communication on phones and the internet.' Such globetrotting has been the norm for the super-rich for some time; when the process expands across society it becomes more problematic, and the potential for conflict is heightened.

Eurabia is somewhat hard to take seriously because the projections deal with such distant periods, and because it attracts wild exaggeration or conspiracy theories. Early in 2009 a video warning of an Islamic takeover of Europe became a huge YouTube hit, watched by 10 million people in a short few weeks, and even leading to a BBC debunking. It was based on glaring factual errors that suggested sloppiness or dishonesty, claiming that French Muslims had a fertility rate of 8.1 per woman (it is well below 3), and that 30 per cent of French children are Muslims, when the actual figure is probably between 10 and 15 per cent. Doubtless Muslim fertility is declining – Pakistani and Bangladeshi total fertility was 9.3 in 1971, and 4.9 in 1996 – and fertility is of course influenced by wealth and female education, so that Iranian immigrant fertility, for example, is at or below that of natives in all

European countries. But immigrant TFRs are often higher in Europe than in their home countries, and in Europe religious Muslims are 40 per cent more likely to have three or more children than non-religious Muslims,[130] so that the overall decline in Muslim growth rates will be down to the more secular having fewer children.

According to the latest Office for National Statistics, Pakistan-born women in Britain have an average of 4.7 children, those born in Bangladesh 3.9 and India 2.3, while mothers born in the UK bore, on average, 1.6 children. That gap is narrowing, but will still remain large for a considerable time, and it's very unlikely that the name Mohammed will ever cease to be the most popular boy's name, a position it reached in 2010. (Although Muslim immigrants have a smaller pool of given names, and Western naming patterns have moved towards greater diversity in recent years, this does illustrate a demographic truth.[131]) And even as Muslim birth rates decline, the advantage stays the same, perhaps even increases, because native birth rates are in free fall. In Austria the total fertility rate in 1981 was 3.09 for Muslims and 1.67 for native Austrians; in 1991 the figures were 2.77 and 1.51; and in 2001 2.34 and 1.32 – meaning that the ratio has grown.

And none of this really makes much difference because natural increase is still bolstered by high levels of immigration, mostly from countries with high fertility rates. While birth rates across much of the second world are falling, and Iran, Algeria, Lebanon, Tunisia and several central Asian and Caucasian countries have below-replacement rate fertility, Afghanistan, Somalia and Nigeria remain at over 5.5, while Pakistan's average is 4. By 2050 Nigeria will have 258 million, Bangladesh 243 million, Ethiopia 189 million and Uganda 127 million, meaning that the external population pressures on Britain will stay strong for the foreseeable future.

By 2030 Britain will have a Muslim population of 5.5 million, roughly 8.2 per cent of the total population. That's hardly Eurabia, some might argue, but that figure will not be spread evenly across the country. By that year Oldham, Bradford, Blackburn and possibly even Birmingham could be Muslim-majority towns. Leicester will already become Britain's first-ever majority non-white city some time in the 2010s. Any tension that ensues will of course be blamed on Islamophobia, and yet no society in history has watched a minority grow from 0 to 8 per cent in two generations without serious problems. And project those opinion poll figures about views on terrorism, sharia law and apostasy onto a population of 5.5 million and Islamophobia does not seem entirely irrational. It has already been speculated that had France wished to join the invasion of Iraq in 2003 it would have been hampered by the threat of urban violence. In a dozen years time would Britain be able to join the US in intervening in a Muslim country, even if its leaders thought it the right thing to do, without risking riots? Would Geert Wilders be able to deliver his address? It seems unlikely.

If that happens it is not because Muslims have outrageous fertility levels, as is often claimed, but because natives have unsustainably low ones. In Austria the Muslim fertility rate of 2.34 is close to the optimum, but on current trends Austria will be the first western European country to be over 20 per cent Muslim before mid-century. As Arnold Toynbee pointed out: 'Civilisations die from suicide, not murder.'

And even in 2030 the fertility gap between British Muslim and non-Muslim will still be 0.8 per woman, which translates as a 40 per cent increase per generation. And that's assuming that the government stops immigration from countries such as Pakistan, with its 256 million people – something no MP for Blackburn or Bradford will vote for. People who scorn the Eurabia thesis miss the point. If Western Europe is 16 to 20 per cent Islamic it might not be Eurabia – sharia law and beheadings in the street or any of the wilder imaginings – but it will not be Europe as Europeans have known it for a thousand years.

Democracy and Diversity

The goal of a multicultural Britain has certainly been achieved, but whether it will bring about the permanent liberal majority its supporters hoped is another matter.

Democracy, parliamentary rule and the jury system all developed in countries that were remarkably homogenous, England, Denmark and Holland, while in the polyglot east the

transition from autocracy to democracy was met with conflict. In
the Ottoman, Austro-Hungarian and Russian Empires ethnic and
religious diversity prevented political liberalisation and progress;
only when those empires were broken into relatively homogenous
nation-states (often following brutal ethnic cleansing) did they
liberalise, Turkey being a prime example. And democratic institutions such as the jury system have always been problematic in bi-
racial areas of the US.

Multi and bi-racial societies do not vote along class lines, as the
British have traditionally done, but line up according to tribal
affiliation. The American South, Northern Ireland and Lebanon
are not fertile grounds for multicultural centre-Left parties; there
are 'centre-Left' parties in these regions, but they tend to acquire
all their support from one group, whether it's Catholics for the
SDLP, blacks for the Democrats or the Shia Hezbollah in Lebanon
(centre-Left, of course, in its economic views, not in its stance on,
say, LGBT issues). And diversity increases this trend; in the US the
higher the share of the black population the higher proportion of
whites voting Republican, with 73 per cent of whites in the South
opting for the party in the November 2010 elections. In the pres-
idential election two years earlier the GOP won the support of
over 85 per cent of whites in Mississippi, Alabama and Louisiana,
home to some of the poorest white Americans; in 2000 George
Bush won seven of the nine most African-American states in the
US because of overwhelming white support.

Where does this leave Labour? Former Cabinet Minister Chris
Mullin revealed in his published diaries that in January 2004 he and
some colleagues had discussed scam marriages that were 'putting
enormous pressure on young Asians'. He wrote: 'The trouble is we
are terrified of the huge cry of "racism" that would go up the
moment anyone breathed a word on the subject. There is the
added difficulty that at least 20 Labour seats, including [Foreign
Secretary] Jack Straw's, depend on Asian votes.' Labour, which
once supported minorities in line with its compassionate, interna-
tionalist philosophy, now actively depends on them; according to
Nick Spencer of the Theos think-tank, British Muslims are three
times more likely to vote Labour than Conservative. But if they do
continue to be the minorities' party, while retaining their traditional

white working-class support, it will be against all historical precedents from other countries. If 'Enoch was right' about anything, it was when he wrote in the Sunday Telegraph in 1968 that 'In the end, the Labour party could cease to represent labour. Stranger historic ironies have happened than that.'

Labour promoted mass immigration partly because it gave it a multicultural following, but in so doing it has bequeathed the poisonous legacy of tribal politics. The 2008 London Mayoral elections were perhaps the most racially divided in English history, showing a marked correlation between ethnicity and voting patterns in wards. Working-class whites in the suburban south tend to vote Conservative, and some of this may be down to an identification with the Tories as the party of their ethnic group over Labour, the traditional party of their class. Most studies suggest that Powell's infamous speech won Ted Heath the 1970 election, and that the Tories' subsequent reputation for being a little bit racist helped to win over voters who saw Labour as the immigrants' party. Certainly Margaret Thatcher took votes away from the National Front when she famously said that the British feared being 'swamped'.

This probably cost the Tories little, except the hostility of people, both white and black, who would never vote for them anyway. Even in the successful 2010 election Conservatives won only 16 per cent of the ethnic minority vote, while Labour attracted 72 per cent of Bangladeshis, 78 per cent of African-Caribbeans and 87 per cent of Africans. There's no reason to suggest this will change in the long term; African-Americans vote overwhelmingly for the Democrats, and it is unlikely that large numbers of black or Muslim Britons will turn to a predominantly white anti-redistributionist party. Labour thinkers who decry working-class Tories as class traitors forget that voting on race rather than class lines is the norm in diverse societies, and that even the relatively poor show increased hostility to social democratic policies. All of which bodes ill for the Labour party; just as poor Protestants in Belfast do not vote SDLP, if parts of England develop similar demography poor whites may switch from Labour. The party may come to resemble the American Democrats, an alliance of wealthy white liberals and minorities.

Or we could get even more nakedly sectarian politics. In areas where Pakistani or Bengali voters are close to a majority we already have public officials with Islamist links. In 2010 voters in Tower Hamlets elected as mayor a former Labour Party councillor who, Channel 4's Dispatches alleged, had connections with the fundamentalist Islamic Forum of Europe. Lutfur Rahman was removed as the party's choice to stand as mayor, despite winning the nomination, and went on to stand as an independent, backed by the Respect Party (Labour had chosen the third-place candidate, who was Bangladeshi, over the runner-up, who was white). Respect may be a sign of things to come; mixing socialism and environmentalism with Muslim issues such as support for Palestine and Kashmir, the party was able to win the Bethnal Green and Bow seat in the 2005 General Election, as well as several council seats, on the back of Muslim disillusionment with Labour over Iraq. Despite having its origins in the European hard-Left, its support is strongest in Muslim areas, especially Birmingham and Bradford, where George Galloway won a by-election in March 2012 with leaflets telling voters 'God KNOWS who is a Muslim. And he KNOWS who is not.' What's to stop an openly 'Islamic' party winning seats in the European elections some day?

As diversity increases, democracy weakens. Faith in democracy declines when people see that they cannot make a difference, and mass immigration, a policy clearly and consistently opposed by most people and yet which no mainstream politician will speak against, has shaken the public's trust in politics. Since politicians will not listen to people's concerns, they come to the conclusion that politics is pointless.

In Bosnia, the introduction of democracy into a complex multi-ethnic region where tribalism had been suppressed first by monarchs and then Communist dictators led to a bloodbath, unleashed by the Orthodox Christian minority who feared losing their position to the growing Muslim population. Between 1961 and 1991 the proportion of Muslims in Bosnia rose from 25 to 45 per cent, while Serbs dropped from 43 to 32 per cent; while this was partly explained by the semantics of census categories, it did reflect genuine demographic change. Just as support for the Far-

Right peaks in areas around immigrants, Serbs in districts where ethnic change was most rapid were most sympathetic to anti-Muslim violence, while Bosnian Serbs in comfortably Serb areas were much less active in ethnic cleansing. Lebanon was over two-thirds Christian when the French carved it out of Syria, but lower fertility rates and higher emigration levels reduced that comfortable status, while the arrival of Palestinians in 1948-9, 1967 and 1973 fatally unbalanced the country's make-up. Across the border Israeli political concerns are dominated by the presence of a 20 per cent Arab minority and a fear that their higher birth rates could one day create an Ulster-style situation, the main driver towards encouraging Jewish immigration. (However the rise in ultra-Orthodox birth rates, and the decline in Israeli-Arab fertility, has helped to calm anxieties and the prospect of peace.)

Bosnia and Lebanon were both former provinces of empires, where diversity was not a problem. Under the Ottoman millet system the sultan's officials dealt with ethnic leaders who in essence policed their own communities, with their own laws. But democracy makes ethnicity and demography matter, and in the absence of a common national culture voting becomes a tribal headcount. Bosnia and Lebanon are extreme examples of demographic instability, as is Northern Ireland. And yet the essential components of Northern Ireland – Irish Catholics and British Protestants – are the same in two other parts of the United Kingdom. In England Irish immigration over a century and a half following the Great Famine peaked at between 3.5 and 5 per cent of the population, and led to total assimilation of Irish Catholics. In Scotland Irish immigration was proportionately much larger, accounting for up to 15 per cent of the population, and was enough to lead to sustained sectarianism and segregation, as Catholics were too large in number to be assimilated. In Northern Ireland an Irish Catholic minority of just over 35 per cent was fatal.

This had a huge impact on integration, so that between 1964 and 1982 only 6 per cent of Catholics in Northern Ireland married non-Catholics, compared to 67 per cent in England and Wales over the same period. As a child of an Irish immigrant who married an Englishman, I can say thank God that more of her countrymen did not come here, so that I have grown up free to choose who I marry, who I vote for and even which football team I support.

The real problem is not so much that parts of England are multicultural but that they are bicultural. While a multicultural society is problematic, a bicultural one is explosive. The most acute points of tension in future years will be those mostly northern English towns that are almost evenly divided between Muslims and, as they may style themselves, Christians. England will not become a Bosnia or a Lebanon by any means, but the interest payments on diversity will continue to dwarf the original loan.

The greatest damage has been done to those aspects of England and Englishness that the Left cherish most; the gentleness and humility, the egalitarianism and social welfare institutions, the secularism of public life, the presence of unarmed police and, most of all, the everyday freedom and easy-going, unobtrusive national identity that did not need to be defined by 'values'. England has paid a heavy price for its experiment in diversity; that 'modest, reticent and peaceful England' may be a thing of the past.

14

When Prophecy Fails
How we can make it better

When Prophecy Fails, the classic work of social psychology from the 1950s, tells the story of a doomsday cult which believed in the end of the world. The book came about after authors Leon Festinger, Henry Riecken and Stanley Schachter read a local newspaper story headlined 'Prophecy from planet Clarion call to city: flee that flood'. It told how Chicago housewife Dorothy Martin had been given mysterious messages in her home by aliens from the 'planet Clarion' telling her that a great flood would cause the end of the world just before dawn on December 21, 1954. A former follower of Scientology founder L Ron Hubbard, Mrs Martin formed a cult around her, with followers leaving their jobs and spouses to prepare for the alien spaceship that would collect them.

It wouldn't be spoiling the ending to point out that the flood never came, and nor did the aliens. But Festinger and his colleagues noted a strange phenomenon; that when the day arrived, rather than the group fading away and its leaders left a laughing stock, it instead grew, as the previously inward-looking members began actively recruiting others. As Festinger noted: 'If more and more people can be persuaded that the system of belief is correct, then clearly it must after all be correct.' In order to avoid the truth that firmly-held ideas were based on false assumptions, and the psychic pain that would cause, Martin sought to convert others to the idea in order to enlist social support. Festinger found that belief *increased* after failure became apparent if the believer had committed themselves to it, and had made important life-changing decisions as a result. The more dramatic such decisions, the more firmly held the belief. But the individual believer required social support to maintain the illusion; while one isolated individual could not withstand disconfirming evidence, if the believer could convince others, who will in turn confirm the belief, the fantasy could be kept alive.

For those who experience disconfirmation, the realisation that an idea on which they banked their entire moral framework, and their country's future, is completely misguided is difficult to take; similar to the sickening feeling of finding out that the plausible young man might not actually be the son of the deposed president of Gabon and doesn't really have US $26 million in the bank. This may partly explain the exaggerated outrage which people show towards any critic of diversity; often people who have advocated mass immigration all along can only respond to criticism by angrily asking what the critic might do, the alternative being presumably mass deportations or mass murder. Yet if it was the proposed alternatives they feared all along, why did they pretend there was no problem? It is a telling response and something one would not expect of a view based on rational analysis, rather than faith. Instead it looks like a subconscious admission that the experiment has left Britain with deep problems.

One strange aspect of the debate is that believers often talk of diversity as being inevitable; yet when people say something is inevitable, it suggests that their enthusiasm is not entirely genuine. 'Inevitable' was the line Bolsheviks used about Communism, and by Euro-federalists to describe their dream of a nation-free Europe. Nothing is inevitable except death – our future may be secular or religious, conservative or liberal, capitalist or socialist, and there is simply no unstoppable one-way direction towards the end of history. One should be wary of any argument that uses the line. People also talk of the achievements of a multiracial society in the same way they talk about a community overcoming a serious disaster. We've got through; we've survived; there haven't been mass casualties. People do not normally talk about good things in this way. Where they do discuss it, it is couched in euphemism; for example the Wikipedia page on 'diversity in the workplace' poses opposite sides of the argument as 'positives' and 'challenges'. And even when promoting diversity, its advocates talk about it in the same language they would about a disability; the calls for American colleges to be ranked according to 'diversity' alongside such standard measurements as exam results looks like a subliminal admission that it is a liability, like counting the number of children eligible for free meals.

Because the case for mass immigration is so weak, the argument often turns instead to the individual. Supporters base their argument on other people's supposed fears, of immigrants and immigration, change or globalisation. To be in favour of diversity is to be positive, optimistic, courageous and decent; to be against implies fearfulness, resentment or hostility.[132] Yet hostility to diversity does not mean hostility to foreigners, and most opponents are clearly not hateful in the slightest. The Pew Foundation's wide-ranging research in 47 countries showed that opposition towards immigration was universally strong, yet significant majorities of people in England, France, Canada and the US had positive attitudes to third world peoples.[133] In the words of Labour peer Maurice Glasman, most people are anti-immigration, but pro-immigrant.

Change is not necessarily positive or negative, yet change for change's sake is exactly the argument used for demographic revolution; that because older and less attractive people are fearful of and hostile to change, we should embrace it. This is not an argument one would present to a climatologist, for instance (and a graph of immigration levels looks far more like a 'hockey stick' than its climatic equivalent) yet any rapid change to the social ecosystem is bound to have unpredictable results. Yet for all the psychological analysis of opponents' motivations, proponents consistently run away from this central question – do the benefits outweigh the costs?

What next?

Diversity came with the best intentions, but beyond a certain degree of immigration the costs to a society, in terms of greater atomisation, inequality, crime, religious tension, government inter-ference and authoritarianism, easily outweigh the benefits. It is a utopian idea: we are not going to start sharing our nations with the rest of humanity anymore than we would share our property, and those who fall below the high moral standards set by the Jacobins of diversity are not deviants. Until this is appreciated England will continue to see mass immigration as a solution to various economic problems that are actually aggravated by immigration, like a delusional hypothermia sufferer taking off his clothes.

The sceptics may be wrong, of course. It is perfectly possible that we may look back at this change and see it as a positive development, but it will not be accepted either way until there is an actual debate. Sixty years after mass immigration began, and ten after it intensified, we have not plucked up the courage to ask – has the cost been worth it?

We do not ask because of the fear of offending people. But criticism of past immigration does not suggest criticism of someone's existence. We are all products of the past. Many of us would not be around had our parents or grandparents had access to birth control; are supporters of the pill suggesting that we should never have been born? Indeed, because of the butterfly effect, most young white Britons would not have come into existence were it not for the impact immigration had on society from the 1950s and 60s. Britain's diversity experiment in many ways resembles a troubled marriage – but not even the unhappiest of spouses regret the precious, beautiful children who resulted from their union.

And we have not asked because we are scared of what the answer will be, and of the consequences. Yet there is no reason to be fearful; perhaps it is because we are past the stage where the children of immigrants fear the spectre of repatriation that we can discuss it more openly. Honest debate need not lead, in the words of Woody Allen, to black-and-white newsreel footage scored by a cello in a minor key. In light of the Holocaust, and the various other atrocities carried out in the name of nation or race, it is understandable why Western societies feel so tortured about immigration, but it is only the West that is so tormented. And while a world free of ethnic conflict is a worthy goal, the mass importation of peoples across continents is a strange way to achieve it. It is paradoxical that those who cite the spectre of racial conflict are justifying a policy most likely to bring it about – mass immigration; like Oedipus, western Europe is, by trying to avoid a disastrous future, doing everything to make it happen.

Alain Finkielkraut, a French essayist whose father was deported to Auschwitz, has warned how anti-racism is the biggest danger facing the West. 'The lofty idea of "the war on racism,"' he has said: 'is gradually turning into a hideously false ideology. And this anti-racism will be for the twenty-first century what Communism was for the twentieth century: a source of violence.' Just as the pacifism that followed the horror of the trenches led the way to the even worse inhumanity of Hitler's war, so Britain and its European neighbours, in recoiling from the idea of nations, may now be paving the way for fresh disaster.

Our inability to distinguish between pathological racism on the one hand and a desire to protect national integrity – a desire we would not dream of denying any non-Europeans – has significantly diminished our quality of life and promises future problems. And in what area of life, political or otherwise, do we even question the wisdom of honestly discussing an issue? Only when it has become a taboo in the most Freudian sense, something we dare not think about for fear of what we might feel. Every society needs taboos, but as a result we have become terrified of expressing opposition to enormous, dubious change in case we are classed as morally abnormal.

How do we make it better? We can start by rejecting the idea of diversity, as it is currently understood, as a euphemism for a world without national sovereignty or borders. This is the opposing extreme to the racial purity fallacy of the late 19th and early 20th centuries, and should be consigned to the same dustbin of stupid ideas. Like most things, diversity is good up to a point; but nothing is beneficial in extremes.

We also need to abandon the Marxist critique of race, and accept that human beings are fallible creatures who discriminate and pre-judge and sometimes fall below the standards required of the anti-racist lobby; and that it is impossible to create a society based on the assumption that people are perfectible. We have to reject universalism, for nation-states provide the most progressive means of human self-organisation, the best environment for democracy, liberalism and economic advancement; and besides which, without national identity some other tribal identity will take its place – most likely religion. We are not entering the post-national age; indeed across the world the agitations of peoples such as the Kurds and the Tibetans show that the nation-state remains as popular as ever. Nor are the states people desire mere geographical identities without shared ideas of culture, history and ancestry, but rather extended families, even if they are families that adopt and marry out. The great manifestation of this illusion, the European Union, also makes it impossible for Britain to control its borders. For this reason Britain must take back all powers over its own borders.

Except to the ideologues, it is not racist to suggest that national ethnic majorities have the right to remain a comfortable majority; different people may have a different idea of comfortable, but Yitzhak Rabin's figure of 80 per cent is certainly reasonable as a lower figure. Not only is this as morally right as the idea of private property, but it is practical too. Such states are more likely to be well-run, free of corruption, secular and democratic, and, most of all, diverse in the one area it really matters – diversity of opinion. And what's more – those benefits are enjoyed by everyone, including minorities.

The most immediate step that any government must take is to restrain immigration, including far stricter rules on marriage, which is the least progressive form of immigration, being almost entirely within ethnic groups.

Eventually we will also inevitably have to withdraw from our international obligations to house refugees, which is both impractical and creates the dubious principle that non-citizens have rights towards another country. We must always provide sanctuary, where possible, although in practice it will always be extremely hard to make decisions over genuine refugees and those simply wishing to avoid a miserable life, an understandable motive. Where possible we should try to offer help closer to their homelands.

There should be a moratorium on developing world migration, except for the most exceptionally talented, and help for those who wish to return home (although realistically no politician, especially a Conservative one, will touch anything that will be portrayed as 'repatriation', even voluntary, which conjurers up images of sideburn–wearing marchers carrying placards that say things like 'Enoch calls a spade a spade'). Ethnic division and hostility to foreigners decline during periods of restricted immigration, and tighter controls will reduce the problems of diversity; over time these problems ease to a certain extent as people intermarry.

In the longer term Britain should restrict settlement from developing countries to only highly-skilled workers, while maintaining fairly open borders with those states possessing a minimum median income of around $10-12,000; this would currently include western Europe, North America, Australia, New Zealand, Japan, South Korea, Singapore and Israel, but if and when they rise above that bar, eastern Europe, Brazil and China could soon be included (assuming there is a reciprocal agreement). Open borders between countries of comparative wealth risks little in the way of social unrest, and genuinely aides the spread of ideas, while fostering ever stronger links between the scattered branches of the human race. Diversity has always existed at the top of society, and should continue to do so. In contrast open borders with countries at lower levels of social and political development brings enormous costs: it creates entirely one-way immigration, and feeds only our short-term hunger for cheap labour which allows us to sidestep the issue of welfare dependency.

And immigration is intimately tied up with the problem of welfare, which will take political courage to tackle, but David Cameron has at last recognised the problem, stating in an April 2011 speech that the blame for mass immigration 'lies at the door of our woeful welfare system'. We need to overcome the idea that natives are unsuited towards low-skilled jobs, somehow too good to do the dirty work. There is so simply no need to import unskilled labour, especially when so much of it is short-term, and when fewer unskilled workers are needed that in previous generations.

The greatest danger remains religious-based strife between Britain's Muslim minority and Christian majority. Perhaps the easiest, or at any rate least controversial, step is blocking the inflow of finance supporting hard-line strains of Islam emanating from Saudi Arabia and elsewhere, by banning the funding of schools and mosques from outside sources. There must also be a total ban on any sort of state funding and promotion of groups that do not explicitly support the primacy

of British law over any other, and which hold beliefs vastly at
odds with the British public. It should go without saying that
public figures of all creeds should criticise whenever possible
anti-social attitudes towards religious liberty, gays and Jews.
Debate will continue over the dangers posed by faith schools,
which will be viewed as a threat to social cohesion in areas
where Muslims and non-Muslims do not meet each other in any
other area, but it is questionable whether their abolition will
seriously reduce segregation. This is a tribal problem and it
seems unlikely that official discouragement of religious identity
will have much effect; even the Soviet Union failed to successfully suppress communal loyalties after 70 years of severe
oppression. Closing a few Church of England schools is
unlikely to make much difference.

The real challenge, and difficulty, is forging a sense of
nationhood that is strong enough to hold the country together.
Multiculturalism has failed, but the replacements currently being
suggested will also fail, because they are built on the same
assumptions of the anti-racist Left. Such beliefs, that British
identity is racist if it does not include some fictional multi-ethnic
past, or that all ethnic groups must have equality of outcomes,
or that racism is institutionalised in any white-dominated organisation, are a recipe for eternal conflict and bitterness. Yet these
divisive ideas are still actively promoted by the race relations
industry, which stretches across all areas of the state. The
government must cut off the oxygen supply to the people with
a vested interest in seeing racism everywhere. Not only are many
of the problems they identify not a product of racism, but such
groups are a cause of huge resentment, and their attempts to rid
the world of discrimination and inequality are not just likely to
fail, but to cause further division. The extent of equality and discrimination laws must be scaled back, so that at the very least
small businesses are exempted, while no business or
government department should have to prove its commitment
to 'equality and diversity'. Neither should diversity be used to
bring radical social change by dismantling British social
structures in the name of reducing 'bonding', something which

has already had hugely negative consequences.

Whatever happens Britain must not continue to sacrifice the liberal institutions and practises it has spent centuries building up in the name of diversity – better to have liberalism in one country than globalised authoritarianism.

Although the Labour party in recent years must shoulder much of the blame for these problems, it is perhaps the Labour tradition that offers the better hope of bringing British national identity back to life. We need to re-awaken a sense of nationhood that does not turn ugly, what the socially conservative 'Blue Labour' peer Maurice Glasman calls a 'generous patriotism', rather than an unpleasant and xenophobic nationalism. It is not just a question of creating an identity that unites different races, but one that unites both white conservatives and white liberals. Labour as a party once came closest to achieving that; perhaps it has the best chance of doing so again. Having said that, plans by the Coalition Government to introduce a new citizenship test focussing on British history and literature are a step in the right direction.

Rather than trying to forge a new identity that will fail to unite us, we should look for inspiration in the old one, starting with a nation-based school history curriculum. A shared sense of history and culture is far more liberal in practice than the creation of state-enforced British values, many of which are not shared by much of the population. A nation does not need official values, it only needs a narrative and a shared past, from which values and loyalty naturally emerge. You do not need to share some artificial government-approved British vision; you only need to love Britain, and that cannot come about until school children are taught the basics of British culture and history; Shakespeare and the King James Bible are a more effective tool of integration than a thousand multiculturalism manuals. We should not fool ourselves that we will create a conflict-free society – France and the United States, even with their strong civic cultures, still have serious problems – but we can, at least, try to minimise the potential for diversity to become division.

Recalling his parents, who willingly raised their son to be an

Englishman, Chief Rabbi Jonathan Sacks once said: 'They were proud to be English because the English were proud to be English. Indeed, in the absence of pride, there can be no identity at all.'

This seems like a good place to start.

Further Reading

Ali, Monica *Brick Lane*

Anderson, Benedict, *Imagined Communities*, Verso, 1983.

Bawer, Bruce *While Europe Slept*. Doubleday, 2006.

Blond, Phllip *Red Tory: How Left and Right have Broken Britain and How we can Fix it*. Faber and Faber, 2010.

Borjas, George, *Heaven's Door*, Princeton, 2001

Brimelow, Peter *Alien Nation. Common Sense about America's Immigration Disaster*. Random House, 1995.

Browne, Anthony *Do We Need Mass Immigration?* Civitas, 2002

Buchanan, Patrick J *Suicide of a Superpower*

Burleigh, Michael *Blood and Rage: A Cultural History of Terrorism*. Harper, 2008.

Sacred Causes: Religion and Politics from the European Dictators to al Qaeda Harper Press, 2006.

Burleigh, Michael and Wippermann, Wolfgang The Racial State: Germany 1933-1945. Cambridge University Press, 1991.

Buruma, Ian *Murder in Amsterdam: The Death of Theo Van Gogh and the Limits of Tolerance*. Atlantic, 2006.

Caldwell, Christopher *Reflections on the Revolution in Europe*. Penguin, 2009.

Chua, Amy *World on Fire: How Exporting Free-Market Democracy Breeds Ethnic Hatred and Global Instability* Arrow, 2004.

Collins, Michael *The Likes of Us. A Biography of the White Working Class*. Granta, 2004.

Conway, David *A Nation of Immigrants? A Brief demographic history of Britain*. Civitas, 2007.

Dalrymple, Theodore *The New Vichy Syndrome: Why European intellectuals surrender to barbarism*. Encounter, 2010.

- The Man Who Predicted the Race Riots. City Journal, Spring 2002.

Davies, Jon Gower, *Mind-Forg' d Manacles*, Civitas, 2012.

Davies, Jon Gower *The New Inquisition in Britain Today*. Civitas, 2010.

Dench, Geoff, Gavron, Kate and Young, Michael *The New East End*

Kinship, Race and Conflict. Profile, 2006.

Dennis, Norman, Erdos, George and A-Shahi, Ahmed *Racist Murder and Pressure Group Politics*. Civitas, 2000.

Diamond, Jared Guns, *Germs and Steel*, Vintage, 1998.

Flanagan, Caitlin *How Serfdom Saved the Women's Movement*. Atlantic magazine, 2004.

Gilroy, Paul *There Ain't No Black in the Union Jack: The Cultural Politics of Race and Nation*. Routledge, 1987.

Glenny, Misha *McMafia*. Vintage, 2009.

Goodhart, David "Too Diverse?" Prospect Magazine, February 2004.

Grubel, Herbert, *The Effects of Mass Immigration on Canadian Living Standars and Society*, Frasier Institute, 2009.

Haidt, Jonathan *The Righteous Mind*

Heffer, Simon *Like the Roman* W&N, 1998.

Huntingdon, Samuel *Clash of Civilizations and the Remaking of the World Order*. Simon & Schuster, 1997.

Johnston, Philip *Bad Laws*. Constable & Robinson, 2010.

Kaufmann, Eric *Shall the Religious Inherit the Earth? Demography and Politics in the Twenty-First Century*. Profile, 2010.

Kriwaczek, Paul *Babylon: Mesopotamia and the Birth of Civilization*. Atlantic, 2010.

Kynaston, David *Austerity Britain 1945-1951*. Bloomsbury, 2008.

Lasch, Christopher *The Revolt of the Elites and the Betrayal of Democracy* W.W. Norton, 1995.

Legrain, Philippe *Immigrants: Your Country Needs Them*. Little, Brown, 2007.

Leiken, Robert, *Europe's Angry Muslims*, Oxford, 2012.

Levitt, Steven and Dubner, Stephen *Freakonomics: A Rogue Economist Explores the Hidden Side of Everything.* Penguin, 2007

Levy, Andrea *Small Island.* Headline, 2004.

Lewis, Bernard, *What Went Wrong?*, Phoenix, 2002.

Lipset, Seymour Martin *American Exceptionalism: A Double-edged Sword* W.W. Norton, 1997

Jones, Owen *Chavs* Verso, 2011

Malik, Kenan *From Fatwa to Jihad: The Rushdie Affair and its Legacy.* Atlantic, 2009.

- *Strange Fruit: Why Both Sides are wrong in the Race Debate.* Oneworld, 2008.

Mount, Ferdinand *Mind the Gap: The New Class Divide in Britain.* Short Books, 2004.

Moxon, Steve *The Great Immigration Scandal.* Imprint, 2006.

Murray, Douglas and Verwey, Johan Pieter *Victims of Intimidation: freedom of Speech within Europe's Muslim Communities.* Centre for Social Cohesion, 2008.

Nazir-Ali, Michael *Triple Jeopardy for the West: Aggressive Secularism, Radical Islamism and Multiculturalism* Bloomsbury, 2012.

Oppenheimer, Stephen *The Origins of the British.* Constable, 2006.

Pearce, Alan *Whose Side Are They On?* Gibson Square, 2009.

Phillips, Melanie *Londonistan: How Britain is creating a Terror State Within.* Gibson Square, 2006.

Pinker, Steven *The Blank Slate: The Modern Denial of Human Nature* Penguin, 2002

Pollard, Justin *Alfred the Great* John Murray, 2006

Putnam, Robert *Bowling Alone: The Collapse and Revival of American Community.* Simon & Schuster, 2000.

Rassam, Suha *Christianity in Iraq.* Gracewing, 2010.

Roth, Byron *The Perils of Diversity: Immigration and Human Nature.* Washington Summit Publishers, 2010.

Rushdie, Salman *The New Empire Within Britain*, 1982.

Sandbrook, Dominic, *Never Had It So Good*, Little Brown, 2005.

Scheffer, Paul *Immigrant Nations* Polity Press, 2011

Sergeant, Harriet *Welcome to the Asylum* IEA, 2001.

Sewell, Dennis *The Political Gene: How Darwin's Ideas Changed Politics.* Picador, 2000.

Shepherd, Robert *Enoch Powell: A Biography.* Pimlico, 2007.

Shepherd, Robin, *A State Beyond the Pale*, W&N 2009.

Scruton, Roger *The Roger Scruton Reader.* Continuum, 2009.

- *The Uses of Pessimism and the Danger of False Hope.* Atlantic, 2010.

Singh, Swaran "All in the Mind". Prospect magazine, September 2010.

Smith, Zadie *White Teeth.* Penguin, 2001.

Steyn, Mark *America Alone: the End of the World as We Know It.* Regnery, 2006.

Stillwell, John *The Internal Migration of Britain's Ethnic Groups* University of Leeds, 2010.

Sunstein, Cass *Going to Extremes: How Like Minds Unite and Divide.* Oxford University Press, 2009

Sykes, Bryan *The Seven Daughters of Eve.* Transworld, 2001

- *Blood of the Isles.* Transworld, 2007

Tebble, Adam James *Exclusion for Democracy.* Brown University 2006

Walden, George *Time to Emigrate?* Gibson Square, 2007.

West, Patrick *The Poverty of Multiculturalism.* Civitas, 2005.

Whittle, Peter (ed) *A Sorry State: Self-denigration in British culture.* New Culture Forum, 2010.

- *Being British: What's Wrong With It?* Biteback Publishing, 2010

Wilkinson, Richard and Pickett, Kate *The Spirit Level: Why Equality is Better for Everyone.* Penguin, 2010.

Winder, Robert *Bloody Foreigners: The story of Immigration to Britain.* Little, Brown, 2004.

Wolfe, Tom, *A Bonfire of the Vanities* Farrar, Straus and Giroux, 1987.

Worden, Blair *The English Civil Wars: 1640-1660* Phoenix, 2010.

Zachary, G Pascal *The Diversity Advantage: Multicultural Identity in the New World Economy.* Westview, 2003.

Notes

1 And not that this will necessarily guarantee a brotherhood of man: Britain, Germany and Russia went to war in 1914 despite their heads of state all being first cousins, and wars between brothers tend to be more vicious than those between strangers.

2 http://www.guardian.co.uk/education/2011/jun/22/quarter-state-school-pupils-from-ethnic-minority

3 Eastern Eye. Britain's Richest Asians 2000 http://www.jsrds.com/images/pdf/htmls/pdf1.html

4 http://www.telegraph.co.uk/news/uknews/immigration/8142176/White-Britons-to-become-minority-by-2066.html

5 http://www.dailymail.co.uk/news/article-1004185/Devastating-demolition-case-mass-immigration.html

6 http://www.guardian.co.uk/politics/2004/jun/28/immigrationpolicy.immigration

7 http://www.prospectmagazine.co.uk/2010/02/transforming-britain-by-accident/

8 http://www.publications.parliament.uk/pa/ld200708/ldselect/ldconaf/82/8210.htm

9 http://www.telegraph.co.uk/news/uknews/immigration/8550197/Immigration-asylum-backlog-led-to-amnesty-MPs-warn.html

10 http://www.telegraph.co.uk/news/uknews/1493122/Blair-accused-on-migrants.html

11 http://news.bbc.co.uk/1/hi/uk/4733777.stm

12 The Origins of the British, p401

13 As far as anyone knows. The largest survey of British Y-chromosomes, which took samples from 1,772 men, failed to find any of similar type to that most frequently found among Africans.

14 http://www.runnymedetrust.org/uploads/EMBESbriefingFINALx.pdf

15 http://www.dailymail.co.uk/debate/article-1249823/IMMIGRATION-Sir-Andrew-Green-decade-deception.html

16 http://news.bbc.co.uk/nol/shared/spl/hi/programmes/analysis/transcripts/08_02_10.txt

17 *Immigrants: Your Country Needs Them*

18 Theodore Dalrymple,*The New Vichy Syndrome*, Encounter, 2010

19 http://www.channel4.com/news/media/2009/06/day08/yougovpoll_080609.pdf

20 http://news.bbc.co.uk/hi/english/static/in_depth/uk/2002/race/results_full.stm#question28

21 This was not an idle boast. Temperatures had reached as low as -20c the previous winter.

22 Among them was Bert Trautmann, whose talent for goalkeeping was spotted while playing among POWs and who would eventually play for Manchester City, winning the FA Cup in 1956 despite breaking his neck during the game. Trautmann remains the only man to have won both an Iron Cross and an FA Cup Winner's Medal, a record he is likely to hold onto for some time.

23 Kynaston, David *Austerity Britain*

24 Interviewed by Daniel Lawrence, *Black Migrants, White Natives*, Cambridge, 1974, pp39-40

25 Many Anglo-Indians spoke a slightly archaic Victorian English. Rather like a Classics scholar going back in time to 3rd century Rome and finding the locals speaking a vernacular proto-Italian.

26 From an investigation by Robert Davison in Nottingham in the 1960s

27 Among them 'Lord of the Beasts of the Earths and Fishies of the Sea' and 'Conqueror of the British Empire in Africa in General and Uganda in Particular'.

[28] Shepherd, Robert *Enoch Powell: A Biography*, Hutchinson, 1996

[29] ibid

[30] ibid

[31] Quoted in the 2008 BBC documentary, *Rivers of Blood*

[32] http://www.guardian.co.uk/politics/2007/nov/04/conservatives.uk

[33] Indeed Nick Griffin's oratorical power is so great that it actually broke the space-time continuum, with his appearance on *Question Time* leading to the murder of a gay man in London a month before, according to one cabinet-backed campaign against the BNP. The United Against Fascism campaign Expose, which was backed by two Government ministers, claimed in a press release that Griffin's comments that the sight of two men kissing was 'creepy' had inspired a murder that had already happened; yet the previous Mayor of London had invited and welcomed an Islamic cleric who actually advocated the murder of homosexuals.

[34] http://www.popmatters.com/pm/review/68903-skins-punks-by-gavin-watson

[35] http://news.bbc.co.uk/1/hi/magazine/6546617.stm

[36] Kynaston, David *Austerity Britain*

[37] Or as one east London resident told the Young Foundation, 'those big-hearted ones who've got their own big houses and make these rules'.

[38] This is explored thoroughly in Steven Levitt and Stephen Dubner's *Freakonomics*.

[39] No relation to the word 'oik'.

[40] Told to the author in an interview

[41] Named after Mike Godwin, who observed of internet debate: 'As an online discussion grows longer, the probability of a comparison involving Nazis or Hitler approaches 100 per cent'.

[42] That's GK, not AK.

[43] Use of the word 'racism' in published English-language books increased 30-fold between 1957-1995, according to Google Ngram Viewer

[44] As discussed in Chapter 6

[45] http://www.nytimes.com/2011/02/08/science/08tier.html?_r=2

[46] Almost everyone knows of someone who has been killed by a car, for instance, but transport arguments must still strike a sober balance between costs and benefits.

[47] Speaking on This Week With David Brinkley in 1991, he said: 'I think God made all people good. But if we had to take a million immigrants in, say Zulus, next year, or Englishmen, and put them in Virginia, which group would be easier to assimilate and would cause less problems for the people of Virginia?'

[48] A contradiction noticed by the blogger Laban Tall
http://ukcommentators.blogspot.com/2010/01/cognitive-dissonance-alert-part-637.html

[49] Quoted in Peter Brimlow's Alien Nation, from interviews with representatives from the US Department of the Interior and offices of American Samoa, Micronesia, Northern Mariana Islands and the Marshall Islands

[50] http://www.telegraph.co.uk/comment/columnists/maryriddell/6533366/Gordon-Brown-should-say-the-unsayable-immigration-has-been-a-boon.html

[51] http://news.bbc.co.uk/1/hi/uk_politics/5273356.stm

[52] http://www.guardian.co.uk/politics/2004/apr/27/immigrationpolicy.speeches

[53] http://www.civitas.org.uk/pdf/cs23.pdf

[54] http://www.wrr.nl/fileadmin/nl/publicaties/PDF-Rapporten/Nederland_als_immigratiesamenleving.pd

[55] http://www.spiegel.de/international/europe/eu-targets-skilled-immigrants-european-commission-launches-new-push-for-blue-card-a-513083.html

[56] http://www.dailymail.co.uk/news/article-1325013/Migrants-took-9-10-jobs-created-Labour.html

[57] http://www.npc.umich.edu/publications/policy_briefs/brief8/

[58] Eric Ruark, *Immigration* Lobbying: A Window Into the World of Special Interest

[59] http://www.telegraph.co.uk/news/uknews/1583501/Immigration-raises-house-prices-say-peers.html

[60] http://www.publications.parliament.uk/pa/ld200708/ldselect/ldeconaf/82/8206.htm

[61] According to the Office for National Statistics. For the past 50 years their population projections at the 20 year range have been accurate to 2.5 per cent.

[62] http://www.telegraph.co.uk/education/1564618/Immigation-drains-Britain-says-Left-think-tank.html

[63] *Immigrants: Your Country Needs Them*

[64] As shown by Ann Brittain in the journal Social Biology: 'Anticipated Child Loss to Migration and Sustained High Fertility in an East Caribbean Population', 1991, and in the 1990 study 'Migration and the Demographic Transition: A West Indian Example', from the Institute of Social and Economic Research, University of the West Indies, Kingston, which looked at birth, death and emigration rates from 1880 to 1967 for the island of St Barthelemy.

[65] http://www.telegraph.co.uk/health/healthnews/8429306/Foreign-trained-doctors-more-likely-to-be-struck-off.html

[66] http://www.un.org/esa/population/publications/migration/execsum.pdf

[67] According to the Dallas-based National Center for Policy Anaylsis

[68] American journalist Steve Sailer was the first to note the contradiction between diversity and equality in a 2000 essay, *Inequality, the Immigration Dimension.*

[69] Christopher Snowdon's *The Spirit Level Delusion* does rather more than this, and is well worth reading for balance.

[70] And neither is poverty the obvious factor. North Dakota and West Virginia are both poor but highly egalitarian.

71 Economists Stephany Gould and John Palmer concluded of the reasons for America' s lower welfare provision that only 'heterogeneity of population and distinctiveness of public philosophy' seem to have explanatory power

[72] In a study discussed in the next chapter.

[73] Goodhart, David 'Too Diverse?' *Prospect* magazine.

[74] Discriminating was, until fairly recently, a fairly positive term, and someone who was 'discriminating' in their choices was able to distinguish good from bad. Only with anti-racial discrimination campaigns in the 1960s did its more general meaning decline.

[75] http://www.migrationwatchuk.com/briefingPaper/document/165

[76] http://www.migrationwatchuk.org/briefingPaper/document/165

[77] Hammurabi's Code introduced the punishment of 'an eye for an eye' and also decreed that if a builder's work collapses and 'kills the son of the owner the son of that builder shall be put to death'. A wet liberal he was not.

[78] http://www.guardian.co.uk/education/2009/oct/25/chicken-run-city-schools

[79] From the Radio 4 programme *Foreigner Policy.*
Available at: http://www.bbc.co.uk/programmes/b00qh0zf

[80] Ethnic diversity, of course, is only one of many factors that affects trust. Kahn and Costa's own research documented higher desertion rates in the Civil War among Union Army soldiers serving in companies whose soldiers varied more by age, occupation, and birthplace, based on military service and pension records of 5,673 black Union Army soldiers. People fight better alongside people like them; this was the thinking behind the ill-fated Pals system in the First World War, in which groups of friends and colleagues from the same towns and villages were recruited into units (the one tiny flaw being that one battle could wipe out an entire neighbourhood, rather than spreading the losses more thinly).

[81] http://www.ft.com/cms/s/0/beee7058-c087-11db-995a-000b5df10621.html#axzz1bjf9uw00

[82] Gaertner and Dovidio 2000, Motyl et al. 2011. From *The Righteous Mind*

[83] K Pickett and R Wilkinson, People Like us: ethnic group density effects on health, *Ethnicity and Health* (2008)

[84] Singh, Saran *Prospect* magazine, October 2010

[85] Of course 'getting on your bike' is exactly what Conservative ministers have traditionally wished the unemployed to do, the free market requiring some labour mobility. The difference now is that many on

the Left now wish people to move across continents rather than towns.

86 http://news.bbc.co.uk/1/hi/wales/6609093.stm

87 The Young Foundation report found many examples of parents who had chosen baptism because local secular schools were majority Bangladeshi.

88 http://www.thedailybeast.com/newsweek/2012/04/01/biologist-e-o-wilson-on-why-humans-like-ants-need-a-tribe.html

89 From the 1916 essay, Transnational America

90 http://www.timesonline.co.uk/tol/life_and_style/education/article6650995.ece

91 Even so, the Government has recently begun promoting curry schools to teach Indian cuisine to natives who wish to take jobs in the restaurant trade.

92 Japan, also, has the largest number of patent applications every year, with South Korea in fourth, ahead of any European country.

93 Alesina, Alberto F and La Ferrara, Eliana *Ethnic Diversity and Economic Performance* (December 2003). Harvard Institute of Economic Research Discussion Paper No. 2028. Available at SSRN: http://ssrn.com/abstract=569881

94 Liddle later admitted he had been wrong to use such phrasing, using a four-letter word to describe himself.

95 As explained in her 1985 book, *Evolution as Religion*

96 Although there is no evidence that our medieval ancestors actually debated this question. Alas the absurdity of 20th century academia was very much real.

97 Singh, Saran *Prospect* magazine, October 2010

98 http://www.city-journal.org/html/12_2_oh_to_be.html

99 Malik, Kenan. *From Fatwa to Jihad.*

100 As Chanu, the elder husband in *Brick Lane*, puts it: 'What they are doing, you see, is co-opting these immigrants into their grand political schemata in which all oppressed minorities combine in the overthrow of the state and live happily ever after in a communal paradise. The theory fails to take account of culture clash, bourgeois immigrant aspirations, the hatred of the Hindu for the Muslim, the Bangladeshi for the Pakistani, and so forth. In all reality, it is doomed to failure.'

101 Mala Dhondy, quoted in *From Fatwa to Jihad.*

102 http://www.thisislondon.co.uk/standard/article-23552199-lee-jasper-black-only-schools-will-beat-gangs.do

103 In *From Fatwa to Jihad* and *Strange Fruit* Malik analysed the similarities between multiculturalism and racism.

104 It is common for local councils to regularly translate documents into ten or twelve languages, and they do not confine translation services to necessary communiqués; the biggest spender on translations, Haringey in north London, has translated and published several documents online which were never read once, including a pamphlet for gipsies translated into Polish, as well as the Haringey Women's Directory in Albanian, Bengali, Kurdish, Somali and Urdu.

105 On the other hand one should not be shocked that a Sikh sides with white extremists against Muslim extremists. A *Newsnight* report on the EDL asked Singh how he could side with the EDL in light of the racism his family must have suffered, yet such harassment would not have been on the same scale as recent Sikh-Muslim violence in India, which reached horrific proportions in 1947.

106 From a 2006 NOP survey for Channel 4's *Dispatches*

107 http://www.dailymail.co.uk/news/article-431316/New-curriculum-make-lesson-politically-correct.html

108 http://www.thisislondon.co.uk/news/article-23386024-ethnic-minorities-more-likely-to-feel-british-than-white-people-says-research.do

109 http://www.equalityhumanrights.com/advice-and-guidance/your-rights/race/what-is-race-discrimi-nation/what-forms-does-racial-discrimination-take/

110 b http://blogs.telegraph.co.uk/news/davidgreen/5575747/Its_time_to_shelve_the_Equality_Bill/

111 http://www.guardian.co.uk/money/2009/oct/18/racism-discrimination-employment-undercover

112 http://www.guardian.co.uk/politics/2005/mar/21/uk.race1

113 A policy that has a disproportionate impact on one group over another, even if it itself neutral and fair.

114 Two of the gang were finally convicted for the murder early in 2012, while in June Home Secretary Theresa May ordered another inquiry into the police handling the case.

115 Polland, Justin *Alfred the Great The Man Who Made England*, page 230

116 West, Patrick *The Poverty of Multiculturalism*, from the introduction

117 http://www.civitas.org.uk/pdf/cs23.pdf

118 If culinary disgust equated to ethnic hatred, England would have been nuked by now.

119 http://news.sky.com/skynews/Home/UK-News/Islamist-Militants-In-The-UK-Backing-Jihad-Activities-Says-Leaked-Government-Doc/Article/200811215147646

120 http://www.timesonline.co.uk/tol/news/uk/article671510.ece

121 http://www.timesonline.co.uk/tol/news/uk/article782242.ece

122 'They only consult to cast him down from his excellency: they delight in lies: they bless with their mouth, but they curse inwardly'

123 Although ironically such anti-Christian desecration may become impossible when Ireland's Islamic population more than doubles in the next 20 years, if Terence McNally's experience is anything to go by.

124 Douglass, like Booker T Washington, was also strongly opposed to mass immigration in America.

125 Caldwell, Christopher, *Reflections on the Revolution in Europe*

126 In the run-up to the 2009 election one of its candidates for the South-West region, the half-Jewish Barry Bennett, was quoted as saying: 'I know perfectly respectable half-Jews in the BNP... even Hitler had honorary Aryans who were of Jewish descent... so whatever's good enough for Hitler's good enough for me. God rest his soul.' (Hitler did not, in fact, have 'honorary Aryans'; the Nazis were quite petty about that sort of thing.)

127 Speaking to the author

128 Kaufmann, Eric

129 http://www.dailymail.co.uk/news/article-2045447/Headteacher-David-Levin-says-London-divided-ethnic-ghettos.html

130 Kaufmann, Eric

131 This is if the eight spellings all count as one name. There is also some debate over whether, if we count all the variations of Mohammed as one name, do we do the same with Oliver, Oli, Ollie, which would push Mohammed back into number two spot. It depends on whether one sees diminutives as new names, rather than as variations.

132 Indeed conservatives are on average more fearful by their nature. A DNA analysis of 13,000 Australians found that liberals and conservatives had marked difference in genes that related to neuro-transmitter functioning, particularly glutamate and serotonin, both of which are involved in the brain's response to threat and fear.

133 Wike, Richard and Horowitz, Juliana, World Publics Welcome Global Trade – But Not Immigration: 47-Nation Pew Global Attitudes Survey, the Pew Global Attitudes Project, October 4, 2007 pewglobal.org

Index

Index

Index